HUMAN GEOGRAPHY

Human Geography

R.K. Tripathi

Commonwealth

Human Geography

First Published, **2012**

ISBN 81-7169-642-2

Published by:
Ajay Verma
For Commonwealth Publishers
4831/24, Prahlad Street,
Ansari Road, Darya Ganj,
New Delhi - 110 002
Ph.: 3272541, 3257835
Fax : 91-011-3257835

Typesetting by:
Stylish Laser Typesetter
Delhi - 110053

Printed at:
Efficient Offset Printers
Shahzada Bagh, New Delhi-110035

Preface

Human geography in the realist mould has as its goal emancipation, the uncovering of the base and superstructure of society so that individuals will appreciate fully the enormity of the exploitative and alienating relationships on which society is based. All human geography is applicable, therefore, all human geography is linked to political practice. The political programme of revolution linked to realist research is necessarily a gradualist one, since the goal is to encourage people to realise their situation and to replace it; to convince workers of the world to unite, since they have nothing to lose but their chains.

The word geography can be used in both the vernacular and the academic sense. With regard to the vernacular, it states that we are socialised into particular spatial structures and interpretations of nature, within which we are enable to produce our own, according to our decisions, but constrained by that context and the interpretive powers that are given to us. With regard to the academic, it states that we are socialised into a particular division of labour which enables us to work in particular ways, according to our choice, but also constrains our thinking by the concepts that we are given. The existence of human geography within an academic division of labour may not be the optimal path to emancipation and the creation of a future.

Editor

Contents

1
Towards Human Geography

In the middle of the 1970s these words from Lawrence's essay 'Democracy' seemed to epitomize the uncertainty of human geography, or at least one of its practitioners. The motivation for a welfare approach to human geography was unashamedly human betterment, consistent with Losch's axiom that the real duty is not to explain our sorry reality, but to improve it. Just as neoclassical economics had provided the conceptual foundations for an earlier generation of human geography in the locational analysis tradition, so welfare economics now permitted the rigorous exploration of the question of what is best, or what should take place in the spatial arrangement of things.

The uncertainty arose from recognition that such heady concepts as social well-being and the quality of life, which were central to the welfare perspective, appeared inconsistent with the analytical trappings of economics and its disdain for value judgements. At a deeper level there was an emerging realization that the development of those laws which geographers had been seeking almost as a passport to scientific respectability implied a world vastly different from that of actual human experience. These uncertainties had already been encountered by nimbler minds and to some extent resolved by espousal either of humanism or of a more active 'radical' stance on social change. They were, however, symptomatic of an era in which great expectations had been aroused by the supposed capacity of the new quantitative and model-building human geography not only to explain reality but also to improve it, facilitated by modern cybernetics and harnessed to the cult of managerial rationality.

Urban and regional planning along with development problems were seen as fields in which spatial reorganization could be used to attain specific goals, with almost a mechanical deliberation. Such expectations foundered not only on the limitations of spatial planning revealed in practice, but also on the inability of what passed for geographical theory to make much sense of a world so apparently unyielding to well-intentioned state intervention.

Changing models of humankind

While geography's reconstruction as spatial science had been closely associated with the adoption of numerical and statistical methods, the role of economics had also been significant. Economics had provided the most convincing model of a law-seeking social science, with an enticing battery of supporting graphics and a mathematical rigour the more convincing by its occasional obscurity. It had even become spatial in its regional science offspring. Equally if not more important was that economics provided a convenient model of man(/woman, but necessarily male in this rational world). While *homo economicus* was introduced originally as an ideal type, this perfectly informed and perfectly able being automatically maximizing personal utility or satisfaction through marketplace choices soon became a substitute for something far more complex. He(/she?) was easily understood, and comfortingly infallible in a world of so many fallen angels. Geographers were by tradition too much empiricist, and engaged in the 'real' world, to be captivated by *homo economicus* for long.

However, the variations which we adopted were not much less dauntingly inhuman, even with a few cultural considerations, personal preferences and random variables thrown in as they tried to maximize their place utility. And when a somewhat more imaginative 'behavioural' geography emerged its so-called actors were little more then inanimate participants in some stimulus-response system. Like *homo economicus,* they were good actors in the sense that they learned their lines and put on a predictable performance, but for the most part it was to an implausible script and a plot tedious in its simplicity. That geography was ready to grapple with a more complex humankind as well as with more subtle processes of causation was signalled by an emerging interest in humanism. But this remained somewhat muted, or relegated to the sidelines of disciplinary restructuring. Much more influential was the radical critique built on Marxism.

However, the model of humankind provided by the Althusserian reading of Marx which informed geography's early dallying with structuralism turned out to have little depth of character. Indeed, *homo marxicus,* in the form of capital single-mindedly extracting the last drop of surplus value from labour or manipulating state policy to its precisely understood purpose, bore an uncanny resemblance to profit-maximizing *homo economicus.* One cardboard character replaced another. But, as in conventional economics and the geography built partly upon it, not only was the characterization inadequate, so also was the plot. Explanation came perilously close to determination.

The quantitative model-building era was yielding to a no less mechanistic account of the world, in which social superstructure was determined by the economic base or substructure and individual human beings (capitalists as well as workers) appeared captive of macro-structural forces. For the more ardent practitioners of Marxism, simply to evoke 'the law of value' or the 'logic of the accumulation process' was sufficient explanation, with human volition reduced to collective class struggle. It took the penetrating irony of E. P. Thompson to undermine such views. He pointedly stated, 'if a mode of production is proposed to entail a regular and rational form of sequential development, and a complex (but uniform) internal relational structuration, *independent of the rationality and agency of the human actors who in fact produce and relate,* then, very soon, the questions will be asked: who is the divine will which programmed this automating structure, where is the ulterior "unconscious power"'?.

The notion of social structures as not fixed and immutable but the outcome of human action or agency helped to bridge the schism which had hitherto separated Marxism and humanism. The resurgence of humanism actually provided a more persuasive platform for the critique of empiricism and positivism (which are by no means inconsistent with crude Marxist economism), and hence for their partial displacement in human geography by an interpretative approach informed by qualitative methods.

The drama of human life

That this concluding chapter should have taken so many paragraphs to reach the substantive content of the book is no oversight. Our authors have addressed a humankind quite different from the actors to-which many readers may have become accustomed in the literature of geography, economics and some other social science. The preceding chapters have in various ways sought to reveal a world of experience, in which the meaning of things and places, and of life itself, is far from self-evident, yet in which commonsense and lay beliefs are as legitimate, as real, as findings of science. It is a world in which human volition is neither determined nor unconstrained, neither predictably responsive to stimuli nor totally lacking in logic or rationality.

A world in which people can contradict themselves as well as others, giving different account of their lives in different circumstances - different versions of the truth. This world is a far cry from that of location theory's optimizing entrepreneurs, distance-minimizing consumers, place-utility maximizers and the like, and it is worth a brief reminder of how at least some of us reached it-how-our own paths (or understanding of them) changed in the unfolding drama of disciplinary development.

We have spared readers the personal biographies which are now being used as explicit accounts of academic experience, having indulged ourselves in that respect elsewhere, so the above must suffice. The analogy of drama repeatedly comes to mind, as these sentences are composed. Perhaps it reflects a hitherto unconscious urge to try to step out from and externally observe human activity, consistent with the traditional expectations of the objective and detached scientist. We may watch a play, but we now recognize ourselves as actors in another broader drama. That all the world is a stage and no person an island may be trite but goes to the heart of the interpretative approach, for we are part of and contributors to that which we seek to understand. The dramaturgical analogy figures prominently in a number of the preceding chapters as a means of understanding. Human life is likened to a drama (sometimes even a game), with a text (or rules), a plot, and roles or parts. Such a perspective helps to illuminate strategies of face-to-face encounters, as Susan Smith explains. Rose stresses that a text may be spoken or written as well as acted out.

The interpretation of a written text after the fashion of literary criticism captures the essence of the practice of distillation of meaning which may not be immediately apparent or conveyed by a superficial reading. Burgess and Wood refer to messages and codes, further to underline the indirect, hidden or even deliberately distorted meanings that a text may convey. A further dimension to this strand of work concerns the role of the media.

The press provide a population with access to a plot which may, convey a greatly simplified or partial view of social life. As Susan Smith puts it, the script 'is an unfinished checklist of cues providing the public with a basis from which to extemporize', for example with respect to how they deal with crime in relation to race. The performance in which people engage ensures the local reproduction of racial categories set up nationally and internationally; 'such a "production" is acceptable because it works: plot and script offer a pragmatic basis on which to conduct everyday life in any uncertain environment.'

Tomaselli's analysis of Afrikaans-language films demonstrates the role of the media in helping people to make sense of and come to terms with a collective historic experience which has a bearing on their present identity. As he explains, contained within plots, characters and social practices, can be found the suppressed traumas, hopes, fears and preoccupations of Afrikaner culture. At a deeper level he identifies an historical materialistic base in what he describes as capital's ultimate defilement of Afrikaner cultural space. The symbolic transformation of the *uitlander* (outsider) from white English capital to blacks across the border is full of resonant foreboding for white South Africa. The study by Burgess and Wood of television advertising is more explicitly geographical in its concern with the production of meanings for places. Their text of visual images and spoken script is composed of signs, which they set out to decode.

The interpretation of signs depends on 'shared understanding of the codes which structure messages'; their analysis depends on being part of the action, in the sense of being able to grasp the subtleties of use of accent and evocation of characters from both the actual Docklands/East End and TV dramatizations. To them, a new place has been created by advertising: 'Nothing in these commercials signifies geographical or cultural realities.' Yet the image motivates action, as their survey of the response of small businesses revealed. And night after night on *TV, East Enders* becomes real enough to captivate a quarter of Britain's population.

In this confused and confusing world where fantasy becomes a form of reality, it is a sense of place which can give people a location, at least in a tangible environment of bricks (or concrete) and mortar. But there is more to place than built form. Places can become symbolic, of anything from a fading way of life, a lost relationship, a sought-after security or sign of status. People seek to preserve them as they are, as in the Chicago neighbourhood described by Jackson, the Howdendyke of Porteous and the widow's house where she was happy with her husband, and in the affluent Vancouver suburb examined by David Evans. Understanding the meaning of place, what it signifies for people and how-the signs are read, are close to some long-standing geographical concerns, even if the route to understanding revealed by some of our contributors is unfamiliar. Keith provides a particularly vivid illustration of how certain places took on a symbolic significance to black people in Britain. It was-in these 'no-go' or 'front-line' places that violent confrontation with the police occurred in the early 1980s, in a struggle for control of crucial territory.

The explicit police policy of desymbolizing particular streets reveals-a degree of lay understanding greatly at variance with the stimulus -response methods of social control which have come to be expected of police dealing with civil disorder. Keith's reconciliation of the dramaturgical approach with semiotics is a useful reminder that the meaning of action played out on British streets has to be reconstructed with some care rather than read directly from what is visibly manifest. With the dramaturgical analogy, semiotics (semiology) has emerged as a -major theme of this volume.

The Oxford *English Dictionary* definition of these terms - a branch of pathology concerned with symptoms -reminds us that signs are but surface manifestations of something deeper. These meanings will be shared by people in a particular locality or otherwise drawn together: devised, articulated, reproduced and possibly changed by discourse, individual- conduct and personal interaction. Symbolic interactionalism 'posits that all objects carry meaning which is socially constructed through group reference' (David Evans). Evans calls on Giddens' notion of structuration to reveal human action and social structure as recursive in a manner which allows for change in the significance of place, in a complex and perhaps contradictory process. He points out that the anti-growth strategy of Vancouver suburbanites would ultimately challenge the foundations of the economic system on which the people concerned depended for their employment and affluent lifestyle.

The place which they sought to protect, with its symbolic semi-rural exclusivity, somehow existed outside of capitalism and its attendant values: captive of their own imagery, they fail to grasp its intrinsic contradiction.

Central to the interpretative endeavour is hermeneutics, or the theory of the interpretation and clarification of meaning. In its original form hermeneutics was developed to explicate and adjudicate contending theological texts, and was then applied to historical sources more generally.

The interpretation of texts involves what Giddens has referred to as a 'double hermeneutic', whereby the analyst attempts to interpret a world which is already interpreted by people living their lives in it. Something of the complexity of modern hermeneutics is explained by Rose in his concluding note on method. It is not simply a matter of finding what lies behind the signs in the text but of looking '*with* the text at what it says to successive generations of interpreters thereby involving the text, the interpreter and the interpretation in an ongoing text-event.'

We interpret other texts in a continuing 'self-encounter', while at the same time being concerned with understanding other people's actions. People's pre-interpretations are important to any explanatory account. They may comprise what are sometimes referred to as 'lay' or commonsense' interpretations (even 'theories'). However misguided, or wrong, lay interpretations may appear to be to others or those who may consider themselves experts, what people believe to be true motivates action. In health, for example, lay theories of how the body works and of what it means to be ill influence how people behave in seeking medical care, as Donovan and Cornwell have revealed, even though such beliefs may be discordant with scientific knowledge of anatomy or with how medical practitioners define illness. Health education which disregards lay interpretations runs the risk of failure.

Commonsense interpretations of life may be

grounded in shrewdly evaluated experience, leading to such conclusions that heavy smokers do not always die of lung cancer and that this complaint can also afflict non-smokers: an intuitive grasp of the distinction between necessary and sufficient conditions. Jackson's assertion in his Chicago study that people 'accurately recognize their own interests and understand the root cause of their problems', however contestible as a generalization, at least reminds us that ordinary people are seldom fools or merely victims of false consciousness - far less playing parts written by others in a drama they cannot comprehend.

Sources, materials, methods and theory

It should be clear *by* now that an interpretative geography has been informed *by* sources quite different from those on which the quantitative model-building (empiricist or positivist) paradigm was built. Economics has been displaced by sociology (and in particular interpretative sociology) and anthropology (especially its ethnographic tradition), as major influences on geographical practice.

The impact of strands of anthropology is notable, for it could be argued that it is in this discipline that the interplay of case study, method and theory has been most clearly articulated. Philosophy in its strict sense has augmented the customary 'philosophy of geography' discourse. Realist philosophy has been invoked by some (e.g. Smith and Keith) and phenomenology, especially that of Schutz, has been a major influence, for example to Rose and Donovan in this volume. Pickles underlines the possible confusion of usage in the term method. This book is about method, Eyles announces at the outset, and so it is in the sense both of philosophy (a way of knowing) and practice or technique. In fact, the collective if not entirely consistent sense of philosophy expounded in this volume conforms broadly with phenomenology as Pickles explains it.

And from this, specific methods (techniques) of observation and data assembly follow. They are mainly qualitative (as opposed to quantitative) in the case-studies, as might be expected of a philosophy not inclined to accept a world of objects with specific measurable properties. But this is not to say that quantitative methods, even statistics, are no longer useful: they are by no means inconsistent with the interpretative approach, as Eyles and Pickles point out, if it is recognized that some aspects of human experience are capable of sensible measurement, formal tests of association, and so on. To be somewhat more specific about research material and qualitative methods as techniques, this volume has illustrated a variety of approaches to textual analysis, broadly defined. This can refer to texts in the literal, literary sense, as in the documentary sources examined by Jackson and Porteous, and the newspapers which were part of Smith's material. Of a similar nature are the advertisements looked at by Burgess and Woods, and the films examined by Tomaselli. Informed by semiotics, the techniques employed resemble the critical reading of literature, or even of a painting or piece of sculpture: interpreting in its most obvious colloquial sense. In other work, the material to be interpreted is the spoken word, recorded (by taking notes or use of a tape recorder) for subsequent analysis following what are often long, informal (but not necessarily unstructured) interviews. The chapters by Mel Evans, Donovan and Cornwell rest on this technique.

The participant form of observation is a particular means of listening to and observing people in which shared experience should enhance access to research material as well as its interpretation, providing, literally, inside knowledge. Both Evans and Porteous show how participation in local life was an influence on the research process. Various of our contributors have emphasized and illustrated the demands of qualitative research. An empathetic understanding of the people concerned is important and this may be conveyed as commitment to a cause of theirs, as in Porteous's study of a community being 'erased'. Establishing empathy may come easily living in and being part, of a community but is more difficult if there are evident cultural, class or gender barriers.

The solution may be unexpected: Donovan found her Jewishness and the shared experience of racism helpful in establishing empathetic relations with blacks. The development of personal skills in communicating (conversation and especially listening), along with verbal improvision, quick thinking and especially knowing when to turn off the tape recorder are essential in informal survey work. So is awareness of self-presentation, including how to dress in a manner which respondents will find acceptable. More generally, Susan Smith stresses the importance of 'an understanding of the active role of the analyst's self which is exercised throughout the research process'. Mel Evans suggests that 'the success of participant observation does not primarily depend on the casual adoption of one set of rules against another but upon a profound level of introspection on the part of the researcher.' The supreme challenge is to step back from the inevitable personal involvement, so as to see more than does the mere participant. Qualitative research raises ethical issues which may not be so starkly revealed in other approaches. Mel Evans's considered use of a hidden tape recorder for covert observation is a case in point.

The identity of respondents and even of the location

of a study may have to be concealed, as in Cornwell's work, if only to prevent the embarrassment of people finding their frankly expressed views in print in an attributable manner. However, Cornwell did feel impelled to show her work to those who participated in the study. So did Porteous, as part of a research strategy designed to elicit their reaction; this was largely unsuccessful but he also felt he owed it to them, for 'one of the ethical imperatives of qualitative social research is the need to give one's informants the right to comment upon and criticize one's interpretations.' The rigours of qualitative research are stressed and demonstrated by a number of our writers.

Geographers steeped in the practice of numerical measurement and statistical hypothesis testing in the positivist tradition are sometimes tempted to dismiss qualitative work as little more than journalism, which fails to conform to conventional standards of scientific practice, or what Mel Evans terms 'the rigour of an imported logic'. But the rigour of good qualitative research has been convincingly set out by Mitchell in an exposition of the case-study approach which has influenced a number of contributors, including Susan Smith who claims with ample justification that 'the logical consistency required to validate case analyses is just as scrupulous as the demands of statistical inference and experimental replication.'

The development of theory is also different from, but no less rigorous than, more conventional approaches. Donovan is explicit in the theoretical implications of her eclectic combination of phenomenology, ethnomethodology and ethnography, which provides 'a methodology which is sensitive and flexible, and which embraces the views and opinions of ordinary people in their own terms.' This leads to 'grounded' theory, generated by a grounding in the data collected instead of arising from a *priori* constructs, and refined in the ongoing interaction of data and theory, in what Eyles in the first chapter describes a theory-informed case-studies. But we should not expect too much grand theory, as David Evans suggests in his exploration of structuration as the basis for a case study. At this stage plausible accounts, the validation of which is internal to the discourse of the perspective adopted (to use Eyles' phrase), would itself be quite an achievement. Wider questions of validity involving choice between macro-theories or competing '-isms' (or '-ations') may be more moral than scientific.

Like all scientific endeavour, the aim of interpretative geography is to understand and explain the nature of reality. But it recognizes that investigation of the social world does not construct the real world anew. In other words, order cannot simply be imposed on the world through the use of scientific methods and constructs because an 'order' already exists.

As Schwartz and Jacobs graphically put it, we are in the reality reconstruction business: the tortuous business of learning to see the world of individuals or groups as they see it. The existence and relevance of the orderings and knowledge of such individuals and groups are accepted and used as the bases of examining the social world. Interpretative geography therefore accords central importance to such definitions and perceptions and how these relate to behaviour.The task of research is, therefore, to uncover the nature of the social world through an understanding of how people act in and give meaning to their own lives.

As Silverman suggests, we cannot put our commonsense knowledge of social structures on the side. Thus not only do observer and observed use the same phenomena to identify meanings but we must also place these meanings at the centre of analysis. These meanings demonstrate the inter-subjective nature of the world: that much of our experience of everyday life is shared and an investigation of this experience and world requires methods which allow the acquisition of 'insider knowledge' through interaction, observation, participation in activities and informal interviewing.

But while interpretative geography searches for and accepts the definitions and meanings of the social world as given—it reconstructs, reality by revealing the taken-for-granted assumptions of individuals and groups in space—another dimension may be identified. This dimension is still concerned with the identification of meanings but does not take for granted the everyday and the commonsensical.

Of course, few researchers end their endeavours with revealing the meanings of those they observe. They also order and interpret, often employing scientific constructs, deriving from previous work, theory, and the relations between theory and observation, so that a scientific ordering is used to give shape to the meanings derived from everyday experience.

Other researchers, however, have emphasized not the specific nature but the system of relations between words and images as sources of meaning. This approach owes much to structuralism and semiotics and is geared to the interpretation of texts in a theory-informed way because the relational nature of the system must be structured by something.

Interpretative geography is in sum concerned with the understanding and analysis of meanings in specific contexts. Its importance derives from the well-known difficulties with geography as spatial science, the critique of which is now well documented in human geography. Further, qualitative methods are not new. Such methodologies have been employed in human geography for well over ten years, particularly in humanistic geography as Ley's study of Philadelphia and Western's of Cape Town's District Six attest. Attempts have also been made to systematize method, pointing to the importance of interpretative approaches which help focus attention on the study of specific locations.

Increasingly, general theories and descriptions are being found not to apply to specific cases or places. Thus, for example, the theory of the relations between local and central states formulated largely from American experience is not so applicable to the contexts of either non-elected bodies such as British health authorities or where the local bodies have a history of vigorous independence as with the Australian states.

Suggestions to study the specific are not to demand a return to the idiography of regional geography. They put forward the desire for specific descriptions from theoretically-informed positions, a strategy differing from the grand theorizing of the conceptualizers, the wide-ranging generalizations of the quantifiers, and the abstracted descriptions of the idiographers.

An emphasis on methodological contributions thus focuses attention on the need for theory-informed descriptions of specific places to enhance our understandings and explanations of the world. Indeed in many ways, a major task which interpretative methods try to address is, how can social reality be represented or described? To the forefront of concerns have come the problems associated with geographical description.

The apparently coherent description of place by much traditional regional geography now seems shallow in that it categorizes the world into broad divisions, i.e. landforms, climate, transport, and so on, while that by locational analysts aims for the representation of the world as numerical generalizations. But the material we use to describe the world are our representations and constructions of other people's representations and constructions of what is occurring in the social world. What Geertz says of the ethnographer is as apposite for the geographer:

> what the ethnographer is in fact faced with— except when (as, of course, he must do) he is pursuing the more automatized routines of data collection—is a multiplicity of complex conceptual structures, many of them superimposed upon or knotted into one another, which are at once strange, irregular, and inexplicit, and which he must contrive somehow first to grasp and then to render... Doing ethnography is like trying to read a manuscript—foreign, faded, full of ellipses, incoherencies, suspicious emendations, and tendentious commentaries, but written not in conventionalized graphs of sound but in transient examples of shaded behaviour.

For Geertz, ethnographic description, in grasping the complexities of context and the significance of local knowledge, is thick description. But the researcher's task does not end there. It is necessary to go on to construct a system of analysis in which the aim is to draw large conclusions from small, but very densely textured facts.

This approach has much in common with induction in which generalizations are developed from information presented in case-studies using refinement, abstraction, typification and categorization. Most field researchers use analytic induction, so as to remain faithful to the data collected and avoid prior categorization of those data. Thus the 'results' at the outset of data analysis are no more than hunches to be revised and refined by repeated checking and combing through the data. The researcher must take particular notice of the data which do not fit the existing version of events.

This progressive categorization and refinement end

when the findings are consistent with the data. Theory is thus based on observations of one particular section of reality. Theory is conceived not in terms of logical deductions but relations between observed phenomena. It is also likely to be less grand than other propositions espoused as theory in geography, e.g. central place theory, laws of migration. This is because theory developed through induction and from thick description is general and contextual.

One way in which the researcher can try to get to grips with the complexity of the social world is by adopting a multiple research strategy. There are different types of such strategies. First, multiple investigators can be used. They may come from different disciplines, although this may create a problem of communication.

It is perhaps useful to have men and women researchers in a team. It is also useful to have researchers of different ethnic origin if the research is to deal with cultural and ethnic issues and perhaps of different ages too. The most noted bias—class— is extremely difficult to do anything about as virtually all researchers are, in terms of their class of destination at least, middle-class.

Secondly, there may be multiple theories. In this all possible theoretical propositions are used even if they are contradictory or inadequate. For example, if we are interested in discovering the effects which state actions had on the lives of the residents in a particular district, we should utilize the varying interpretations of the role of the state, inter alia, as an agent of consensus; as a way of resolving competing, often equivalent claims; as a vehicle operating at the behest of the ruling class; and as an institution with relative autonomy which must though reproduce the conditions for continued capital accumulation.

The researcher may then discover all the empirical

relationships that pertain, interrogate these with the possible range of interpretations, identifying the degree of fit, and select those relationships where data are theory-related. Such an approach avoids empiricism and unnecessary replication. It may, however, lend itself to theoretical eclecticism; a useful if difficult to control characteristic of much human geography.

The multiple theory strategy does not absolve the researcher from the need to assess the relative explanatory merits of the theories. In this assessment, it is necessary to divorce substantive considerations from assertions based not on the scientific but the apparent moral worthiness of a theory.

It may, however, be argued that all social theories have a moral foundation and that scientific claims to the 'truthfulness' of their foundation are specious. Research must be theory-informed (to avoid the error of empiricism) and it must search out counterfactual cases, but the power and acceptability of its theories may eventually be based on argument and moral suasion.

Finally, there can be multiple sets of data, requiring different methods. It is possible to obtain different data relating to different phases of the research process, different settings and different informants. It was indeed the early anthropologists who advocated and practised such strategies.

Malinowski, for example, noted the need for statistical coverage for the organization of the people under investigation; observation to discover the behaviour and conduct of individuals and collectivity; and ethnographic description based on conversation and interview to elicit the 'mentality' of the people. Thus, statistical surveys and quantitative analysis remain relevant for interpretative research.

Sieber shows how the quantitative dimensions obtained from survey or sociometric analysis may be useful correctives to ideas gained from conversations in field research. They can correct the notion that all aspects of a social setting are congruent; demonstrate or refute the generality of a single observation or field observations in general; and cast new light on field observations.

We should add that field research may also cast a different light on survey results. Thus, for example, the specificity of findings from such survey instruments as the Nottingham health profile and scales of health and health care satisfaction dissolves when people talk about their health and illnesses and connect them with their work, families and neighbourhoods.

Perhaps, though, it is best to conclude with Trow when he argued: 'different kinds of information about man and society are gathered most fully and economically in different ways. The problem under investigation properly dictates the methods of investigation'—a remark both apparently trivial and profound.

The possible range of qualitative and interpretative methods would, therefore, seem vast, and the interpretative geographer a methodological eclectic. 'The field researcher is a methodological pragmatist. He sees any method of inquiry as a system of strategies and operations designed—at any time—for getting answers to certain questions about events which interest him'. But the methods must be appropriate to the research problem at hand: hence, the great variety of approaches.

Further, reality is reconstructed: it is not simply there. This has, as Rock points out, implications for methodology which 'neither mirrors not mines reality, it works towards its manufacture'. Such manufacture implies emerging interpretation of a changing world which has implications for the validation of such research. For the present, however, we shall examine those methods that rely on interaction which individuals and groups to elicit meanings and actions and then those that are more explicitly interpretative through being textual or hermeneutic exercises.

Interacting and talking to people may take many forms, ranging from formal survey instruments with their multiple-choice checklists and closed questions to participant observation. There has been interesting recent work to rehabilitate the survey method. For example, Blaxter argues that it may be possible to develop survey instruments from qualitative research so that generalizations and policy implications may be investigated on the basis of representativeness.

A spirited defence comes from Marsh who attacks the schism between two different methods appropriate to either causal explanations (surveys) or meaningful explanations (participant observation). In survey research, the process of testing causal hypotheses is often an indirect matter of drawing inferences from already existing variance in populations by a rigorous method of comparison. But while the correlations are produced by the survey, the interpretations are not.

Often these are supplied by the researcher more or less systematically. Yet it seems more plausible that these interpretations should come from the data rather than outside. This has been a powerful argument for asking the people being studied to supply meanings.

A correlation from survey analysis may be elaborated by introducing intervening variables to show the possible effects between the initial variables. More and more refinement can be applied in the form of the researcher introducing more subtle interpretation through further intervening variables. When a plausible account of the actions involved is obtained, the process may stop. Marsh's solution is thus not a 'retreat' to participant observation, except when people are not capable of 'communicating the meaning of their actions validly', but extensive piloting of data collection, procedures and trial analysis of results.

It is, however, possible to suggest that the validity of meanings is context-dependent, and while people obviously know what their actions mean to themselves, they may not always be clear on what they mean to others.

To illustrate such a point we need only refer to the somewhat outmoded notion of 'latent function'. In Merton's example, were all the Hopi aware that their rain dance had the functions of ideational and social solidarity as well as of trying to make rain? Marsh's argument suggests, therefore, that we should not reject outright the survey method; rather use it in circumstances where people seem able to communicate what they are doing and what it means.

There is though a method or approach which 'lies between' the survey method and participant observation: the interview. Of course, social surveys are usually carried out by interview but there are different approaches. Moser and Kalton divide interviewing into formal and informal types.

In the former, questions are asked and the answers recorded in a standardized form. It is thus assumed that the researcher knows already that which the interview is designed to uncover. With the use of this knowledge and piloting, the researcher must ensure that the questions are phrased unambiguously and that they are not intimidating to any respondent. The question must, therefore, be understandable and the standardized answers, as found in many questionnaire schedules, must be meaningful in terms of the respondents' experiences. These answers must also be mutually exclusive and cover all possible replies. While such schedules are useful in eliciting information of a routine nature, as with the General Household Survey, they tend to force replies into particular categories which respondents may or may not have thought about. They also tend to assume an unproblematic relation between words and deeds. This relationship may be complicated by individuals wishing to emphasize their adherence to societally perceived good and minimize their commitment to what is seen as bad.

In the latter—informal interviewing—the questions asked, their sequence and wording are not worked out beforehand. In this case, the interviewer tries to tailor the wording of the questions to each particular individual and ask the questions in an order appropriate for the interviewee.

The aims are to ensure that the questions have the same meanings for all respondents and to engage in 'conversation' to set the respondent at ease. Such interviewing requires great skill on the part of the researcher who must not only be an empathetic listener but a good conversationalist, able to keep a dialogue going; and a social theorist, linking responses and meanings to a broad body of knowledge.

With informal interviewing, it is not assumed that appropriate question phrasing and style of answer are known in advance. These emerge as the interview progresses in the process of interaction between researcher and respondent. Such research is also referred to as depth interviewing and is portrayed in this volume by Porteus, Donovan and Cornwell. In it, the researcher must become sensitive to which questions are relevant and meaningful.

The researcher does not, however, approach the task without any framework. There is usually a checklist of topics to be covered by all respondents. In this sense, it is wrong to call such interviewing nondirective. The researcher must, if need be, encourage talk along certain avenues.

Non-directive interviews are more the preserve of psychoanalysis than social research. Nor should such interviewing, be called unstructured because, as Hammersley and Atkinson point in their discussion of 'ethnographic interviewing', all interviews, like any social interaction, are structured by both researcher and informant.

Such interaction takes the form of a conversation and this allows the researcher 'to probe deeply, to uncover new clues, to open up new dimensions of a problem and to secure vivid, accurate, inclusive accounts from informants based on personal experience'. Informal interviews allow the recording of everyday life. They allow people to describe and talk about their own lives in their own words.

In introducing his talks with West Indians in Britain, Cottle argues that 'without allowing people to speak freely we will never know what their real intentions are, and what the true meaning of their words might be.' People may still not tell the researcher the 'real' and 'true' as they 'really' see it. Even if the researcher and respondent gain mutual respect and recognition, it may still be thought that it is the researcher who is talking, who is in control, who is intrusive.

Another approach which also raises these issues is participant observation, which is illustrated in this book by Mel Evans and Susan Smith. 'The participant observer gathers data by participating in the daily life of the group or organisation he studies. He watches the people he is studying to see what situations they ordinarily meet and how they behave in them. He enters into conversation with some or all of the participants in these situations and discovers their interpretations of the events he has discovered'. There are, however, a variety of ways in which a researcher may engage in participant obser-vation.

Four ideal types have been identified, ranging from complete participant in which the observation role is concealed; participant-as-observer, in which the relationship between the researcher and others is defined by the research; observer—as participant, in which the distinctiveness of the researcher's role is made clear from the outset; and complete observer, in which there is no contact between researcher and researched. Most participant observation falls into the middle two categories, the separation of which in practice may be difficult.

In fact, Gans suggests three: total participant, researcher-participant, total researcher. He goes on to say that he was almost always the researcher-participant involved in research, but not the participation: 'I played the required participant role, but psychologically I was outside the situation, deliberately uninvolved in order to be able to study what was happening'. In his study of Levittown, he found it sometimes difficult not to become involved in political affairs in conversation with neighbours.

The participant-observer has to be both inside and outside the group, institution or community under investigation; and must be immersed but remain a critical commentator able to see a complete pattern or process with daily or routine interactions and events. This relation between involvement and detachment is a determining factor in the nature of the research produced by participant observers. It is possible though doubtful that a forceful researcher may alter the situation being studied.

Total immersion may lead to the researcher ceasing to research, while many pieces of such research usually have appended what Schwartz and Jacobs cruelly call a methodological confession which may throw doubt on the reported findings. But participant observation can bring a neighbourhood studied by survey analysis to life.

It provides an insider's account with an outsider's detachment. In concentrating on a small place or a few individuals or households, participant observation is a case-study approach, allowing theoretical generalizations to emerge from its detailed investigation of a selected dimension of reality. The case study shows well some of the main features of the qualitative approach, namely that typicality and representativeness are unimportant and that the validity of interpretation depends on 'the cogency of the theoretical reasoning'.

In many cases of depth interviewing or participant observation, other data are sought, analysed and interpreted. Documentary evidence, to build up a picture of the relevant past, or to obtain statements, views and meanings unobtainable through interaction, illustrated in our book by Porteous with planning documents, and David Evans with community newspapers, may also be used, although they do present particular problems concerning their authenticity, availability, selectivity and meaning. One particular type of document is the life history which is the account of a life, completed or ongoing, the use of which can present an individual's evaluations of experiences and give the context of experience. Thus far, its main use in human geography has been in an autobiographical way as part of self-reflection to pose the values on which life and work are based.

The use of documentary evidence points also to the more explicitly interpretative approaches and the examination of 'texts'. While appearing to have much in common with hermeneutics, particularly as originally conceived as the interpretation and clarification of meaning through the philological analysis of texts, these approaches share elements of the structurallist perspective.

Indeed, the approaches of Rose and Pickles in this volume have strong links with the hermeneutic and phenomenological traditions, while those of Burgess and Wood and Tomaselli are more closely related to structuralism and semiotics. There is of course a relation between rather than separation of phenomenology and hermeneutics and structuralism. This relation may lead to phenomenology being regarded as the context of method (philosophy as method) rather than a method per se (method as technique).

If we turn to the structuralist-semiotic dimension, it must be noted that structuralists construct the human subject in a particular way within an interrelated system of signs and significations. These signs are dependent for their meanings on their place within an articulated system; they are not arbitrary but possess no outside origin or unity; and they bring together a concept and image.

But although the system of signs is relational, the relations between signs and between signs and meanings are not fixed. Recent research has concentrated, on how meanings are fixed and articulated: 'language is the domain of articulations and meaning is above all a cutting-out of shapes. It follows that the future task of semiology is far less to establish lexicons of objects than to rediscover the articulations which men impose on reality'.

This rediscovery has been based on different 'texts'. Indeed, the 'text' may be seen in dramaturgical terms. Language itself—conversation or descriptions—can be examined, but for the meanings of places to individuals and groups it may be that paintings and plans, film, advertising and television are as appropriate.

All such interpretations of meaning, however, are based on internal analyses of the 'text'. Such analysis seeks to establish and deconstruct the realities the text itself sets out. The subjects derived from such an analysis are not arbitrary or commonsensical but are determined by the text itself.

Validation and beyond

With their emphases on meaning, it is trite to say that qualitative and interpretative approaches differ from those of natural science and 'scientific' geography. This implies that the criteria of validation are also somewhat different. Interpretative geography does not stand outside its subject-matter: it is part of the investigation and of the discourse itself. This may be clearly seen with the textual interpretative analyses.

Principles of validation are internal to the discourse itself. Hirst suggests that the criteria of appropriateness and adequacy are specific to the objectives of the discourse and practice. Interpretations must be justified in terms of the presented evidence, so much depends on the coherence of argument and the reason, consistency and honesty of the theorist. The theorist, whatever his or her approach, must therefore reflect on the nature of his or her research, interpretations and role.

Questions of validation may thus involve ethical questions about researcher role and the purpose of the research. In any event, theoretical reasoning must be exposed to full and critical gaze to evaluate its relevance and cogency, examples being provided by Mel Evans with respect to ideology and David Evans to structuration.

The conventional, often taken-for-granted, view is that the gaze belongs to the community of scholars, including the researcher. This view supposes a certain distance between the interpreter and the object of interpretation, 'as a reader might engage a text, rather than in terms of a metaphor of dialogue'. Indeed, these authors suggest that dialogue is a more accurate reflection of how interpretation occurs in fieldwork.

Dialogue suggests an insider's account or description of the social world as opposed to, or as well as, the more usual outsider's one. While interesting attempts to present accounts based on dialogue are reviewed by Marcus and Fischer, little attention has yet been directed to how such descriptions may be validated.

But in qualitative approaches, the relationships between theoretical constructs and empirical observation must also be validated. As is perhaps well known, this relation is usually seen in terms of empirical indicators and theoretical concepts. Does the indicator really measure the concept it is intended to measure? While there are no unambiguous rules, three procedures are commonly discussed.

First, there is face validity in that on the face of it the indicator measures the concept. This seems similar to the idea of the plausible account developed by Carrier and Kendall in the context of welfare developments. Does the relation between concept and indicator seem plausible? In essence the appeal is to a commonsensical, consensual understanding of a relationship in which these characteristics may be based on lay or scientific commonsense or rules. In all this, it is important not to suppress the evidence that does not fit: the interpretative geographer must also search for evidence that refutes the assumed relationship between phenomena, just as statistical geographers try to avoid spurious correlations. Disconfirming evidence and the search for counterfactual arguments are important procedures in the process of validation. Comparative or cross-cultural analyses may also assist in steering clear of easy explanations.

Secondly, there is criterion validity whereby a new indicator can be compared with an existing, generally accepted one. Such a procedure would be useful in replicating research or in refining an established relation between concept and indicator.

Thirdly, there is construct validity which depends on listing whether propositions are confirmed when the new indicator is used. We might suggest that the addition of intervening variables to the assessment of a relationship is an example of a search for construct validity. Some of these claims to validity lend themselves to quantitative and qualitative research. The outlined approach to validation assumes that theory and evidence are unconnected or related in some unproblematic way. But inductive, reflexive research means that concepts and indicators are developed simultaneously. If, further, the behaviouristic assumption of standardized response to the same stimuli or events is dropped, the possibility of identifying standard indicators becomes doubtful and a search for them unnecessary.

What may emerge, however, is a typology, often in the form of a set of ideal-types of, say, actions or meanings, which represents sub-types of a more general category. Ideal-types emerge from the specific case under investigation but have a more general applicability in determining the validity of theoretical concepts. Eyles produced ideal-types of sense of place to inform on the relationship between the individual, the individual's identity and materiality, and ultimately the theory of structuration. Ideal-types and typologies allow systematic thought to be addressed to the nature of each type of category and the relations between them, although they should not be pursued 'beyond' the data or their analytic value. Part of their value, however, is that they may enable a development of alternative links to be made between theory and data. They may assist in the search for counterfactual argument or falsifying evidence to address the emerging theory.

Further, the identification of ideal-types, second-order typifications, allows the employment of Schutz's postulate of adequacy for scientific knowledge. To be valid, a second-order typification must allow the observed to understand an action as it is described by the construct. This construct must also possess logical consistency and allow subjective interpretation in that the observed's ideas must be used in the model that account for the 'facts' observed: a possible means of validating insider accounts as well. These ideas are taken further and exemplified in a study of health and health care by Eyles and Donovan.

It is also possible to analyse data using multiple theories, with multiple strategy becoming a basis of validation. Bensman and Vidich approached their study of Springdale by utilizing many different perspectives, each yielding different orders of data. This multiple theoretical strategy, called theoretical triangulation by Denzin, is but one basis of this form of validation.

All are predicated on the notion of triangulation which itself derives from an analogy with surveying. It is possible to use different research workers on the same problem or data from different sources, e.g. respondents, phases in the fieldwork, social contexts and times.

Inferences from one set of data can be checked against those from others. But data from different sources do not necessarily provide a more complete picture. As Lever notes, it is not a matter of checking whether inferences are valid but of finding out which ones are. It should also be noted that differences between data-sets may be just as illuminating as similarities.

Further, many of the qualitative approaches have developed their own specific criteria of validity. All rely on the significance of the 'insider account', whether theoretical or lay. But just as we have not reviewed all the technical problems connected with how to do qualitative research—e.g. gaining access, listening and asking questions, note-taking and recording data, using documents and analysis and evaluation—because good texts already exist, we do not intend to rehearse these criteria separately because again, good sources are easily found.

2
Geography of Life

For many geographers, the failure of phenomenologists to produce rigorous empirical phenomenologies casts a dark shadow over the whole enterprise, and other qualitative research approaches are to be sought. Among those geographers who still find the phenomenological project of interest, many have begun to argue that we need practical examples of phenomenological geography carried out in concrete situations.

In part the slow development of sound exemplars of phenomenological method is a product of the difficulty involved in understanding the complex and varied claims made about it, and in part the difficulty of the method itself. But there is another reason why we have seen-only limited application of the phenomenological method in the discipline: this has to do with what we normally think 'method' entails, and what 'the phenomenological method' actually is.

Despite the apparently limited success of phenomenological approaches, phenomenological terminology and much of the spirit of its early advocates have found acceptance and continue to exert a strong influence on a discipline which now takes the life-world and the taken-for-granted world as important areas of study, and qualitative or interpretative methods as serious alternatives to naturalistic methods. Such claims alone suggest that something important is embedded here. But what could it be? Previous attempts to give an account of the phenomenological method have encountered severe difficulties. Central among them is the need to use language which presupposes the phenomenological project, but which is either uncommon or now means something very different in everyday language. Thus, in commenting on *Phenomenology, Science and Geography,* Johnston complained that some of the words used—apodictic, factical, incompossible—were neither in his personal vocabulary nor his dictionary. This points to a basic requirement for the student of phenomenology. These words are in the *Oxford English Dictionary,* and the reader of phenomenological works must be prepared to keep a vocabulary list of such words.

Partly this is a necessary condition of beginning any new scholarly endeavour. Partly it is because in the phenomenological project, in trying to overcome the traditional metaphysics of subjectivism and objectivism, everyday language use often is not appropriate. Translators of phenomenological works have been forced to use terminology which is exact, but which does not evoke this traditional metaphysics. This attempt at careful language use has not been entirely successful, and this points to the second requirement for the student.

Words such as 'universal', 'essential', 'subjectivity', 'objectivity', have particular meanings in current everyday parlance, but these are not what they originally meant, nor what phenomenologists mean by them. This problem is concatenated on the one hand by geographers' seeming reluctance to adopt philosophical language, and on the other hand, by their persistence in dealing with philosophical issues regardless. For our present purposes it is important to bear in mind that: (a) it is necessary to use language carefully and exactly when we are trying to avoid the many philosophical pitfalls that have confounded previous attempts to understand the human sciences; (b) this careful use may well have resulted from careful consideration of alternatives, and not from the wholesale adoption of jargon; and (c) the meaning of a term should as far as possible be taken from the text and the tradition to which that text points, and not from a cursory reading of secondary literature or the imposition of other meaning.

Before we begin discussing the phenomenological method let us think about 'methods' as we normally understand them. The *Oxford English Dictionary* defines method as a mode of investigation, a procedure for attaining an object, or a special form of procedure or set of rules and practices adopted in any branch of mental activity or in pursuance of a particular goal. More specifically 'method' refers to certain specific procedures in mathematics and the experimental sciences, such as least squares, experimental method or the deductive method.

When turning to a book on qualitative methods one might assume that methods are procedures or rules which, like tools, permit us to construct an account of the way some aspect of the world is. Modern social science often views method in this way, as a series of approaches or techniques, each of which fulfils its function in permitting the researcher to construct another piece of a broader project: an account (or a geography) of intra-urban mobility, an analysis of capital flows in the city, an explanation of settlement patterns in Pennsylvania.

Interview and questionnaire schedules, participant observation, archival research, multi-dimensional scaling, correlation and regression techniques; these and others are often seen to be the methods of social science. Thus, when we turn to 'the phenomenological method' we might at first assume it to be of a, similar character. Indeed, most of the literature in geography which makes reference to the phenomenological method treats it in this way; it is applied to methods which are descriptive and interpretative, and which are therefore assumed to be qualitative.

In evaluating claims about phenomenology, geographers have consistently demanded examples of the use of the method as if it were like all these other methods. Calls for doing phenomenology have been calls to put the method into practice in investigating some empirical problem or other. But this view of method is too narrow for our present purposes: method here will not be a tool or a technique, but will involve a philosophy, an approach to inquiry, and only then specific procedures for the actual conduct of research in a particular science such as geography. Nor will the phenomenological method tell us very much about the kind of techniques we need to use in empirical research, for the very reason that phenomenology does not deal with empirical research as such, but with the essential or invariant structures which found the objectifications of empirical categories.

In making such a strong claim, the aim is not to dissuade students and researchers from pursuing phenomenological research'. It is to say that, while there may be no straightforward technique to be picked up, the adoption of the method (as we shall come to understand that term henceforth) will be much more productive than any single technique could be. In this sense the 'phenomenological method' is not, nor can it be made into, a method (i.e. a technique) like many others in this book. In large part this is because the phenomenological method, unlike other qualitative methods in this book, does not address empirical issues.

Phenomenology indeed tells us how we should go about 'doing' things, but in regional ontologies not in empirical (or positive) science. Thus, calls from geographers for phenomenologists to demonstrate the efficacy of their approach through practical and concrete examples completely miss the point. In this sense the phenomenological method is much closer to what we might call 'ontology of science) than it is to what we call 'empirical research'. Having said this, it is none the less the case that working through the phenomenological method will radically transform both the questions of empirical inquiry and approaches to them.

Phenomenology is at once a philosophy and a rigorous science, and thus its scientific character is very different from that of the sciences of nature, life, mind and society. Primarily it is method of philosophy whose aim is to clarify a *priori* and ungrounded assumptions in order to permit phenomena (including things, concepts experiences) to be shown as they show themselves, and to do so in a way which does not show them in any other way than the way in which they show themselves.

Phenomenology thus turns away from the objects themselves and to the way in which the objects are given to their *objectness.;* to their being as phenomena, i.e. objects of experience. With this apparently confusing beginning, phenomenology establishes four important principles often ignored by the social sciences: first, that the objects of science cannot be specifie *priori;* second, that all knowing is intentional; third, that the task of science is the precise and accurate description and account of the phenomena we encounter in the world; and fourth, that the task of phenomenology is methodically to permit this, and to avoid the distorting influence of a *priori* and unclarified assumptions.

Much effort has been expended to apply phenomenological principles to the empirical study of society, but we must be careful with such applications.

First and foremost phenomenology is, as Heidegger says, the method of ontology; it seeks to be rigorous and scientific in the sense that it does not want to take its basic concepts for granted.

When phenomenologists provocatively call for a return to the things themselves it is a call to arrive at the primary presuppositions, beyond which we cannot go and which do not need to be clarified because they are immediately evident (i.e. apodictic) in direct intuition. Phenomenology is thus an attempt to construct a science of 'ultimate' (not 'unchanging' or 'absolute') grounds: that is, a science based on rationally derived grounds. Such a study of primary presuppositions is different from the other sciences. It is not concerned with things, which in everyday life (or the natural attitude) are given to us as unquestionably obvious, nor does it take these things as given.

Phenomenology is concerned with the way in which objects are constituted; that is, with the conditions or horizon of meaning within which objects have the meaning that they have for us (be we concerned with physical things or non-physical objects such as consciousness, society, place or power). To understand what this means and what implications it holds for our discussion of the phenomenological method, it will be necessary to make a distinction between the natural attitude and the philosophical attitude.

The first step in the phenomenological method involves the 'bracketing' of the 'natural attitude': 'that is, suspending the naively held belief that mundane objects exist in themselves in such a way as to be strictly transcendent to our consciousness of them'. Husserl makes a clear-cut distinction between the natural and the philosophical attitudes. Much confusion exists as to the nature of this distinction, and the failure to recognize it has greatly influenced the way in which geographers have viewed the phenomenological method and its possible applications in geography.

Kockelmans has described the natural attitude in the following way:

> in the natural attitude one tacitly assumes that we are in a world through *which* our mind can roam at will and in which we can consider any part we want, without changing the objective nature of what we consider. According to this view, the object-pole of our knowing is an objectively existing, fully explainable world that can be expressed in exact, objective laws. This 'objective' world exists wholly in itself and possesses a rationality that can be fully understood.

Philosophy begins from a different position since it cannot begin as the positive sciences do, naively taking the pre-given world of experience for granted. The philosophical attitude requires that we must return to the original experience in a special way. It is this turn from the natural attitude to the philosophical attitude which is at the root of the phenomenological method, and which, because it is overlooked by geographers, causes so many problems in understanding the phenomenological method.

In part, the phenomenological method is this turning to experience not as naively and uncritically given, but as the object of reflection. This is the eidetic reduction (which takes us from the world of facts to the world of ideas), and is what is sometimes called the procedure of 'bracketing': the reduction of the relativities of the cultural world to the invariant or universal structures of the life-world. A second reduction (actually a set of reductions)—the phenomenological reductions—take us from the world of facts to meaning. In this way the phenomenological method is a problematizing of the everyday, taken-for-granted world. Instead of dealing with the world at the level of facts, phenomenology seeks to deal with the constitution of those facts from and in the pre-scientific life-world. Phenomenology operates at several 'levels'. For its founder (Husserl) it was to be a philosophical method.

The need for a philosophical (phenomenological) foundation for empirical science arose because of the way in which empiricism reduced the world to natural and biological phenomena, and the way in which it forgot that its objects were not real objects naively given to immediate perception, but had been constituted through long processes of abstraction and idealization. At this level, phenomenology is the science of regional ontology, which clarifies how the objects of the sciences are constituted; for example, with what space, time, distance and place mean for each domain of the sciences.

The regional ontologies thus seek to establish the essential structures of meaning from which each domain of the sciences constitutes its particular view of the world. Such 'essences', it should be noted, are not transhistorical or immutable, but are transformed in the on-going project of scientific inquiry and the changing structure of everyday life. But, it must also be stated that this transformation is itself a bounded one; bounded by the nature of the phenomena taken as objects for each of the sciences. Phenomenology is thus also concerned with the processes by which the sciences transform experiences of the life-world into scientific claims: with the processes of distanciation, thematization, idealization, objectification, abstraction, formalization and possibly quantification, by which science constitutes its objects.

Since the everyday world is itself not an object of immediate perception but is also constituted, it too has to be investigated as to its constitution. Here phenomenology is both thick description of the structures of signification which constitute the life-world and an ontological analysis of the constitution of those significations. It is at this level that social scientists have focused most of their attention, and at this level that phenomenology comes closest to ethnography, interpretative sociology, or to the qualitative methods with which this book is concerned. However, this level only makes sense as an inquiry into the constitution of the life-world when situated in the context of the other three levels. Only then is phenomenology a critical enterprise in which life-world descriptions are developed along with the explicit analysis of the constitutive processes adopted by the geographer. Fact (ontic world) and horizon of meaning (ontological world) are thus joint poles of the phenomenological project.

Philosophy, science and everyday worlds are tied together by the investigation of the constitution of objects or objectifications. Because phenomenology seeks to clarify the limits of such objectifications—i.e. to clarify the way in which the world is given to these domains of experience—it is inherently critical.

The issue of phenomena and masked-phenomena

The humanist sees in the individual's striving to make sense of the world the foundation for a phenomenological geography of experience: a world of cognitive maps and developing complexity of representation; a world of social contracts which form a web of social interactions; a system of signs and symbols whose meaning constitutes the lived world of the individual. These and other claims found the humanist's belief in the integrity of individual perception and understanding, and the importance for geography to begin with this subject as the building base for any humane geography. Few would argue with the intent behind such claims: the need for science to incorporate the dignity of human beings; the meaningful nature of human action; the symbolic structure of cultural life. This fabric of daily existence fills out a human geography and avoids the bleached bones of many analytical approaches to human behaviour.

Since Freud pointed to the unconscious as a crucial element in the explanation of certain behaviour, the issue of masked or hidden phenomena is one with which any phenomenology must deal from the beginning. Its corollary in the social realm is found in Marx's claim about the relationship between bourgeois culture and its economic foundation. In geography its current form is clearest in the relationship between structure and agency, and studies dealing with ideology, power and culture.

The game

Phenomenology claims for itself the role of philosophy of science. What could this mean, and how can it be so? To answer this question, and to clarify the nature of the phenomenologist's interest, let me discuss the issue in terms of the nature of a game. A game, say a game of soccer, can be 'experienced' in several important ways. First, of course, is the experience of the players in the game. Here immersion in the game is a prerequisite for effective play: only the players who 'give themselves over to the game' can play effectively and well. Here the players immerse themselves in the act of playing, and, much like the conditions of social life, the rules under which they play are present to them only as limits on what constitutes playing and not playing the game.

The fully immersed player does not necessarily recognize these rules in the act of playing, but instead may feel that the play of the game is governing his actions. There is a necessary tension between the play of the game carrying the actions of the player and the player controlling the outcomes of parts of the game. Both are necessary for the game to succeed as a game. The player who is unable to concentrate on the game in this way (who is unable to immerse himself in the playing) may find that the attempt to move a spherical object from one end of a field to another, and to shoot it through three pieces of wood, is a less than meaningful activity. Such a player does not submit to the rules and we say he is 'no longer playing the game'.

There are other participants in the game besides the players. The referee in a sense is playing a different game since he is interested in the limits of permissible play; that is, he is interested in the intersection between the game being played and the rules within which it is played. The spectators are also participants in the game, and they like the players must immerse themselves in the game and its rules. To step out of that context is suddenly to find the game to be a rather odd activity.

Several perspectives on the soccer game are independent of participation in it. The investor who has an interest in the success of the club may see the game as a means of financial security or loss. The sociologist who studies the game may see it as an outlet for pent-up aggression, a diversion from unpleasant conditions of work or home, a means of entrenching class interests through the generation of profit and the absorption of surplus on the one hand, and the creation of a large, interest group supporting the perpetuation of existing economic relations, on the other hand. These and other perspectives may be valid claims about the game of soccer. In each the 'object' is 'soccer', but each claim takes that object to mean something different depending upon the framework or horizon within which the claim is situated.

In each the object of discourse is constituted differently, and the relations within which it is analysed are also different: for the players these relations are those of each player to all the others and to the rules; for the referee they are the relations of players to the game (that is to a set of rules); for the spectator's they are the relations of the players and/or the teams to the game (that is, the rules and the symbolic function that each team plays); for the sociologist the relations are those of the game to broader issues of economy or society. In each of these the objects so constituted may or may not be constituted accurately in terms of the phenomena themselves, but where they are so constituted each of the claims about the game may be valid claims.

We have a set of objects (soccer in each of the different frameworks of analysis) which take their meaning from the horizons within which they are situated. All social science is of this type. The phenomenologist aims to refocus attention on the rules and the horizons within which each social experience is given to us. The horizon of the players is only one, albeit important, possible horizon. We have many possible perspectives on society. But are we to accept each of them as equals in the attempt at explanation? This depends to some extent on our purpose. If we want to understand individual and group action then each of the contexts sketched briefly above (and many possible others) describes the elements of such an understanding, and the way actors in each setting understand their actions.

What is missing from each of the descriptions is an analysis of constitution, both conceptually and historically. When we turn to such a constitutive enterprise we immediately recognize that experience itself is constituted through its historical formation. As such actions may arise from, and maintain in place, social structures and relationships, which are unintended consequences of those actions. Description is thus inadequate where the horizons of meaning have been limited to the intended and examined consequences of 'playing'. These actions may only be intelligible in the context of their origins and unintended consequences. Thus, to refuse to extend ethnographic description to its broader critical base seems to have little justification given science's prior claim to be critical and rational.

The logical tension of phenomenology's claims to describe the phenomena as they show themselves is then that some phenomena show themselves as symptoms of underlying causes, or as phenomena which appear as one thing but really are something else. Phenomenology must be able to deal with such masked phenomena. It cannot restrict itself merely to the immediate experience and its context of meaning. This second task is for Geertz 'specification' or 'diagnosis': stating what the knowledge social actors have of their actions demonstrates about the society in which it is found and, beyond that, about social life as such.'

> Our double task is to uncover the conceptual structures that inform our subjects' acts, the 'said' of social discourse, and to construct a system of analysis in whose terms what is generic to those structures, what belongs to them because they are what they are, will stand out against the other determinants of human behaviour.

The phenomenological method and geography

Phenomenology has been greatly misunderstood within geography as to its essential premises and one of its major aims. Phenomenology is not concerned only with naively given experience, neither is it anti-scientific nor a criticism of science. Indeed, one of the major aims of phenomenology is to provide a rational foundation for the sciences as well as for life more generally. It would be a mistake to reject phenomenology at this stage because it is inappropriate to spatial analysis, cultural geography, participant observation methodologies or critical geographies. Because it is about the ontological, and not -

unlike these areas of inquiry themselves—about the ontical, it will have much to say about each.

Phenomenology, science and life-world

When Eddington raised the question of how we are to understand the fact that the scientist always deals with two tables: the table of atoms and empty space, and the solid table at which he eats or writes, he pointed to an important problem for all the positive (i.e. positing) sciences, be they theoretical or empirical.

As scientists pursue their inquiries, the objects of their scientific research become increasingly removed from the same objects in the everyday world. This occurs to such an extent that Eddington is forced to ask whether the two tables have any relationship to each other. The objectifying tendencies of modern science should neither surprise nor horrify us. Empirical science operates as a positive, that is to say positing, science by setting up (or positing) a framework of meaning within which the world is seen in a particular way; as physical, biological or cultural, for example.

In so positing a framework of meaning and its corresponding objects (or objectifications) the community of physicists, biologists, anthropologists, is able to penetrate and explain the abstract relationships between phenomena. These sciences of phenomena are sciences of facts, and to establish their claims they need special languages, methods and procedures. That is, for the most part, what this book on qualitative methods seeks to achieve for aspects of geographic research.

The actual procedures of any positive science thus involve methodological procedures for distancing the observer from the observed (distanciation)—and this is equally true, albeit differently so, for participant observation methods and other forms of social analysis.

In order to deal with this issue, Geertz has suggested the use of Heinz Kohut's concepts of 'experience-near' and 'experience-distant' to capture the difference between the actor's frame of reference and the frame of reference established by the scientist. These involve agreed-upon principles and methods, in terms of which the world of everyday experience is constituted as a 'world' of objects for quantum physics, evolutionary biology or descriptive ethnography. These procedures include idealization and thematization, abstraction and objectification, and in certain cases they may include formalization, functionalization and mathematization. Each procedure entails, to a greater or lesser extent, the distancing of the observer from the observed, or, to be more accurate, each entails the researcher standing back from lived involvement and treating the world as a set of objects (but not necessarily things) of theoretical reflection.

Consequently positive science is necessarily forgetful of its origins, or what Whitehead called the 'fallacy of misplaced concreteness', where science forgets that its concepts are abstractions and not concrete objects. In being forgetful of their origins in this manner the sciences lose touch with (a) their own processes of abstraction and concept formation, i.e. with the way in which they constitute their objects of study; and (b) the origins of their abstractions in the everyday world of experience (the life-world). The project of phenomenology—as a philosophy, a science and a method—is to clarify the way in which objects are constituted in the sciences, the arts and everyday life, and to show how these objects relate to the pre-given life-world.

In regard to the mathematical and natural sciences, phenomenology may thus function to provide their rational ground by dealing with the constitution of objects and their relation to the everyday world. In spatial analysis the regional ontology of space, time, place, distance,... can thus be clarified. In modern human geography the domains of conflict, power, production, social interaction and sense of place are to be clarified in this manner. In ethnographic geographies the task of phenomenological analysis is the clarification of the structures of signification within which action is meaningful and intelligible. In each of these cases the essential or invariant structures that constitute a particular phenomenon are sought: the essence of the phenomenon.

Defining the eidos

The notion of the eidos or essence of a phenomenon has created much confusion, and a good deal of heated debate. Much of this disagreement is founded on a misunderstanding. The eidos is nothing more than the essential structure that constitutes the being of a particular phenomenon. We can begin most easily with the geometrical figure. What do we mean when we say that we see a circle'? What is it that we see? On the blackboard we see a diagram of a circle, but we know this to be a mere device for aiding our discussion. When draw a landscape of glacial deposition on the blackboard we do not presume the sketch to be the landscape.

Similarly, the sketch of the circle is not what we mean when we refer to a circle. The eidos of a circle is thus necessary for each blackboard sketch to be intelligible as a circle, but the sketches themselves are insufficient to capture the eidos of 'circlehood'. Even given a blackboard full of circles we could not inductively derive the essence of circle, for we might just as select the *aspect* of white, of unevenness, of something drawn, of shape when viewed from the side. We need some understanding of the eidos of circle—in this case an axiomatic understanding of a geometrical principle—a figure whose sides are all equidistant from its centre.

(This, incidentally, explains the problem with those aspects of geography which assume that method is learned by doing independently of clearly specified principles about what constitutes the essential characteristics of the objects under study and the methods of dealing with them.

Without such principles the novice has a wide range of possibilities from which to derive the 'essential' characteristics of the enterprise; a factor that very often leads to intense frustration on the part of graduate students as they are apprenticed into an approach, rather than educated about it.) Such a notion of essence does not invoke any absolute (sometimes called Platonic) essence, although in this example the mathematical, is transhistorical in the sense that it is invariant over time and space. Such a geometric figure is by definition invariant only within a particular framework of meaning: that of Euclidean two-dimensional geometry.

In the case of social phenomena their essence is not transhistorical, and it is for this reason that we need an interpretative phenomenology. Phenomenology depends upon this notion of eidos, and it is to be applied to all phenomena if they are to be rationally grounded in a science of objectifications and in a life-world of original experience. Such an eidetic knowledge permits us to distinguish the essential and the accidental in empirical relationships, and thus influences the practice of research in the natural attitude.

Above all, such eidetic knowledge raises serious questions about the amount of time and effort that positive social science is spending analysing relationships and testing hypotheses about phenomena which are and can only be related accidentally, not eidetically. To put this another way, meaningful empirical research requires a foundation in ontology, or a preliminary understanding of the essential characteristics of the phenomena with which it deals. Perhaps we need an example to clarify some of these claims. Social scientists and geographers among them, have suggested that human behaviour in complex urban environments involves spatial search strategies by which route selection occurs and habituated travel paths are established. Such search strategies are often linked to other forms of spatial searching, such as finding an object in a complex array, or to the performance of animals in maze experiments.

The links are obvious ones, and have been useful heuristics by which we conceptualize behaviour in space. But is such conceptual linkage phenomenologically valid? If we envisage human behaviour as if it were adapted maze behaviour, or some other stimulus-response relationship, won't we in fact find such a relation? What would we find if we began with several fundamental, but different principles? For example:

1 Human action is intentional, and is thus always to be conceived in terms of its correlate - its object, or in some cases its objective.
2 The intentional structure of experience is not unidimensional or simple. It is layered and complex, composed of multiple intentionalities, where switching between objectives is the norm, not the exception.
3 Human experience is ambiguous in two senses: first, in that the objectives of action may be only partly defined, or they may be satisfied when only partly achieved; second, these objectives are situated in the context of human learning and may thus be transformed in the process of their being consummated.

To begin with principles such as these is not to deny the possibility of operationalizing and formalizing relationships in science. The issue is prior to such formal processes, and indeed the point of the example above is that its thematization and formalization is possible, but would lead to very different conceptual and theoretical accounts of spatial behaviour than those with which we currently work. What would happen, for example, if we added a fourth principle?

All human action is social in nature, and social action by its very nature produces and reproduces contexts with intended and unintended consequences. Or a fifth: human action occurs within a context of socially produced meanings, which in turn renews and reproduces those meaning structures.

Phenomenology and the thematization of scientific knowledge

Phenomenology operates in a different domain from the natural attitude to which the positive sciences are confined. The difference between phenomenology and positive science is hinted at here in the introduction of the qualifier 'positive' science. This is not the philosophical position known as 'positivism', but describes the essential characteristic of modern science: that it is a positing science.

Modern science posits a framework of meaning within which the world is given as a set of relations which can be thematized and formalized. This positing process occurs as a domain of phenomena is taken as an object for a particular science. The positing of the framework of meaning involves the thematization of the everyday world a particular world for scientific investigation, and this entails the objectification of that world, i.e. it involves procedures by which the world is taken as the object domain of a particular science.

Thematization and objectification constitute the first levels of the abstractive reduction, where the everyday world is reduced and abstracted from. The result is a series of idealizations—the state, the economy, the market, exchange value, profit-maximization—each of which has a correlate in everyday experience, but each of which is transformed into an analytical and formal context. This is the process of formalization, and it results in the problematization of the everyday, taken-for-granted world.

Degrees of formalization are possible, one such being the formalization which results in establishing relationships which can be expressed as functional relations (functionalization) or in mathematical terms (mathematization). While phenomenology indeed uncovers these procedures of-science, rather than rejects them, it is vital that we recognize the attendant claim that phenomenology always makes: that we must deal with the phenomena as they show themselves to be. It is precisely at this juncture that the debate between quantitative and qualitative approaches to science has arisen.

The debate is misspecified if it is seen to be a denial of the validity of quantitative methods. The question is, instead, which levels of formalization are appropriate to the phenomena of human action and behaviour. The choice is not an arbitrary or conventional one, but is conditioned by the phenomena of human behaviour as such. Nor is the decision between the two a fixed solution to the question: one could readily envisage a situation (and time) where social relations were of such a kind that simple or complex mathematics described accurately those relations.

Furthermore, we must not forget that the choice of methods, and hence the type of solution to this question, is in part a function of the interests which underpin research, and here we may also readily envisage a situation where quantitative methods served certain interests better than qualitative methods. But in both these cases - where social systems take on the character of linear mathematics, or where science is characterized by the interests that underpin it, nothing is said about the fundamental relation of science to the phenomena it studies. It is this about which phenomenology has something to say.

The claim that phenomenology provides a rational foundation and an overcoming of distorted views of phenomena has received much criticism in the literature of the social sciences, and particularly in geography. It is argued that such a project is 'foundational' in nature, by which is meant that it is an attempt to establish solid grounds where we now know none to be possible. In claiming to achieve something like a 'return to things themselves' (that is, a turning back to the consideration of the phenomena as they present themselves—the turn to the philosophical attitude) it is argued that this is an 'essentialist' claim which ignores the social and linguistic construction of reality in favour of something like direct access to phenomena. But both arguments misunderstand the claim to deal with phenomena.

Indeed, both arguments show just how far we have gone down the road to irrationalism in science (where the dominance of the fact prevents us from turning to the grounds from which the fact is derived) - a path Husserl warned against taking, and which underpinned his attempt to develop phenomenology in the first place. (It is difficult to understand how scientists can deny that the project of science deals with the way the world is known by man, that science seeks to comprehend these phenomena without distortion, and that the truth of a scientific claim is founded upon the actual state of affairs. It is again a characteristic of the loss of understanding that such truisms have to be restated again, and in such a way that today will probably not be universally accepted.) The misunderstanding rests on the confusion of the term 'phenomena'. Where the arguments of foundationalism and essentialism have been made, 'phenomena' have generally been confused with 'things'. In fact, phenomena refer to the way in which things and objects which are not things are given to us; the way they are constituted.

The use of the word 'phenomenon' thus implicates both object and subject, and again places at the centre of our thinking the intentional structure of knowledge and experience. Understanding 'phenomena' as the correlate of intentionality thus removes the criticisms of essentialism and foundationalism. Knowledge is socially constructed, and it is precisely this phenomenal realm of socially constructed meaning that the phenomenologist seeks to describe. This is not, however, an easy or a straightforward matter.

The one thing the phenomenologist cannot do is to accept the naive description of the world. That is, we cannot: (a) assume that appearances give us access to the phenomena, since some phenomena may be masked (social relations under capitalism), distorted (the advertising media in regard to product differentiation and effectiveness), or they may be intended to disseminate; (b) take the world for granted in the way we do in the everyday natural attitude; and (c) describe the world (phenomena) in terms of some other phenomena, to which we ascribe some similarities of appearance.

Science without an explicit phenomenological underpinning frequently makes use of analogy in the construction of its objects in precisely this way. In this view, while analogy may be a useful tool of scientific inquiry, it is a fundamentally distorting one because it is based on the assumption that phenomena can usefully be treated as if they were other phenomena: people can be treated as if they acted like animals; economic agents can be treated as if they operated as independent atoms, and so on. Such analogical models are common in science and they are productive stimuli to thinking about the world. But they are dangerous because they sacrifice the rigour of phenomenological description for a much easier, and sometimes more readily applicable model: the education of children is like the manufacture of goods; human communication is like the interconnected flows within a physical system (cybernetics); geographic migration is like the flow of water over a surface with barriers (diffusion); the shipment of goods across land and sea is like the refraction of light through two media (social physics).

For the phenomenologist each of these (possibly 'productive') analogies is distorting because it fails to investigate the phenomenon itself as it shows itself: as educative experiences; communicative action; human interaction and movement; the interaction of social, political and environmental contexts with an economic system. The importance of qualitative methods (i.e. techniques) in empirical research should be immediately apparent; participant observation, diary keeping, in-depth interviews, etc. permit the researcher to attempt to understand selected domains of experience, behaviour or action which more 'distanced' methods do not.

Investigating the phenomenon as it shows itself is, however, far from straightforward, especially where analogical thinking dominates our encounter with the world. In encountering any new phenomena, or any phenomenon with which we have long been familiar, we give an account of it in terms of the experiences we already have. This claim raises two problems. First, it suggests that science cannot help but think as people do in their everyday worlds, striving to make sense of the world through the already-known world. But is this claim true of science? At one level it is a truism that cannot be denied - we only have the known world from which to explore the unknown, and we make the unknown known through the language, concepts and categories of the known (at least initially). However, we cannot be satisfied with this claim as it stands.

Science claims to be a 'fully transparent', rational and critical enterprise. That is, in principle, all its claims are open to challenge (transparency), claims are made on the basis of accurate evidence and sound argument (rationality), and the intersection of the community of scholars and rational methods permits the commonly assumed, taken-for-granted explanations to be challenged in favour of counter-intuitive accounts of the state of affairs (science is critical). The criticism of the Ptolemaic geocentric theory of the universe by the Copernican heliocentric theory of the solar system was one such massive shift from an immediately perceptible account to a counter-intuitive account.

Similarly, when, Galileo postulated in a 'thought experiment' the free-fall and the friction-free surfaces, he introduced counter-intuitive accounts of what had previously been intuitively obvious explanations: the property of all substances to achieve their proper place. Or again, when Baran and Sweezy argue that there is a natural tendency towards crisis (stagnation) under conditions of monopoly capitalism which results from the inability of the economy, to absorb the surplus it produces, our naive impression is challenged by what at first glance appears to be counter-intuitive. It is precisely this ability to problematize the taken-for-granted experience which permits science to arrive at new and critical understanding. Second, however, the claim has a deeper truth to it, and one which Husserl, in attempting to found phenomenology as a pure science of primary presuppositions, may not have fully realized. It is with his student, Martin Heidegger, that the problem is raised and solved. Phenomenology as the return to the things (read 'phenomena') themselves is vital to rational science and philosophy. Such knowledge is, however, always hermeneutical or interpretative, because Dasein (read 'the human being') is always historical, finite and interpretative.

The seeming contradiction between these two claims: on the one hand, that phenomenology seeks rationally to ground empirical science, and on the other hand that this is an interpretative project, raises apparent problems of relativity and loss of precision. But they are only apparent, and not real problems. They remain problems only for those who cling to some absolute conception of the truth, or for those who wish to deny all truths in favour of a radical relativism. The point is that we cannot avoid the hermeneutic aspect of knowledge, but that this does not remove the necessity for, nor the possibility of, establishing rational grounds for empirical research. Descriptive phenomenology indeed has a foundational task in that it intersubjectively explains basic assumptions for doing science.

In the case of human and social sciences interpretation and critique are necessary where communities or individuals attach meaning to social actions in the historical situation in which they find themselves.

Aim

Since concrete, factual propositions belong to the special sciences, the goal as expressed in phenomenology is the... foundation and clarification of the essential structures which underlie knowledge and (known or experienced) reality. In many ways the whole issue of phenomenology has become more complicated than it need be. The most important elements of this method have been in partial use all along, and Husserl's task was partly the clarification and natural extension of generally accepted procedures.

Two basic elements are found in all discourse: reflection and essences or universals. The task of phenomenology is to analyse these thoroughly as issues which are prior to all special regions of discourse and the concrete, factual propositions of the special sciences. With these remarks we can conclude with a brief summary description and definition of phenomenology. The aim of the phenomenological method is the rigorous description of the essential structures that constitutes objects in their various modes of givenness. These modes thus include the modes of givenness of scientific objects, but also include the modes of givenness of everyday objects, objects of memory, objects of political discourse, etc. Such a method is not a method concerned with the ontical (that is, the way of things and facts), but with the ontological (that is, the way of being of things, facts, objects, experiences, etc.).

Phenomenology thus does not concern itself with the everyday (or natural) attitude, which naively accepts the givenness of the world, but with the philosophical attitude, which asks critically about the intentional structure of experience. This is not, however, a search for transhistorical essences, nor for subjective impressions of the everyday, but it is a search for invariant and universal structures (understood carefully). It is not a retreat into solipsism and consciousness, because from the very beginning the principle of intentionality establishes the intersubjective nature and otherness of all experience, and thus its social construction. Of necessity, then, phenomenology is an interpretative enterprise: it is hermeneutic phenomenology.

In dealing with phenomena, phenomenology must penetrate the differences between phenomena, symptom, distortion and lie. Such an enterprise is a critical one, and is, an essential foundation for any science which claims to be rational, and any method which claims to be scientific. The turn from the natural to the philosophical attitude, bracketing and the reductions, and the description of essences or universals, have been specified. These form the basis of the phenomenological method. But, since phenomenology addresses the ontological, rather than the ontical, the actual practice and achievements of the phenomenological method may be more difficult to specify in the abstract.

3
Geography of Education

Geography was perceived very much as part of general education, promoting awareness of environments and peoples, at home and abroad, and the academic discipline was geared to that end. Because they were in universities, the academics were encouraged to do research; the amount done was relatively small. From the 1950s on, this cosy, closed system was changed as the result of a number of interacting factors. The expansion of higher and further education meant more students and, since geography was a large, popular subject at schools, the demand to read for geography degrees grew.

There were more academics as a consequence, employed in universities (and later polytechnics and other institutions) where a greater emphasis was being placed on research—and where personal advancement was closely linked to research records. At the same time, the pro-science ethos saw the growth of systematic studies, at the expense of regional geography (the staple of the education-oriented syllabuses), and the beginnings of the positivist revolution. No longer were the academic discipline and the school subject tied together in mutual symbiosis, though a large number of graduates still entered teaching as a career.

Geographers were finding other outlets for their knowledge, particularly in the fields of spatial planning (urban and regional, town and country etc.). The foundation for this rapidly expanding activity was survey of what was done where, especially what the land was used for, which fitted well with both the empiricist orientation of much academic geography at that time and its strong environmental underpinnings.

The work of Dudley Stamp on land use and capability received wide official recognition, and it was through his efforts and those of a few others that not only was geography accepted as a useful discipline but also geographers were able to fill senior positions in the planning hierarchies. The particular skills of local fieldwork (careful observation, recording, and presentation, accompanied by discursive analysis), developed by academic geographers to promote the educational role of their discipline, found other major outlets. With the development of spatial science in human geography, the academic discipline enhanced the analytical contribution that it was able to make to planning activities - and no doubt the close links (professional and personal) between geographers and planners helped to ensure that those contributions were in demand.

Human geography developed as the academic discipline whose applied outlet was in the field of spatial engineering. (Physical geography developed in the same way, though somewhat later, with respect to environmental engineering.) In this way, the research and teaching activities of academic geographers became increasingly divorced from the discipline as it was taught in the schools: there, the awareness goal of general education remained dominant. This produced tensions: what sort of geography at schools for what sort of geography at universities, polytechnics and colleges? Those tensions underline much of what is discussed in this chapter.

The link between academic geography and town planning remains, but is now much weaker, especially in terms of recruitment of geographers into planning. In part this was because of the professionalization of town planning itself: it now has its own degree courses (mostly postgraduate, with geography graduates major recruits) and professional institutions.

More importantly, by the mid-1970s its period of booming growth was dearly over. For academic departments of geography, therefore, other outlets for graduates had to be found. If the discipline were unable to 'sell' its graduates on an increasingly tight labour market, then it would not attract students—a crucial issue since in large measure the number of academic jobs available is a function of student enrolment. Geographers had to ensure their own future, by preparing for that of their graduates.

The career-oriented outlook is seen as necessary in order to ensure the vitality of the academic discipline: human geography must be 'relevant' to the demands of the world. Academics needed to tailor their offerings accordingly. Concern about output was only part of the issue, however. There was also concern about input, for the contents of academic geography and school geography were becoming more and more apart: the former was promoting utility and positivism; much of the latter was still promoting awareness and regional empiricism. Should the two be brought together again? How? And which should yield? Given the absence of a guaranteed market for their graduates, therefore, academic geographers (human and physical) are much concerned about the content and the image of their discipline: their careers depend on it. So, too, are school geographers, though for somewhat different reasons. Thus all geographers are engaged in political battles, promoting their discipline externally while debating its nature internally. The remainder of this chapter looks at those battles, from three perspectives..

Human geography in higher education

The goals of a degree programme in geography are rarely stated very explicitly, and the same is certainly true of individual courses within those programmes. Institutions advertise their offerings in terms such as

> our courses offer opportunities for you to develop practical skills in field, laboratory, library, archive and computer settings.
>
> Study environmental and social problems in an informal atmosphere. A sound professional education giving direct entry to stimulating careers.

and

> a wide choice of Human and Physical options, plus subsidiary subjects, which develop skills of collecting, analysing and presenting information about Man and his environment in order to provide an education suitable for many careers.

All potential degree-level students will have studied geography for the last five years of their school careers; it is assumed that they know what geography is and have defined their goals for a degree in geography, so all that is needed is to emphasize the nice place, choice, and career-orientation. University, polytechnic and college departments have adopted the consumer sovereignty model, and orient their offerings to what they believe the students *want*.

No doubt in general the academics believe that it is what the students *need*, as well, but survival depends on filling places. One can speculate unendingly about the reasons (a) for the acceptance of the consumer sovereignty model, and (b) for the lack of very explicit degree programmes. With regard to the latter, for example, it may well be that it is the only way to obtain consensus among a very disparate group of academics, with very different definitions of science, applied orientations etc.

Educational research has shown, for example, that most university departments (in all disciplines) are far from homogeneous, and that their members' main academic contacts are within the 'invisible colleges' of like-minded researchers in other places. Their reference group of peers is not the people they work with daily, so it is perhaps not surprising that they lack a collective, departmental view. This is perhaps especially so in most departments of geography in which the main goal when making appointments is to broaden the range of subjects covered rather than to develop specialist research teams. Each department is thus a disparate body of individuals, working as individuals. They perceive the need to present a departmental image, but do this by stressing breadth and choice rather than cohesion, by promoting themselves in general rather than in specific terms. And yet in many the breadth is constrained very largely to a particular view of geography.

Just as many academic staff are not very precise at defining the goals for their degrees and courses, let alone spelling out the curricula to be followed (exceptions to this in Britain are those whose degree schemes are validated externally, notably by the Council for National Academic Awards), so students are not necessarily the rational buyers assumed by the consumer sovereignty model.

Many select geography as a degree subject because they liked it at school (often reflecting as much on teacher as on content) and because they performed relatively well at it. The choice of where to apply to is often based on very partial information, employing no clear criteria with which to evaluate the various offerings. And once in a degree school, the choice of optional subjects is often little better than haphazard. Geography—and perhaps human geography more then physical geography—is not necessarily a subject taken by drifters, but it is one which many select by default rather than by positive choice. Many are not very clear what they expect from a degree in geography—either before, during, or after.

Within most degree programmes, the implicit goals are those of the three types of applied geography: technical control, mutual understanding and emancipation. Of the three, the first (implicitly) receives by far the majority of attention, reflecting not only the dominance of empiricism/positivism among human geographers at present but also the ideology of the dominant forces within society and the general demands for education-cum-training that is relevant, both to the solution of current societal problems and to the preparation of graduates for careers. Given the absence of a major career market—geography is not a vocation—then students must be given the basis for competing in a wide range of job markets.

Human geographers are clearly not alone in this, for careers advisors report that nearly half of all employers seek graduates without specification of the degree subject. They want educated people, and will provide the on-the-job training themselves; but in that context what sort of education should a degree in geography provide?

In promoting their degree courses human geographers emphasize that within the context of disciplinary interests they provide a range of general, transferable skills. Indeed, it is usually the skills element of the programme that are compulsory. Thus all undergraduates are practised in the application of literary skills, in the written and spoken presentation of materials. This focuses very substantially—in some places almost entirely, and obsessionally so—on the writing of essays: most degree results are based not just on the ability to write a structured piece of prose, but to do it in about 40 minutes, without any recourse to reference material, responding to an unseen question.

The ability to react almost instantaneously to a literary stimulus is, to many, the *sine qua non* of an educated person. And that stimulus may be obscure, ambiguous, contorted: it is all part of the test. But the testing of that skill in other contexts, let alone the testing of other skills, is resisted by many: instant recall, and the ability to structure relevant material in a very stressful situation, is still the prime test of an undergraduate's ability. Alongside this, human geographers increasingly promote numeracy as a necessary skill for their undergraduates—though ability in it is much less comprehensively tested.

Virtually every first-year undergraduate course now contains a compulsory element on quantitative methods, and most second-year courses do too: in addition, many provide instruction in computer use, if not programming. This is justified, validly, on the grounds that: quantitative analysis is central to so much contemporary human geography that without an understanding of the techniques employed an appreciation of the discipline's content is impossible; quantitative analysis is increasingly important in many areas of society, and a well-educated citizen should be able to evaluate the presentation of numerical material; and, following on from the last point, numeracy is a skill that employers increasingly demand. Such arguments, though valid, are self-sustaining and, to a considerable extent, conservative.

If geography can only be understood by those with a knowledge of quantitative methods, then the type of geography produced in that way is likely to be sustained to the detriment of others. Further, if a substantial number of academic human geographers have followed this route themselves, and are extending it in their own researches, then the definition of disciplinary progress is very much tied up with increased technical sophistication. This increases the volume of material that students have to appreciate, which means even more technical training. (In general, students are unwilling/unable to tackle this, and as a result most departments do not press them too hard—the consequence for student recruitment is too unpalatable.

There is a growing gulf between the small group of researchers advancing the technical sophistication of their work, the bulk of their colleagues who are 'left behind'—many sticking with, and frequently misusing, the simpler procedures—and the vast majority of students who hardly start up the road.) Numeracy is necessary; but not too necessary because the sovereign consumer may protest.

Literacy skills are developed in all social sciences and quantitative skills in most—in several (economics and psychology in particular) to a greater extent than in human geography, but again with problems of consumer resistance. A third set of skills developed mainly for geographers alone is graphicacy: the ability to present and interpret information in graphical and, especially, cartographical form. After some years of neglect, these are becoming more prominent in degree offerings, to a considerable extent aided by technological developments in data acquisition (notably remote sensing), collation (geographical information systems), analysis (spatial statistics), and presentation (automated cartography). These must be supplemented with direct observation and the acquisition of particular data-collection skills, however, and the fieldwork component is another particular feature of geography degrees.

Within many degree programmes, some of these skills—notably those of numeracy and graphicacy—are taught separately from the' substantive courses. For numeracy it is argued, with a great deal of validity, that this is necessary because quantitative procedures must be taught as a linear sequence; one needs the basic groundwork prior to the applicable routines, and prior to an appreciation of the techniques used in the cited research papers. And then, once the groundwork has been laid, students can use the techniques in an independent study (a project, dissertation, or thesis), in which they combine a range of skills: problem definition, data collection, analysis, and report.

The skills taught are very much oriented towards work in the empiricist/positivist tradition, and most student independent studies have a positivist flavour to them. This, indeed, is the implicit goal of most degree programmes, for many of the substantive courses—a majority of which are systematic, with titles such as industrial geography, historical population geography etc. —have a similar orientation and, as the quoted advertisements show, a major aim is to turn out graduates with basic skills in empirical description and pragmatic problem-solving. To some this aim must be expanded, with greater attention to the provision of skills that graduates can apply.

Although departments vary in the relative stress they place on various skills-training courses, all place them at the centre of their degree programmes: they are as basic as the introductory courses provided (usually one each in physical and human geography). In their substantive courses they are, with a few exceptions, much less prescriptive, largely as a consequence of appointment policies.

Most departments have appointed staff in order to

provide a breadth of topical coverage, and have then allowed the individuals concerned to develop their own substantive courses. Apart from some attempt to provide basic courses in generally popular subjects, such as urban geography, in general what—is taught in the substantive courses reflects what the staff want to teach, which in most cases is their research interest; there is little attempt to provide a coherent degree structure—perhaps because it is impossible?

Most degree programmes are set in the empiricist/positivist mould, therefore, preparing students to be problem-solvers and reflecting the fragmentation that is typical of the systematic fix. Alongside this focus on technical control, via skills and their application, the other goals of geography—mutual understanding and emancipation—receive relatively little attention. A degree in human geography is increasingly a general training rather than a general education.

Many students receive virtually no exposure to the humanistic and structuralist philosophies: they are denied access to what one might term the regional cultural geography that would be part of either a humanist or a realist programme. Their experience of the world is that of the outsider; their insights into life in places - even home or next door, let alone the rest of the world - are few. Thus it is not the concentration on skills *per se* that is the problem, but the context—the systematic fix and the spatial (distance only) fix—in which they are taught; the applications are biased towards particular types and uses of geography.

Two rationales can be offered for this 'bias' in the structure of degree programmes in human geography. The first is the consumer-sovereignty argument. Empiricist/positivist spatial science rose to dominance in the 1960s, and has remained there, because this was what society in general wanted; it has brought status to the discipline and enabled it to prepare graduates for useful careers, which is what they want. (Interestingly, and much to the chagrin of some spatial scientists, many students opt, where the choice is available, for courses that promote awareness of places—not traditional regional geography, but still largely empiricist—rather than systematics.) From this position of dominance (one which is increasing with the retirements—early in an increasing number of cases of people socialized into different views of geography and with a lack of recruitment to replace them), the spatial scientists are able to manipulate the reproduction of the discipline. Academic freedom allows those in post to reorient their work, but relatively few do. Demography is on the side of continued dominance by the empiricist vision.

Secondly, and linked to the first, there is the argument that human geographers cannot change society and therefore they must prepare people to survive in it; to do otherwise is to lose credibility. The sort of training programmes just described at least give graduates the foundation for a career. What would a programme built around greater mutual awareness provide; a better quality of life? But in late capitalist society, quality of life is firmly linked to economics, so what use is a 'good liberal education' if you can't get a job? And as for emancipation, this provides a foundation for nothing in the short term (as well as being, to some, potentially subversive). Its goal is to demystify the mechanisms. But what do people do when they are demystified, when they understand why they are unemployed?

The pragmatism of these arguments is hard to gainsay, for people do need to be able to live after they graduate, and their ability to advance themselves is likely to be enhanced if they have been provided with transferable skills. (Although, as noted above, potential employers are increasingly unconcerned with the substantive context in which those skills have been learned, when there are fewer jobs than graduates it is always safe to have followed a programme in which the substance is potentially useful too.) This is a depressing prospect, for it provides a major straitjacket to education and the development of applied science.

The case for applied geography as the promotion of awareness is a powerful one. Given what we have already done to the earth, what we are now doing, and what we have the potential to do, the need to appreciate ourselves, each other, and our environment is pressing. The case for emancipation is equally strong, for people should be liberated not caged, should be enabled to subject their society to criticism and to work for its improvement, not confined to a particular ideology of development and progress. Therein lies the nub of the problem. Mutual awareness is acceptable, because it is non-threatening; it is not useful though.

Emancipation is threatening, because it seeks to unmask the ideology. Capitalism is robust enough to withstand many such threats from ivory-tower academics —because sooner or later their disciples must live in the 'real world'—and so can tolerate a few radical social scientists, but no more. Clearly human geography occupies an intermediate position between the professions - e.g. medicine, law, architecture, engineering - whose degree programmes are carefully organized to meet the requirements of outside bodies, and the humanities (plus some social sciences) which are clearly providing an education with very little in the way of training (other than in literacy).

The general trend in human geography is towards the former, however, though as yet without the institutionalization. (When it still had a substantial number of postgraduate training awards available, the Human Geography Committee of the Social Science Research Council did conduct an accreditation exercise, which most departments passed.)

There has been little argument for the provision of structured training programmes and outside certification, but the overall drift is for the provision of transferable skills that can be used in future careers. This is at the expense of education. Human geographers have isolated themselves and their students in their own degree schools, restricted access to the wider strands of thought and debate in the social sciences, and focused their work along empiricist/positivist lines. Most would claim that they are not being prescriptive, and yet in aggregate they are. Education is being sacrificed for a particular form of training.

Further and higher education institutions are centres for research as well as teaching; indeed for disciplines such as human geography they are the only places where research is carried out, except in a small number of research institutions whose work is closely tied to the needs of clients and sponsors. It is part of the ethos of such institutions that there is a symbiosis of research and teaching, and that it is the contact with people on the research frontier which gives the teaching its particular qualities. In some areas of empiricist/positivist human geography this is no longer the case, however, for the research frontier is way beyond the final-year undergraduate in its technical sophistication—which is seen by some as providing the rationale either for more undergraduate courses or for postgraduate training in order to produce problem-solvers with the needed expertise. This widening gulf between the research frontier and the teaching task is only to be expected.

Career opportunities for academics are determined

largely by their research performance, and so there are strong demands for them to move forwards in acceptable directions. The lead time needed for students to catch up with them must become longer: more skills must be learned; more textbooks assimilated etc. This is recognized in other disciplines by the introduction of longer degree courses and by the growing numbers who take postgraduate degrees. But this means that training dominates. Is this the way in which human geography should go?

Several alternatives are canvassed. More of the introductory material could be taught in the schools, perhaps, but this makes the school a place of training rather than education. Departments could become more specialized, with research teams focused on particular subject areas, with students able to transfer once they are clear what they want from their final year(s) as undergraduates. But in the end, they all point to the same conclusion: human geography in higher education is biased towards training rather than education, and that bias seems to be growing. There is a need for a new balance, one that allows - though does not prescribe - less emphasis on techniques and on fragmented systematic knowledge and more on the promotion of awareness, at both the actual and the real level. Education should draw people out, not constrain them.

Human geography in schools

The nature of human geography in the schools is closely linked to what is being done in the universities etc., though usually with a lag of a few years. In Britain, this has been because school curricula from the age of 14 on have been oriented to examinations (O- and A-level) set by outside bodies dominated until recently by the universities. A major function of those examinations has been to assess pupils' potential for further and higher education, and so the subject syllabuses have been devised for that purpose, by the people who will be teaching the successful pupils. Because of this, changes in university orientations have been reflected in the school examination syllabuses.

For geography in general, and human geography in particular, this was the case in the 1970s when the empiricist/positivist approaches replaced the empiricist/regional approaches, especially at A-level. What are known to some as 'concept-based' syllabuses replaced those that were 'location-based', and the implicit universalism of positivism was introduced. Places no longer mattered, except insofar as they had physical features which might 'distort' the models; they were merely the testing grounds. Thus school geography, like university geography, has been linked to the notion of training in the solution of empirical problems.

More recently, these developments have been challenged, largely by those who teach in the schools. (There were always some reservations about the changes and the demise of regional geography, but largely on the grounds that the 'new geography' was hard to understand and teach.) That challenge is founded upon a belief in the role of human geography as a necessary part of an *educational* experience for all, not as a training programme for a few. The outcome of these challenges can be seen in recent developments. With regard to syllabuses to be used by examination boards for pupils in the 16+. age group, for example, the introduction to the *National Criteria for Geography*, which all syllabuses must apply, states that:

> Geography is concerned to promote an understanding of the nature of the earth's surface and, more particularly, the character of places, the complex nature of people's relationships and interactions with their environment and

the importance in human affairs of location and the spatial organisation of human activities.

Geographical education may be seen in terms of knowledge and understanding, skills and values. The term 'values' is included to indicate that important topics in geography syllabuses have obvious social and political dimensions and cannot properly be understood without taking account of the attitudes and values of those involved.

Similarly, the *Core Syllabus for A-Level Geography* identified seven points in answer to the question 'What ought a student to have gained as a result of taking an A-level course in Geography?':

1 An awareness of certain important ideas in three areas: in physical geography; in human geography; in the interface between physical and human geography.

2 An appreciation of the processes of regional differentiation.

3 Knowledge derived from a study of a balanced selection of regions and environments, linked with a broad understanding of the complexity and variety of the world in which the student will become a citizen.

4 An understanding of the use of a variety of techniques and the ability to apply these appropriately.

5 A range of skills and experience through involvement in a variety of learning activities both within and outside the classroom.

6 An awareness of the contribution that geography can make to an understanding of contemporary issues and problems concerning people and the environment.

7 A heightened ability to respond to and make

judgements about certain aesthetic and moral matters relating to space and place.

Do these documents not show a better balance of education and training than is typical of higher education? Statement of such goals is insufficient, however; it is their implementation that is crucial, and how this will be done is not clear.

Certainly existing syllabuses do not substantially promote the awareness—let alone the emancipation—that might be anticipated. In general, the cultural variety of the world is ignored, except insofar as certain cultural stereotypes (often implicitly, if not explicitly, racist and sexist) are used to 'explain' why some people do not act as 'rationally' as they would if they understood Weber, Christaller et al. But whereas cultural variety is relegated to an inferior position, environmental variety is not. In the late 1970s, for example, the Northern Universities joint Matriculation Board introduced a new syllabus C, which aims to:

> educate students so that they can arrive at an understanding of regional systems at a variety of scales of analysis . . . against a background of:
>
> (i) an understanding of the effects of physical constraints and stimuli on development;
>
> (ii) an understanding of the historical perspectives relevant to the present situation;
>
> (iii) an appreciation of the influence of institutional factors in shaping the growth and structures of regions;
>
> (iv) a training in the basic skills needed for the application of these ideas in terms of geographical enquiries and investigations.

Within the syllabus, the themes of urban and economic development were to be studied against a background of:

the environmental setting, the historical perspective, the effects of institutional factors' in either the EEC or North America; and the themes of agricultural development, settlement pattern and economic growth were to be studied in one region of the humid tropics and lands under the direction that:

> The characteristics of the environment should be studied as a background to the themes and as relevant to their full understanding.

All of this suggests a regional geography that promotes awareness of cultural variability. But in its interpretation, the physical environment is taught and examined as 'classical' physical geography, whereas there is no separate teaching (let alone examining) of the history and institutions (i.e. culture).

The environmental fix maintains a strong hold. So does the spatial fix, for 'location theory, network analysis, quantitative methods, the use of models and so forth should be used as appropriate...' And the systematic fix, for parts are stressed rather than wholes. Furthermore, the choice of regions to study excluded 'difficult' areas, such as China and the USSR, which do not necessarily fit the definitions of development.

The basic problem underlying issues such as this is the historical' constitution of the discipline of geography, with the continued strength of the environmental fix and the recent dominance of the spatial and systematic fixes. Those who teach geography in the schools are unprepared by their experiences in the universities for a discipline with links that are as strong with the social sciences as they are with the physical sciences.

The intentions of the JMB syllabus cannot be fulfilled because people lack a realist understanding of society, and the best that they can offer is a voyeuristic awareness of 'other sorts of people' in other places. Physical geographers like Gregory and Worsley may feel that their discipline is badly served because students are inadequately prepared in the sciences. At least they could be, for the problem is that pupils doing geography do not select scientific courses too, not that they could not. For human geographers the position is much worse, since the general social science background is not available. Economics is now a major subject in the schools, but it is neo-classical economics which is as empiricist as the industrial geography based on it.

The whole structure of British education is such that a full appreciation of societies is not available, except through the study of history, which is rarely social scientific in orientation. Although there are blueprints for change, therefore, it is doubtful whether the current constitution of geography can meet them. If we interpret the national criteria and the core syllabus as presenting a major case for human geography as the promotion of mutual awareness, then is the orientation of the subject correct? Is the link with physical geography too strong? Are we offering a holistic view which studies societies in their environmental contexts rather than studying environments and then putting people in them? If the latter, then are we not in great danger of promoting environmental determinism and cultural imperialism?

The key problem is the degree to which we are prepared to go beneath the surface appearances, to plumb the empirical and the actual to reveal the real. Most of the 'new' regional syllabuses, such as that described above, do not, because they study regions in isolation. It is accepted that regions differ, but it is assumed that the reasons for that are entirely internal to those regions. They are not placed in their global context, in a world-economy which respects no political borders. To study places in isolation is to tear them out of context, and it leads to what Peter Taylor calls the 'myth of developmentalism', the belief that change can be generated internally and independently of any wider context.

The regional geographies being promoted do not take account of his important identification of three scales —experience, ideology, and reality; almost all of the attention goes to the first, and virtually none to the last. One of the problems of promoting realistic understanding via school syllabuses is clearly that it is perceived as subversion, because it promotes a critical stance towards capitalism and its ideology. Sir Keith Joseph's presentation of desirable values in geographical education has already-been noted, and elsewhere, in a Green Paper on The Development of Higher Education into the 1990s, the Secretaries of State for Education and Science, for Scotland, for Wales, and for Northern Ireland warned those in higher education:

> to be concerned with attitudes to the world outside higher education, and in particular to industry and commerce, and to beware of 'anti-business' snobbery. The entrepreneurial spirit is essential for the maintenance and improvement of employment, prosperity and public services... higher education needs to foster positive attitudes to work

Thus while the efforts of groups seeking to unmask the racial and other prejudices in syllabuses may be provocative (and, to some painful) they are no more than that. (They are, of course, extremely valuable in at least drawing attention to the Eurocentric paternalism of much geography.) Others are, however. Huckle, for example, has proposed a socialist approach to school geography in which:

> lessons can not only sustain prevailing beliefs and attitudes but may also allow pupils and teachers to examine alternatives openly and critically. There is scope for committed work in schools and the current crisis of

> capitalism provides geography teachers with significant opportunities. They teach about industry, towns, developing countries, resources, pollution, and world trade and are therefore well placed to explore the mounting contradictions of a mode of economic and social organization based on inequality and exploitation. By dealing with unemployment, inner city decay, underdevelopment, resource depletion, environmental deterioration and the global economic order in a manner which acknowledges conflict and seeks political literacy... requires politically aware geography teachers who recognize their role as agents of social change.

And the Association for Curriculum Development in Geography has launched the journal *Contemporary Issues in Geography and Education,* including objectives:

> to examine the ideological content of geographical education in relation to its political context,
>
> to demonstrate the relevance and importance of humanist and radical ideas for teaching and research in geography,

and:

> to encourage the realisation of the links between critical understanding and the active transformation of the world in which we live.

These, very clearly, are set in the 'applied geography as emancipation' mould. They promote geography as the study of the insider's as well as the outsider's world, *and* as the study of how those worlds are created. To many, such manifestoes are the work of radicals—but not dangerous radicals, just annoying ones, because they are unlikely to have much impact on the ruling ideology. But their thrust is hard to reject. In school education today geography is unbalanced: just as in higher education, it is empiricist, emphasizing training for problem-solving and, despite many good intentions, avoiding understanding.

Within human geography it underplays mutual understanding and the important role of place in the constitution of society. More importantly, it fails to explore what it is that produces geography, other than variation in the physical environment. By not seeking to understand societies, only describe them, however sophisticatedly, it fails to educate people, falls to help them see what it is that governs their lives. It is part of the ideology of capitalism, promoting the ruling ideas of that mode of production.

Organisation of an academic discipline

Academic disciplines are basically collections of individuals most of whom—the great majority in human geography and like disciplines—teach in a collective context (a department) but conduct their research individually. In addition to their teaching and research, both required of them by contract, most are involved in academic administration at a variety of levels, within their department and institution and in a range of related bodies (research councils, learned societies etc.).

The prospects for individuals and small groups in mass societies are relatively slim, unless they have access to powerful positions within economy and polity. Thus in a variety of ways they need to act collectively in order to protect and promote themselves and what they do. One way is through trade unionism, which promotes the interests of all undertaking a particular role (assuming that the union is able to win bargaining rights), such as teaching in a school or university.

For academics this activity covers contractual issues (salary levels, terms of service etc.) and promotes the elusive concept of 'academic freedom', but is not involved with the detailed nature of the work done nor with the promotion of particular disciplines; a union can promote all academic activity but not some aspects of it to the detriment of others. (Academic unions are notoriously weak and poorly supported. In Britain, the

Association of University Teachers negotiates with Vice-Chancellors over pay and conditions; but many Vice-Chancellors are AUT members.) Each discipline needs its own equivalent of a trade union, therefore, to promote its members' interests. For most disciplines this involves (a) promoting the educational role, to ensure a guaranteed place and size within school and higher education curricula, and (b) promoting the research role. Until very recently, in Britain the two have been treated as one within the university system.

Now there are attempts to decouple them, to allocate resources for research separately from those for teaching: the latter provide baseline funding for all and the former are allocated according to proven excellence and 'relevance'. As yet, separate 'unions' for the two roles have not been proposed. Within academia in general there are two types of 'trade union' for individual disciplines (or groups of disciplines; or subdisciplines). The first is the professional association, which controls both the teaching activities by defining what should be in the syllabuses and by validating degree and other programmes and the professional activities of the individual practitioners, academics and others. Medicine and law are the best examples of these, with their professional associations (e.g. The British Medical Association and The Law Society) operating closed shops: they are recognized in law as the validating bodies, so that only those who meet their criteria are allowed to practise, that is, to call themselves doctors; and they set standards of professional conduct which members must adhere to, and which if broken can lead to the miscreant being 'struck off' and banned from practice.

The last few decades have seen many attempts to extend the range of professional associations, to create more closed shops and so gain monopolies over the Provision of certain services for example, accountancy.

The second type comprises the *learned society*, which is a voluntary body open to all who wish to join and who meet fairly minimal criteria. Fellowship of the Royal Geographical Society is open, for example, to:

> all those who wish to promote its object, defined in its Royal Charter as 'The Advancement of Geographical Science'.

The Institute of British Geographers has a similar broad brief, stating to would-be members that it:

> exists to further the discussion and advancement of geography, and to promote the interests of professional geography and geographers on a national and international basis through its publications, its Annual Conference, its active promotion of Study Groups devoted to specific issues and topics in the discipline, and its encouragement of international symposia.

For these societies, promotion activities are less easy than in the case of professional associations because they cannot claim to speak for all practitioners - no body can claim to speak for all geographers in Britain, for example, in part because it is very difficult to decide who 'all geographers' are, though it can claim to be representative of all geographers employed in certain occupations. Such learned societies have two major roles: (1) to act as pressure groups; and (2) to provide collective services.

As pressure groups, they make representations on behalf of the discipline; their success depends very much on the qualities of the individuals making the representations. As providers of collective services their main roles are in the organization of conferences and other meetings and in the publication of journals, monographs and other materials.

In Britain, there are three learned societies which represent geographers nationally, plus several regional ones. The longest-established is the Royal Geographical

Society, which in the past has promoted a particular type of geography (exploration, scientific as well as voyeuristic) but which now, from its London base and its contacts in the House of Lords and elsewhere, acts generally in the interests of geographers—of whom practising academics are a relatively small minority. The next oldest is the Geographical Association, concerned almost exclusively with geography in education and an increasingly successful pressure group for geography at schools.

Finally, there is the Institute of British Geographers, much the smallest and—despite its wide membership criteria—almost exclusively focused on the interests of academic geographers. It was founded in the 1930s to provide an institutionalized publication outlet (because the RGS was perceived to have negative attitudes to certain types of geography, mainly human) and to organize conferences. These have remained its major functions, though in recent years pressure-group activity has increased, some of it in concert with the RGS and the GA.

There are other bodies, such as the Conference of Heads of Departments of Geography in Universities and the Conference of Heads of Departments of Geography in Polytechnics and Colleges, each of which meets regularly., if not frequently, and occasionally makes representations on' behalf of geography teachers in higher and further education. (They do not-promote research into educational practice, however, a field only thinly populated—despite the excellent Journal of Geography in Higher Education.) But those representations must take a particular form, since they must be acceptable to all members: thus in framing a response to questions from the UGC in 1984, the officers of the University Conference received strong negative reactions to draft comments which implied that some small departments may not be viable. They could not claim to speak 'for university geography', but only for a group of vested interests. Such a situation will undoubtedly frustrate a proposal of Brunsden's (1985) to create a National Coordinating Committee for Geography. He notes that each of the societies and conferences has been sensibly active, indeed 'assiduous in ensuring that matters of national importance are considered', but notes that the fragmentation makes the coordination of responses cumbersome, 'so that the impact of a whole profession speaking with one voice is reduced'.

Geography is not a profession and, except in the most general terms, one voice to represent (or to speak without checking whether it is representative of) geography is virtually impossible. Brunsden's National Committee would need the following brief:

- to identify problems of national concern to geographers; to approach societies (and to receive advice from societies) on issues of concern;
- to identify the correct body and/or individuals to respond to these problems;
- to approach the Education Committee of the Royal Society and the British Academy on these issues and request their help in advising government;
- to ensure that a response is made within the timescales relevant to the problem.

It, too, sounds cumbersome and time-consuming. More importantly, it assumes a professional consensus which is not, will not, and should not be there. Geographers should and will respond, individually and collectively as appropriate. But 'geography' cannot respond. Because it is possible to be an active academic geographer without belonging to any of these learned societies—to be a freerider—what they do, and how they present geography to outsiders, depends very much on the interests of those who chose to join and to be active. The context will be a strong influence on what people want from a society, however. Within the IBG, for example, the current problems with regard to the allocation of resources to higher education and research in general and to geography in particular lead to demands for active promotion of the discipline, as a 'relevant' discipline (i.e. one that trains people to solve problems and undertakes useful, control -oriented, research).

In the 1960s and 1970s, when expansion was taking place, the main focus was on the internal activities—more meetings, especially specialized ones (organized by the specialist Study Groups), and more publications (a greater frequency for the main journal, Transactions, and the launching of a new one, Area). There is a difficulty for learned societies such as the IBG in performing these two roles. On the one hand, they have to undertake external posturing, promoting the discipline as a whole and claiming to speak on behalf of all, while on the other there is a need to ensure the academic freedom of the individuals. For the former, it is necessary to present a united front, to promote geography as a whole, but if the attitudes developed for this are carried over into the second role it carries the risk of the creation of what is termed the *guardian ethic*, a variant of 'the cult of the expert'.

For outsiders, it is necessary that the officers and other elected representatives of a learned society promote their members as the best (if not the only) people within society qualified to advise on certain subjects and to undertake certain tasks. But it should not be acceptable that those same elected officers and representatives seek to govern the activities of the members themselves, deciding what is and what is not acceptable for discussion at a conference, what groups can and cannot come together, and so on. This is to create a monolithic professional association out of a learned society; it implies paternalism and censorship, and is likely to be alienating and discourage membership.

To outsiders, therefore, a learned society must present a united front, in order to speak for geography. For its members, however, it must *promote anarchy. This is* not a synonym for chaos (except in the vernacular usage!) but a description of a particular form of social organization in which individuals are free to associate in communities, to shift around, to dissolve and reform them etc., with the minimum of central control. (The desirable minimum is zero—but financial aid is always welcome.) Maximum flexibility is the goal. It is messy but by far the best way of structuring Academic life: it creates problems when anarchy within has to be promoted beyond as united, but it is necessary.

The guardian ethic is inimical to a discipline such as human geography, because it involves attempts to professionalize what should not be professionalized. A realist social science must be based on the maximum freedom of thought, expression and association.

Freedom of expression is a difficult issue for learned societies, both oral expression—the right to speak at a meeting—and especially written expression—the right to publish in its journals etc. Most societies publish Journals covering the entire discipline, such as the Transactions and Area of the IBG, Geographical journal of the RGS, and Geography and Teaching Geography of the GA. Within the IBG, Transactions is relatively unpopular with the members. Because of its breadth few find many of the papers of interest and prefer more specialist journals, almost all of which are produced by commercial publishers. For geographers today there is a wide range of journals produced and the problem discussed in the previous paragraph is not seen as serious by most. Much more importantly, there is the problem which faces all journals with regard to what is, in effect, 'academic censorship'. In almost all cases, individuals have no right of publication, even in the journals of the societies to which they belong. (The major exception is that most publish the Addresses of their elected presidents 'uncensored'.) To get a piece published you must pass a series of gatekeepers, the journal editors and the 'expert' referees that they consult.

In most cases decisions are made on: (1) the govelty of the piece—is it saying something new?; (2) its quality—is what is said the result of good research?; and (3) its presentation—is the material presented effectively and efficiently? The biggest problem is with the second of these, for what is good research? In some technical areas absolute criteria are available—or are they, for there is considerable debate over many gatistical procedures? But in general it is a subjective judgement.

Subjective judgements can amount to censorship. Very often this will be without malice; the referee makes an honest attempt to provide an 'unbiased' report, but it is nevertheless a restriction on freedom of expression. But most academics have anecdotal stories of explicit censorship, too, of papers being dismissed because of their approach. (In periods of major shifts within a discipline, this can lead to wholesale 'suppression' of certain points of view. The consequence is usually a new journal, such as Geographical Analysis and Antipode.)

Although explicit censorship may be rare, there are plenty of recent examples of worrying events, such as authors having papers rejected because they are of interest to only a minority of the members of a learned society. The gatekeeping role is a difficult one, but if not operated as liberally as possible it is equivalent to imposing an orthodoxy - which in the long term is likely to be self-defeating. But to be too liberal may be self-defeating too, because it will undermine the commercial viability of a journal, whether produced by commercial publisher or learned society. The result then may be the 'nonconventional' or 'underground' publication—the circulation of papers by individuals to others; this is not censorship, but it may mean that certain materials are much more difficult to access than others.

Similar gatekeeping takes place with regard to the publication of books. Academics are involved in the production of the following six types.

1 The instructional text, providing introductions to needed skills at particular levels; for human geographers, statistics texts are the main example of this type.

2 The synthesis text, which summarizes knowledge in a particular field (e.g. the whole of human geography) or, more usually, some part of it (e.g. urban geography).

3 The reference book, such as an atlas or dictionary.

4 The research monograph, which reports in full detail on the results of a programme of research.

5 The essay, which aims to stimulate interest in a topic.

6 The reader, a collection of new or reprinted essays either intended as an alternative to the synthesis text or providing a collection of brief research monographs or essays. (A subtype is the volume of conference papers, loosely linked around a theme and close to the collection of research monographs.)

Of these six, the first three are the most popular with publishers because they have the largest potential markets—especially if they are written for the large, introductory undergraduate classes. (American publishers will invest a great deal in the production and promotion of such a book, and are not very interested, in general, in those aimed at smaller, more tentative markets. Some, it seems, would rather have a competitor for an established book in a field than a new book seeking to develop another field. British publishers are more liberal, and are much more prepared to back small-market books - places matter?) Types 4 and 5 are the more risky, especially if they are by unknown authors, though publishers do seek to promote quality, even in small markets, and some are prepared to back 'promising' authors.

Once again, the strategy is—necessarily, in the context of a capitalist system—conservative. It is supportive of the status quo and promotes conformity rather than freedom. It is valid for a professional discipline, but is it always in the best interests of a realist social science? As to freedom of oral expression, most societies run more or less open conferences with only limited constraints on, for example, time. (The Association of American Geographers allows all who apply to present *one* paper at its annual meetings, but in most cases little more than 20 minutes for the presentation.) To some this lack of any censorship (or, in the politer language, of refereeing of proposed contributions) is detrimental to the quality of the conference—though it is not always clear whether they are criticizing the mode of presentation (which often leaves much to be desired) or the material presented.

Clearly, 'open house' presents organizational problems—too many complaints about overlapping concurrent sessions; too many small audiences—but organizational complexity (even chaos?) is surely preferable to subjective censorship. There are, of course, other gatekeepers who play important roles in the direction of a discipline's development, such as those with influence on the allocation of research grants and studentships and on the making of permanent academic appointments. It is hard to assess their importance, just as it is difficult to evaluate how influential journal editors are. Certainly, the discipline of human geography in Britain is too large for the views (whether dogmatically conservative or agnostically liberal) of a few to dominate, unlike the situation in the past when there were many fewer geographers. But some individuals are clearly more influential than others, and their views, though not decisive, could well be steering the discipline in particular directions.

4
Applicable Geography

The internally generated pressures reflect the responses of human geographers as citizens to the economic and social problems that they perceive, and which the development of welfare geography has impressed upon them. Not unnaturally, some human geographers have been moved, perhaps by perceptions of self-interest but more likely as a moral response to the evidence, to orient their work in some way towards the solution of those problems. In so doing, by acting in what they perceived as a relevant and desirable way, they may have been concerned that what they did was so scathingly treated by some of their fellows. David Harvey, for example, told them that their proper programme of work

> does not entail yet another empirical investigation . . .In fact, mapping even more evidence of man's patent inhumanity to man is counter-revolutionary . . . There is already enough information.

He called on them, to develop a deeper awareness of the processes that produced such inhumanity, and apply that not in support of the proto-fascist, corporate state but rather, as he expressed it a decade later, to:

> Create an applied people's geography, unbeholden to narrow or powerful special interests, but broadly democratic in its conception . . . [as part of] a political project that sees the transition from capitalism to socialism in historico-geographical terms.

Nor were they pleased when Zelinsky concluded in his Presidential Address to the Association of American Geographers:

> how woefully deficient we are in terms of practitioners, in terms of both quantity and quality, how we are still lacking in relevant techniques, but most of all that we are totally at sea In terms of ideology, theory and proper institutional arrangements.

But these were isolated, though powerful, voices. Others were urging them forwards, though cautioning care in not offering more than could be delivered. The external pressures resulted from government interpretations of the economic recession and theories of how to emerge from it. In both the United Kingdom and the United States, the solution to the problems advanced by governments since the late 1970s has been based on firm beliefs in free-market capitalism.

The task of the state is to promote accumulation by controlling inflation and the money supply, encouraging enterprise and investment, and legitimizing a relative decline in the provision of public services and the welfare state. Further, governments have been convinced of the need for massive investment in research into and development of new technology. To achieve these goals, the higher education budget has been cut and there has been a redirection of the available resources towards science and technology.

Universities and other institutions have been encouraged to emphasize the training of students (the provision of 'saleable' skills) over the promotion of general education, and seek a greater proportion of their income as research contracts and commissions from bodies other than the state. Members of all disciplines have been affected by these trends, but some—like human geographers—have felt more vulnerable than others because of their generally poor performance, as they saw it, in terms of fund-raising and producing saleable research and graduates. They have felt the need not only to reorient their work (emphasizing, for example, technological expertise in: data acquisition—remote sensing; collation—geographical information systems; analysis—spatial statistics; and presentation—automated cartography) but also to polish their public image and present themselves more forcefully to the public, to business, and to educational policy-makers. Applied geography is being presented today as both necessary to the future of the discipline and as a contributor to the solution of economic—and social problems. Geography is being placed in the service of society. But is it not a rather narrow definition of service that is being promoted? The present chapter seeks a broad evaluation of applied human geography.

Applied Goals

The term 'applied geography' implies utility, that work is being conducted in a context that involves its immediate use by and for society, hence the emphasis on training rather than education. But what is useful, and for whom? Before evaluating applied geography it is necessary to take a wider look at how science might be applied. For this, science is divided again into three broad types: empiricist/positivist, humanistic and realist.

Positivist Science and technical control

Empiricist science operates in the world of experience only, and most of it is based on an assumed neutral, outside observer. Positivist science uses the data obtained in this way, and structures it into general laws. The goal is explanation, interpreted in this context not just as 'providing an account for' but rather as 'accounting for individual events as examples of general classes of such events'.

The laws that provide the explanation identify the antecedent causes of the observed events, thereby equating explanation with prediction: one can account for a phenomenon because one can say in what circumstances it will occur. Use of knowledge produced in this way is associated with an ideology of technical control.

The laws can be used to predict (estimate or forecast) events, so that it is possible to evaluate the consequences of certain actions and to work backwards from a particular goal to a set of processes that will lead to it. With such laws, therefore, it is possible (a) to avoid certain types of event by ensuring that their preconditions do not occur, and (b) to ensure that other events happen, by engineering their preconditions.

When such an approach involves applied social science then the product can be termed social engineering, the manipulation of society towards certain ends and away from others. Such application of knowledge is inherently conservative, since it takes the empirical superstructure of society as given, identifies its empirical laws, and uses them to reproduce society. Change is excluded, apart from that change which conforms to the laws. Policies of technical control based on empiricist/positivist science are thus based on an acceptance of the current structure of society.

Humanistic science

The goal of the humanistic sciences is to achieve an understanding of events, the thoughts behind the actions that produced the world of experience. The only explanation that it seeks is the account provided (directly or indirectly—through texts) by the actors themselves. There is no future—oriented goal, only appreciation of what created the present—when it was created. Such sciences have a clearly defined applied goal, however: to increase both self-awareness and mutual awareness. Self-awareness is brought about by assisting people to reflect on their situation; mutual awareness by promoting appreciation of the situations of others. Thus hermeneutics are involved in the transmission of information. In such applied work, the role of the researcher is not that of a technician, one who promotes a certain solution, but rather that of a provocateur, one who promotes thought and reflection.

The goal is non-prescriptive, because people are not being directed towards a particular end; self-control remains unimpaired, but its information base is influenced by disinterested outsiders. A major problem in this is in communication. Language itself is a barrier, as Gunnar Olsson has (infuriatingly!) demonstrated. But the expression of ideas is even more of a barrier.

Different perceptions of the same thing can lead to much unproductive debate, as frequently illustrated in international and industrial relations. As a consequence, 'solutions' are often only achieved when a more powerful group imposes its will on others. 'Resolutions' require mutual understanding, through processes of mediation each party learns more fully about the others and itself, whether through the offices of shuttle diplomats, industrial conciliators or marriage guidance counsellors—people who assist others to make decisions but do not make them for them.

Realist science

The mutual understanding promoted by humanistic science may be mutual appreciation of mutual ignorance (though the 'fact' that it is ignorance is, of course, not appreciated). People have their perceptions of the world and how it works, and these can usefully be transmitted to others. But if those appreciations are at best cloudy, at worst false, then becoming aware of each other's ignorance may be interesting and perhaps beneficial, but ultimately unproductive. Much more vital, according to the realist conception of science, is removing the falseness, dispersing the clouds, and promoting real understanding. Distorted views of those structures (probably ideologically created and promoted) must be removed and replaced by real understanding, by explanations of events that can account for their occurrence as individual operations of the mechanisms, but not as examples of general empirical laws. Such understanding must be achieved by those 'working with the tools of the academic trade' but then transmitted to members of society, who should be involved in development of the understanding.

This is the goal of *critical theory*. It, too, uses hermeneutic procedures to increase awareness, but of the real as well as of the actual and the empirical, and of the links between the three. As Bernstein expresses it: 'We cannot understand the character of the life-world unless we understand the social systems that shape it, and we cannot understand social systems unless we see how they arise out of the activities of social agents.' The other two ideologies obscure rather than reveal: that of empiricist/positivist science suggests that societies can control their futures and produce 'better worlds' through empirical manipulations; that of humanistic science suggests that people, as individuals, can create their own futures.

Realist work is emancipatory, releasing people from these false ideologies by identifying the mechanisms, indicating the constraints that these impose, and showing that only a replacement of the mechanisms can remove those constraints. The goal of emancipation its social change—neither the cosmetic social change associated with technical control, which reproduces the mechanisms, nor the romantic social change associated with the voluntarist ideal of awareness, which ignores the mechanisms' existence. It aims for fundamental social change, through the replacement of the mechanisms.

There is, then, not one but at least three types of applied science. All of them are relevant to the practice of geography, as the next sections will illustrate.

Applied geography and technical control

Much explanation in the positivist sciences is expressed as causal laws of the 'if x then y' variety. In most cases, these have been derived in laboratory situations, with contingently related conditions held constant. In the 'real world' many such laws are operating, separately and in combination, so that explanation of empirical events necessarily requires complex models of systems of interacting laws. To apply the results of positivist science, therefore, it is necessary to go beyond the task of abstracting one or a few links from such systems and conducting laboratory experiments.

The systems as wholes must be modelled, and their total operations subjected to experimental work. Only then will it be possible to answer questions such as:

> If we change the value for this element in the system, and the strength of that link, what will be the effects (direct and indirect) on all of the other elements and links in the system?

and

> If we want to reach a certain goal—a predefined value for a given element in the system—what other elements and links will have to be altered, and what will be the other consequences of those alterations?

The first sort of question is asked by those evaluating the impact of an increase in the release of radioactive effluent from power stations, for example, whereas the second is asked by those considering how such effluent might be decreased. Positivist natural science is organized to tackle such questions through its law-seeking procedures. It models the systems, identifies the basic interrelationships within them by experimenting on the parts in artificial conditions, and uses the laws discovered to build up models (usually sets of equations) describing the systems as wholes. There are many difficulties en route, and the separate claims of reductionism (that a system is merely the sum of its parts) and of holism (that there are laws of the whole systems as well as of the parts) are the cause of much debate. But there is a strong belief that full explanation is possible, if hard to achieve.

Physical geographers have adopted this perspective in large numbers in recent years, with a shift away from the description of forms and from essays on the long-term evolution of landscapes (built on the Darwinian roots of geology) and towards the elucidation of contemporary environmental processes. As such, it has been able to develop an applied orientation, providing evaluations of the likely impacts of interruptions to, or changes in, environmental processes. These are based on careful experimental work, in laboratory and controlled field situations, the results of which are fed into larger models of environmental systems. Development of explanations as particular laws and of calibrations of system models has been slow, because of the complexity of the subject matter.

The number of elements and links operating in the physical environment is so large, and the nature of the inter-relationships so complex (involving not only the quantitative change associated with linear models but also the qualitative change represented by models of discontinuities, such as catastrophe theory and bifurcation), that it is very difficult to identify a rational abstraction, a part of the system that can be treated as if it were closed, that is, with few salient external links. So many things have to be held constant in the abstraction that the utility of the results of laboratory experiments is frequently dubious, whereas the results of field experiments are often inconclusive because contingently related conditions could be neither held constant nor eliminated. Climatology illustrates this well.

Laboratory experiments are mainly irrelevant, and it has been necessary to develop large models of a complexly interacting, global system. Field measurements designed to contribute to the calibration of those models cannot take account of contingently related conditions, and so it is difficult to obtain reliable parameters for the many links in the systems. Simulations can provide general understanding, but the number of possible combinations of contingently related conditions is so large (and crucial to the weather produced, and hence to prediction) that full understanding of particular events is still a long way off. The task is feasible, but massive.

In physical geography, positivist scientific explanation leading to prediction and thence to environmental manipulation and control is the goal; it is possible, if unlikely to be fully successful. Is such a goal feasible for human geography too? Is it possible to identify the laws of human behaviour, integrate them into models of societal systems, and so develop the practice of spatial social and economic engineering? The answer widely held within contemporary society to the last question is yes. There is a general belief that such social engineering is possible.

We live in what can be termed a *pseudopositivist world*, one in which the general tenets of positivist science are applied to human actions and societal operations; this is a belief in what Keat has termed scientific politics. Thus governments and their advisers have models of the operation of economic systems, for example, which contain many elements and links and are represented by large sets of simultaneous equations. They then ask questions of the models like the second one above, and from the answers deduce what their economic policies should be: which elements in the system (the money supply, the rate of interest) or which links (types of investment, saving or spending) should be manipulated to produce a desired goal (low inflation, low unemployment, increase in GNP etc.). And this belief in scientific politics by those who practise it is conveyed to society as a whole through the state ideology, creating a widespread belief not only that the government should do something about the issues facing society but also that it can.

Such activities are normally encapsulated in the term planning, which for human geographers implies planning of spatial organization and environmental use. There is a long record of geographical contributions to such activity, largely involved with collection of the data on which planning could be based. With the development of a positivist human geography and the representation of spatial organization in systems terms, geographers have become more fully involved in providing the tools for planning as well as its information base. Brian Berry has identified four types of planning activity in this context.

1 *Ameliorative problem-solving*—or planning for the present. This involves the identification of a problem which requires immediate action—serious overcrowding of housing in an area, say, or a major traffic bottleneck—and the relevant local parts of the system are manipulated to provide a ready solution, without much attention to the likely feedforward and feedback consequences. It is likely that the problem will reappear, perhaps in a slightly different form,

perhaps elsewhere, soon, but meanwhile the immediate issue (and its possible effect on government legitimacy) has been removed.

2 *Allocative trend-modifying*—planning toward the future. In this activity, major trends within a system are identified, and resources are then allocated so as to accentuate their more desirable aspects; the system is steered in the general direction it was heading for in any case. Thus likely problems are identified (a demand for new routes, for example) and avoided.

3 *Exploitative opportunity-seeking: planning with the future.* This is similar to the previous type, except that little attention is paid to the possible deleterious consequences of the identified trends. Whereas trend-modifying suggests the articulation of a clear goal -in the context of current events, opportunity-seeking aims merely to reap whatever benefits are available, and is inclined to let the future take care of itself.

4 *Normative goal-oriented planning for the future.* Unlike the other three, this does not start with the present and project forward: it starts with the future and works back, identifying what needs to be done in order to reach a predefined goal.

All of these activities involve creating the future. But there is also the need to monitor the future, as it happens. Geographical involvement includes the following activities:

1 *Analysing intended policy impacts*, which involves asking whether a policy has worked, in terms of the goal set. Much of this is relatively straightforward (the policy intended a certain outcome; did it eventuate?), although there are problems of knowing what would have happened if the policy had not

been enacted - what is the datum against which the policy should be evaluated?

2. *Analysing spatial variations in policy implementation and impact*, which is an extension of the first type, looking more specifically at distributional aspects. Many policies involve the public provision of goods and services at fixed places; others involve their provision by areas (perhaps by local agencies to which responsibility is devolved). And many policies are aimed only indirectly at the individuals who are supposed to benefit; they are the targets but the implementation is only to the area in which they live (the aspirin approach). To what extent, then, are they successful in reaching the intended beneficiaries, or do some people, in some places, get an advantage over others that was not intended.

3 *The analysis of unintended consequences* which come about because all of the impacts of a change in the system have not been evaluated before policy implementation (as in ameliorative problem-solving). This requires a properly specified model of the system involved.

4 *The prediction of future policy impacts*, which involves prior evaluations similar to the first three (except that they are posterior evaluations).

The existence and promotion of all of these activities implies that technical control is possible in this context, that one can have an applied positivist human geography involved in the creation of the future. There are several arguments against this, however. The first is not a fundamental one, but only operational. It is similar to the case presented above regarding the difficulty of modelling climatic systems and hence producing accurate weather forecasts, but it is more defeatist. In human geography, everything is linked to everything else and everywhere is linked to everywhere else, so that abstraction of a part is at best very partial and at worst an entirely counter-productive chaotic conception. To study just one piece out of context is to misrepresent reality grossly, and serve no purpose, because the external links are so important, and yet unconsidered, that any forecasting and prediction is (logically) impossible. To accept this argument is to agree that much planning cannot be undertaken in the positivist context. But are all abstractions from socio-economic systems necessarily chaotic conceptions? To study one town's economy without reference to movements beyond its borders certainly is; to study its traffic problems may not be.

A second, more fundamental, argument is that planning through the use of statistical laws and mathematical models uses a machine metaphor which is irrelevant to the analysis of human societies. Humans are thinking beings, not automatons, and to treat them as programmed responders to stimuli denies their humanity. Furthermore, and more practically, to model them in that way is counter-productive because future behaviour cannot (or should not) be constrained by present behaviour. People can and do change, and social engineering should neither assume that they do not (with consequences for the validity of the models) nor ensure that they will not (either physically or ideologically). And because they do seem to act habitually in a taken-for-granted world should not cloud the fact that they are also rigorous hypothesis-testers.

Following from this argument is a third, that indeed people are changing all the time. Every action contains within it elements of change, and the society is not the same after that action as it was before. And, crucially, the nature of that change is not predictable, unless a great deal is known about the contingent conditions, now and in the future—as the steel company closure example showed. Thus modelling, even dynamic modelling, of society is irrelevant because it refers to an historically (in time and place) specific instant. One can learn from the past, but no more. Nevertheless, there is much planning and planning-related activity taking place, and human geographers are being encouraged to get fully involved in it.

The pseudo-positivist world is in operation. Furthermore, many argue, even though one accepts the force of the above criticisms it is necessary to act in this way, because the consequences of not doing so would be a much worse society than we have and are getting. We need to be prepared, whether for a massive flood of migrants (who might not eventually come) or a major increase in road traffic, for example. The information on which we base those preparations is imperfect, but it is not useless (except where it is self-defeating, as in traffic forecasts and the consequent road provision). And the work done in recent years does indicate habitual behaviour, especially in certain contexts.

Some people will undoubtedly 'deviate' from model predictions, but then the models were only supposed to be valid at an aggregate level. Such responses may well be bolstered by reference to the sorts of work that human geographers are involved in. Much of it is concerned with the local scale of experience only, with aspects of daily life which are important to individual short-term well-being but trivial in terms of the trajectory of the mode of production.

Access to shopping centres, the provision of country parks, and the details of a bus route are of local, transitory importance only, but nevertheless attention to them is not entirely irrelevant, since if planning can improve access and provision it will help to maintain social consensus and thus aid the state in its legitimator role. Thus many human geographers who work on problems relating to everyday life can claim that they have a valid role as positivist-technicians because it is better for society to operate on the as if assumption that the pseudopositivist approach is valid than to be both unprepared and in danger of social dissent if everyday difficulties are not attended to.

This is a conservative position to take. It accepts the basic structure of society, and seeks to manipulate certain aspects of its superstructure only; it accepts the need for a strong state to implement planning; and it realizes that its major contributions are likely to be in ameliorative problem- solving only. It is involved in patching-up the future, rather than creating it. And yet, it could be argued, such an approach to date has had massive benefits, for life expectancy levels have never been higher and the standard of living/quality of life never better. There are still major inequalities in the world, but the success of capitalism is slowly raising everybody's life chances. We would do well to give the market as free a rein as possible, so that this can continue.

Against that is the argument that relative inequalities are not being reduced very much, that immiseration continues on a very large scale (currently in much of Africa), that the environment is continually being degraded, and that the end of optimism is nigh. To treat the symptoms rather than the cause of problems not only simply redistributes the problems it also aids and abets the interests of those within the global economy who would suffer from the effects of fundamental changes which tackled the problems at source. We can suggest how central government money should be allocated to local governments in order to meet felt needs, but we are not able to tackle those needs themselves and eradicate them.

Choice of the role of applied human geographer as technician is necessarily an ideological one, therefore. If the scientists claim that they are neutral and that the use of their work is a decision of others, that the work is applicable rather than applied, then they are bolstering the status quo. By could be being positivist scientists they are creating knowledge which can be used.

Whether Sennett's proposal is workable is very dubious, but in any case it is not applicable at larger scales. And yet the tension between places at the state scale is of even greater potential importance. Today, much more than ever before, an eruption could lead not just to war, not just to the destruction of societies, but to the destruction of the whole of humankind, and indeed the earth itself as a sympathetic environment for human life. We have the capacity to destroy ourselves many times over at the mere push of a button, and that event could be triggered by a chance encounter, bred in a climate of ignorance, fostered by immature behaviour, and stimulated by nationalist ideology.

How, then, do we reduce the tension, promote accommodation, create maturity, and defeat xenophobic ideologies? At the local and even national scales, people can learn to appreciate diversity, to accept differences and coexist in harmony, through contact. But at the larger scales, this is impossible. Accommodation must be promoted by education, by creating positive attitudes to peoples and cultures, not negative ones. For this task, human geography has a clear role, as the discipline best able to display and describe the diversity that is the cultural geography of the world. A human geography should be humanitarian.

Human geographers—British human geographers in particular in my context—are very myopic in their research activity at the present time; as we have expressed it elsewhere, they have disengaged themselves from overseas research. There is a clear need for much more research into other places, not in the positivist mould of seeking to account for what happens there in terms of general laws, but in the humanistic sense of seeking to appreciate how societies are structured and to transmit that appreciation to others.

The world is our oyster, but unless we promote its proper study it may soon be nobody's. As an aside at this stage, there is a major applied task for physical geographers in a similar context, promoting awareness of environmental constraints. The positivist approach to the environment implies technical control; it is associated with what O'Riordan calls a technocentric ideology, built on so-called professional expertise, presenting itself as rational, objective and efficient, but in effect arrogant and elitist, and believing in the positive value of objective science and intervention. Against this he sets the ecocentric ideology, based on humility in the face of environmental processes, which recognizes that humans cannot control the environment, only destroy it. The sorts of environmental education linked to these ideologies are very different.

The one promotes a vision of control, the other of accommodation; the former dominates, but its optimism is proving unfounded. The foundation for such an educational enterprise will be a 'new regional geography'. This will not be the descriptive trivia and catalogues of earlier regional geographies, but an engagement with the cultural diversity of the world in the context of the realist approach in which places matter. By promoting awareness, it may also stimulate emancipation. Mutual understanding at all levels—individual to international—may promote relative peace and harmony, counter tension and conflict, and reduce military posturing. Thus an applied geography which advances mutual understanding is to be welcomed and sustained. But the ignorance that it dispels is at the empirical and the actual levels only; what of the real level?

The cultural geography of the world reflects the development of separate societies in relative isolation and their subsequent contact with others, with many hybrids as a consequence. They have developed in the context of not only the environmental and societal interpretations but also the containing structures that they have put in place and subsequently sustained—their modes of production. Full understanding of societies, then, should involve seeing them in their historical context, as interpretations of the imperatives of one or more mode of production.

The goal of emancipation involves revealing to individuals, and thus to societies as a whole, the forces that underpin how their own and other societies operate. Those forces are not directly apprehendable; you cannot observe the accumulation imperative any more than you can see the law of gravity, all you record are events that are consistent with both. Thus appreciation of the structure of society involves: (1) the construction of adequate theories of the world of mechanisms; (2) advocacy of a non-determinist, non-voluntarist approach to understanding and explanation; and (3) development of the skills of story-telling, integrating their study of the real, the actual and the empirical in a coherent narrative. In this way, research results can be used to reveal not only the workings of our own social formation but also those of others, portraying them not simply as interesting 'deviants' but as separate interpretations of the same basic forces. In such an approach the role of empirical and actual investigations is not just to provide illustrations of the distinctness of separate social formations but also to bolster the theoretical appreciation of the mechanisms in the real. For example, the Sheffield steel closure case illustrates the map of choices available to the state in such situations and provides a framework for studying which choice was made.

Comparative analysis with other cases can be used to illustrate: (a) how different choices result from different contexts; (b) how whatever choice is taken, the longer-term goal of the state is to promote and legitimate capital accumulation, so that the differences between the cases are of means, not ends; and (c) how the contingently related conditions are therefore crucial for the form of the choice but not for its rationale. There is, then, a great need for comparative work, in the style of the 'new regional geography' advocated above, with the goal being not just to show that things are different in different places (or at different times in the same place) but rather to show that the world is a mosaic comprising spatially separated (though linked) groups of people working out solutions to similar problems.

Every capitalist state, it is argued, needs to promote and legitimate the accumulation imperative and to maintain a social consensus accordingly. Applied geography as emancipation seeks not only to promote awareness of how this is being done in different places, but also why. A major problem facing the emancipatory task is that the mechanisms at the real level are difficult to comprehend by many not only because they are not empirically apprehendable but also because ruling ideologies interpret them in particular ways which are consistent with the promotion and legitimation roles of the state. As already noted, an ideology comprises a core set of beliefs with associated principles to guide action. It provides a world-view, a framework for living, and it is assimilated by individuals as part of their socialization. In many ways it is comparable to the ideal-types that people use to organize their daily lives, in that it is a simplified picture of the world created to facilitate living in it. It differs from those ideal-types, however, in that it is concerned with abstractions rather than concrete instances, and also in the way it is moulded. Ideologies are the ruling ideas of societies. They develop through social interaction in places, but their development and maintainance is closely controlled by the ruling forces in society. Thus all societies have an ideology which promotes the dominant class interests: under feudalism, for example, the divine right of kings was such an ideology in some places; under capitalism, it is the necessity of accumulation. Such ideologies are presented as representing everyone's interests, however, so that in Britain the necessity to accumulate, to have successful free market operations in which profits are made as a reward to enterprise and risk-taking, is advanced as in the interests of all.

The major beneficiaries, of course, are those who reap most of the profits, so that the class goal is being presented as a general goal. To this extent, therefore, the ideology distorts reality, presenting a view which is not entirely consistent with the mechanisms that are being advanced. The goal of emancipation is to unmask that distortion, to reveal the ideology for what it is, a set of ideas constructed to promote a particular mode of production and its local interpretation. The ideology promotes a false consciousness by focusing attention on the empirical; emancipation removes that, by exposing the real.

The goal of emancipation is not simply promotion of theoretical awareness; it is to free people from the hegemony of ideology and to give them greater control over their lives through the revelation of how their societies really work. From this should come constructive social change, engineered by people fully aware of their situation. Emancipated individuals are those in full control of their own lives, not slaves to a structure, however tolerant that structure may be in terms of allowing choice and however successful it may be in providing material benefits.

Thus the theoretical understanding that this form of applied geography provides is to be used not simply to deepen the awareness that could be gained through greater mutual understanding but also to provide a practical guide for the reconstruction of society.

Applied geography In this context is directed towards the general interest, not in the sense advocated in capitalist ideology but rather in a constructive critique of that ideology and all that it represents. It promotes the general interest by generating the conditions in which people themselves will decide what it is, not have a definition imposed on them. Human geographers' involvement requires creating what Harvey calls a 'common frame of discourse', a means for understanding through which 'the myriad masks of false conflict be stripped away and the real structure of competing rights and claims be exposed'. There may appear to be no particular geographical role here, but

> There are many windows from which to view the same world, but scientific integrity demands that we faithfully record and analyse what we see from any one of them . . . The intellectual task of geography. . . is the construction of a common language, of common frames of reference and theoretical understandings.

and thereby to show how space and place are integral parts of the continued restructuring of the world-economy. Indeed, space and place are used to promote capitalist ideology, to assist in the creation of false consciousness by implying that the world is divided into many independent parts. The empirical validity of that view must be challenged, not just through empirical analyses that show the many inter-connections between all parts of the global world-economy but also, and crucially, by theoretical analyses that reveal the oneness of the underlying mechanisms. Space and-place do matter, but as resources to be manipulated, not as independent variables.

Quo Vadis?

Applied geography is almost invariably associated with technical control: the applied geographer is a technician, not a provocateur let alone a catalyst for radical change. This definition, as illustrated here, depends on a particular view of the interests that applied work is to serve. Mutual understanding is presented as in the general interest because it creates conditions in which tensions will be relaxed; but it neither tackles the sources of those tensions nor seeks to remove them.

Emancipation is presented as in the general interest because it promotes real understanding by all, the unmasking of ideology. It tackles the sources of the tensions by demonstrating their origins and creating the conditions in which people will use their knowledge to remove those origins and create a new, non-exploitative, non-alienating mode of production in its place. Any approach to applied geography cannot be neutral, therefore. It involves a choice and that is a political choice regarding how knowledge is to be produced and used. Further, it is not a choice that is unconstrained. In some countries, notably those of eastern Europe, the practice of geography is determined by the state's identification of national goals. Elsewhere, in the liberal democracies the main centres of geographical work are the universities, polytechnics and colleges that adhere to the concept of academic freedom, which implies that geographers themselves choose how they will practise their discipline. Nevertheless, the geographers are not self-employed; they must act within a constrained environment largely structured for them by the state, which is also the architect of national ideology.

Direct interference is rare (though recall that in the late 1970s the government of Chile dismissed all non—monetarist economists from its universities) but indirect pressure is sometimes great, especially in periods of recession and restraints in public spending. As Peter Taylor has demonstrated, geography only flourishes through patronage—either state or private—and that patronage has to be 'earned' by winning favour with the patrons.

The need to demonstrate an applied expertise is thus especially important in periods of recession. In a booming economy, accountability will be less, and 'pure geography' is better able to flourish. The present recession is clearly a period for an ascendancy of applied geography, serving the interests of the state and those which it supports. Of the three types of applied geography outlined here, technical control is by far the most acceptable, since it advances the promotion of accumulation.

Mutual awareness is both acceptable and needed, since through communication it promotes appreciation of how societies work. It is part of the legitimation role of the state (especially with regard to matters within its own borders), and the promotion of its ideology, as Sir Keith Joseph clearly recognized when addressing British geographers about the relevance and value of their subject:

> Pupils need . . . [an] understanding [of] what is significant about a particular spot on a map or globe and why, as well as knowing where it is. It means understanding why particular changes are taking place and what their effects are likely to be, as well as knowing that they are happening.

He went further, however, in saying why geography should occupy a place in the school curriculum:

> Pupils can be helped to consider the application of democratic values and the rule of law and the consequences of their absence.

The emancipation that would be advanced through the third type of applied geography will not be encouraged, however. It is unlikely to be suppressed directly, but the lack of encouragement, and the denigration of radical ideology and goals, would be sufficient to ensure that it did not flower. (And it might be studiously ignored, as is the case with 'radical' geography in South Africa.) This, after all, has been the fate of sociology in recent years. As Short overstated it: 'criticism of sociology is *de rigueur* for Conservatives who want to get on in public life'.

Today, 'pure sociology' is in decline, but 'applied sociology as technical control' (i.e. social work, social policy, and social administration) is acceptable. The choice set for geographers is a hierarchical one. The initial choice is between either politically and ideologically acceptable or unacceptable applied geography, between technical control and/or mutual understanding on the one hand and emancipation on the other. The former is clearly the popular choice, and for many reasons—not the least of which is self-interest. Within it there is the sub-choice of technical control or mutual understanding. Again, the former is both the more popular and the more likely to win patronage, notably in terms of research support. It has many implications for the practice of geography, not least its emphasis on technical training rather than liberal/general education.

To choose applied geography as emancipation is to choose the geographical wilderness, it seems. Such activity, with its potential threat to the social consensus, is unlikely to succeed because it must counter the strong, well-supported ideology of the other two applied geographies. It may succeed in emancipating a few geographers, encouraging them to realize that to act as either technician or provocateur is to underpin that ideology and the mechanisms that it supports, a task that they may decide is unacceptable: if we believe that under capitalism.

> a problem solved somewhere is a problem created elsewhere, that all winners are compensated by losers, then to retreat to image processing, factor analysing and phenomenological contemplation is to be irresponsible. We need to process images, to analyse factors, and to contemplate—but to a purpose. Without that purpose, we are part of the problem, not the solution.

In the final analysis, the choice must be a personal one, and it poses a moral dilemma. An emancipated geographer is one convinced that radical social change is needed, and is tied to a manifesto aimed at winning the hearts and minds of people by emancipating them, in turn, from the negative ideology of technical control and preventing them from falling into the trap of believing that individuals can create their own worlds; only collective action can succeed, through a long-term programme of political education.

But what happens while this programme is being undertaken? Presumably the inequalities, which are the empirical outcomes of the mechanisms the applied geographers want to reveal, will continue to be reproduced, with many people suffering acute deprivation and premature death as a consequence. (Premature death can be expressed in the 'neutral' language of capitalist ideology as 'low life expectancy'. In realist language it could be expressed as the outcome of 'structural violence', the exploitation of some to advance the life expectancy of others.) Presumably the negative stereotypes, the nationalistic clashes and the military posturing will continue, bringing the threat of nuclear annihilation ever closer.

5
Responsive Methods

There are methods for the study of landscapes and places that are both systematic and responsive. Unfortunately the methods that are systematic are insensitive, and the methods that are responsive cannot be reduced to simple handbook procedures. Landscapes and places are the contexts of daily life, they are with us as we walk down the street or look through the windshield; we manipulate them in gardens, add to them with our purchases, use them as residents and tourists, and give meaning to them in our imaginations and memories.

Scientific and systematic methods, on the other hand, are standardized, objective, capable of being used by others and producing results that can be checked. Their essential merit is that they make a complex situation intelligible by imposing an abstract framework on it.

Trying to investigate places and landscapes by imposing standardized methods is like studying ballet by putting the dancers in straitjackets, or judging wines by measuring their alcohol content—the information obtained may be accurate but it seriously misrepresents the subject matter. This comparison is not exaggerated. There are people who measure what they call landscape quality and attachment to place by means of a complex apparatus of photographs divided into grids, psychological tests, questionnaires and statistical analyses. The results of all this have the same mathematical form as a measurement of alcohol content and are therefore enthusiastically received by bureaucrats and others who prefer a whole number to a clear thought, but as the entire procedure is based on arbitrary definitions of the landscapes and places being studied must where do you draw a boundary around landscape? the results can in fact mean anything one chooses. This must be the sort of approach the philosopher Ludwig Wittgenstein was referring to when he wrote of psychology that it has 'experimental methods and conceptual confusion'.

Systematic and scientific methods are imposed on a subject matter, wringing information from it. Responsive methods —they might also appropriately be called phenomenological or artistic—are adapted to the form and character of the subject.

Actually, when put this bluntly the distinction between the two is overdrawn, It is the responsive methods which are suitable for investigating and teaching about landscapes, human geography, or indeed any phenomena in which particularity and meaning are paramount.

Such phenomena have to be approached with the sensitivity and imagination that are commonly found in those methods of art that reflect uniqueness and cannot be reduced to universal sets of procedures. This might seem to imply that there is nothing in these methods that can be clarified or practised, that they are egoistic and their results are tritely subjective.

Responsive methods can be classified, though not reduced to handbook knowledge; they can be rigorously practised; and we consider them to be an alternative and an antidote to the programmatic and often destructive methods which are widely used for the analysis and manipulation of human environments.

One of our worst imagining is of a society in which most people drift around in a detached haze of abstractions and borrowed opinions, noticing nothing of their surroundings for themselves. They know of few places, or ways to get to them, on the basis of their own experience, but rely on street guides, the suggestions of others and directional signs.

The only words they have to describe the world around them are vague, abstract ones like housing, dwelling unit, central business district, retail facility, or recreational resource; their only aesthetic responses are to cliche picturesque scenes designated for them by markers or historical plaques; they mistrust the evidence of their own eyes and thoughts but regard the opinions of remote experts as sacrosanct.

In all previous cultures everyone needed some direct knowledge of their environments in order to survive. The fact now is that many people, at least among those who live in cities, can exist with a minimal direct experience of their surroundings, relying on packaged information or second-hand advice.

This sort of detachment from the world one lives in should not be encouraged. First of all, it opens the way for the political and commercial manipulation of attitudes. Second, it is our conviction that landscapes and places matter. They are not just incidental visual backgrounds to other social concerns but are part of our being that enter directly into the quality of our lives by providing countless small pleasures, by stimulating our thinking, and even by providing the context for moments of profound revelation. If the abilities to attend for oneself to the qualities of landscapes and environments are missing, then life is greatly impoverished. Accordingly, much of what we do in teaching and writing is generally directed toward the humanist aim of achieving a reasonable, we use the word in its exact meaning— independence in observation, thought and judgement, both for myself and for our students, and is more specifically directed toward an appreciation of landscapes and places.

Seeing, thinking, describing

Investigating actual landscapes requires three closely related activities: observing or seeing, thinking about what has been seen and description. We look carefully at the landscapes we encounter, we reflect on why they are as they are and what they disclose to us and we then attempt to give a straightforward account of what we have seen and thought. These activities are rather more difficult in practice than this simple summary suggests, and for advice and direction we find myself turning repeatedly to the writings of John Ruskin, Martin Heidegger and Ludwig Wittgenstein.

Ruskin was a 19th-century art critic with enthusiasms both for landscapes and for seeing clearly. He cultivated his ability to observe carefully and precisely by making studies of clouds, mountains, geological strata, trees and buildings. He then wrote eloquently about the necessity for and practice of clear seeing. He chastised artists who saw as if in a state of visual confusion, painting either minute details far beyond the range of human vision, or generalized trees and animals. 'It is just as impossible to generalise granite and slate,' he wrote 'as it is to generalise a man and a cow. An animal must be either one animal or another animal: it cannot be a general animal or it is no animal'.

Heidegger's philosophical writings are a phenomenological exposition of Being, of the experience of existence. His work is a demonstration, and sometimes an explicit discussion, of how to think about subtle questions of meaning and responsibility. From Heidegger we learn and releam the possibilities offered by phenomenological ways of thinking which do not impose methodological systems but instead respond to their subject matters and to experiences of these. My understanding of description derives in part from Wittgenstein's philosophical accounts of language. He concluded that the most important aspects of life cannot be explained scientifically; all one can do is describe them in their context and that might clarify their meanings.

The word 'description' can mean many things, including what is usually understood to be interpretation, and indeed in so far as any description is selective it must offer a point of view. We understand description and interpretation to differ only in emphasis — description is rather more concerned with presenting observable facts, for instance of a landscape, whereas interpretation stresses some perspective or context which suggests the meaning of these facts. In both cases the chief aim is to put together pieces of information in a way that makes sense; it is of course the case that somebody else might put together those same pieces in a different way to convey, a different sense.

Description and interpretation differ from explanation because explanation seeks causal mechanisms and processes, and digs beneath the surface appearance of things to try to establish what these causes are and how they work. Because the primary feature of landscapes is their surface appearance, trying to explain landscapes in this way is no better than a biologist killing an animal to find out what makes it live. In practice the three activities of seeing, thinking and describing rarely occur in an orderly sequence.

Observations in an unfamiliar city can stimulate new ideas, or the process of writing may raise questions that stimulate thinking and the need for further looking, and so on. They are mutual and continually repeated activities which we undertake with reference to the landscapes we live in or encounter for a variety of reasons, including travel, field trips and chance. We do not self-consciously and systematically select specific landscapes for research investigations.

Landscapes and their significance

Landscapes are many-sided phenomena. In their most obvious sense they are visible environments which not only have aesthetic and symbolic properties but also serve many purposes, some of which are immediately apparent, like car parks and tree-houses, while others are more subtle, such as property speculation. They can also be an entry point for addressing social and political issues, because they are as much a source of information about social conditions as documents, interviews or censuses.

Considerable expenditures of time, effort and money are required to make and modify built environments so it is unlikely that their appearances are mere accidents. Even mess and dereliction inform us about values and priorities; the abandoned buildings of the Bronx or the rational order of a public housing project tell us no less about the values of contemporary society than the skyscrapers of Lower Manhattan.

Landscapes provide us with something that we can observe directly, and to that extent our work has more in common with a physical scientist than with a social scientist grappling with the chimeras of markets and class systems. On the other hand there is no scope for experiments, and we do not try to explain landscapes in terms of some theory or model, or to give measures to their qualities. Like a junior weighing evidence, we attempt only to give an accurate interpretation of what we have seen, read and thought about, and to allow the form of this account to reflect the character of the landscapes with which we are concerned. In much of our writing we have not been concerned with particular landscapes only for themselves, but have attempted to look through them to identify underlying processes and patterns of thought, such as the placelessness and rationalism which infuse most modern environments.

What is, the practical value of such landscape studies? Note first of all that little of this fits with the currently prevailing paradigm of how the world works, which is as a great machine-made up of lesser intermeshing machines usually called systems—ecosystems, social systems, economic systems, urban systems and so on.

In the context of this paradigm practical application means developing techniques to improve the efficiency of systems of operation. Responsive methods have little or nothing to contribute to such applications; they have no panaceas to offer for either small or large problems. What they provide, to borrow an apposite expression from the phenomenological psychologist Erwin Straus, is not knowledge 'meant for mastering the world, but rather for unlocking it and making a world that is mute speak to us in a thousand places'. This is not unlike the specific claim of J.B. Jackson that landscape study makes for 'alert and enthusiastic tourists', though he appends to this the Socratic comment that by knowing more about the world we come to know more about ourselves.

Joe Powell, a geographer concerned with the qualities of landscapes, has written that the role of geographers is to be 'interpreters of our world: to bear witness to its variety and significance, its beauty and its horrors... by affirmation and protest'. Writing and teaching about landscape can promote independence in thinking and judgement, can help to develop an understanding of the complex and open-ended processes that characterize all human-environment relationships and, perhaps, in the very long run and through an emphasis on responsiveness and responsibility, they might contribute to the discovery and acceptance of ways of living on the earth which are less technically violent and more sustainable than the ones which now prevail.

Artistic methods

Regardless of its merits it may still appear that landscape study has no methodology other than, in C.W. Mills phrase, some type of obscure 'intellectual craftsmanship'. Appearances can be deceiving. While it is not possible to elaborate a complete methodological system, there are explicit techniques that provide a foundation for the study of landscape within geography.

Donald Meinig, writing with reference to geography, has suggested that there is a significant difference between humanism and the humanities, and that in rejecting humanism as a confused body of sentiments it is not necessary also to reject the various insights and methods that are part of the humanities. Accordingly he argues that geography can be approached as an art. This interesting Idea is worth exploring.

Is there method in art? Are we to assume that painting and writing are mysterious, magical processes involving no techniques which can be taught and learnt? Those with narrow scientific minds might be inclined to think so.

For them any procedure not capable of being set out as a sequence of rules which can be applied uniformly and guaranteed to produce standardized results is both mysterious and of doubtful merit. In art there is no universal equivalent to scientific method, nevertheless artists and novelists and poets do communicate their ideas. In fact all forms of art involve techniques which can be elaborated and self-consciously practised, though these techniques often remain latent. And when they are made explicit they are usually developed in ways which, unlike the methods of science, disclose rather than deny individuality.

The abstract painter Paul Klee, much of whose work consisted of repetitive experiments with line and colour in order to find the most effective ways of conveying his experiences of nature and of landscapes, was asked to give a talk about his methods. He acknowledged the force of the admonition that the painter should paint, not talk, but also found that he could indeed give words to hitherto 'nameless processes' and 'Instinctive gestures' which he employed.

However the purpose of these processes and gestures was, for him, not to encourage great acts of self-indulgent creativity. The artist, he wrote, 'does nothing other than gather and pass on what comes from the depths. He neither serves nor rules—he transmits, His position is humble'.

Truth and accuracy are no less important for the artist than for the scientist. John Ruskin devoted much of his early adult life to demonstrating the accuracy of Turner's paintings in terms of the closeness of their observation of rocks, trees, light. These paintings were reviled by most contemporary critics who considered Turner to be wildly fanciful or to have thrown breakfast at the canvas; Ruskin demonstrated that it was the critics who were wrong, for they saw the world through cliches and contrived artistic conventions, and it was Turner who represented accurately what he saw.

Nevertheless there is a difference between art and science in their concern for truth. Art usually seeks to convey the truths of the world as mediated by experience, science usually seeks the truth of the material processes of nature as though independent of human experience. The paintings of Klee and Turner represent landscapes not as law-governed systems of natural processes but as expressions of continually changing experiences.

Painting and writing are not instinctive and spontaneous activities. The special talent some individuals may have for them has to be developed by training in sketching from life, in techniques of shading and brushwork, in grammar and composition, in style, etc.; this requires self-discipline, commitment and practice.

The techniques of the arts and the humanities are, however, not as overt as those of science, and except for some school exercises, they are not usually treated in isolation but are learnt, practised and improved in the context of substantive work on particular topics. There is no general method for the arts and the humanities that is equivalent to scientific method, and while on occasion there have been precisely established conventions which artists have followed, for instance religious symbolism in medieval paintings or rules of perspective, these soon become sterile.

Instead of hunting for a clean distinction between art and science which can only lead to false oppositions and acrimony, we think it is more valuable to look for a distinction between good and bad forms of art and science. This too is intellectual marshland, but at least thinking about this distinction can set us on a worthwhile path toward more solid ground. Ruskin provides some hints on how to proceed. Writing about painting, he proposed that great art was characterized by its embodiment of great and noble ideas, and by its accuracy of observation and refinement of perception; bad art was poorly observed, factually incorrect, superficial and dealt with trivial subjects.

Almost identical comments could be applied to science, with the additional qualification that bad science depends on programmatic, repetitive methods such as those used in corporate research (set 100 hypotheses, test them all and with a bit of luck one will result in a marketable product). These involve no creativity, no thou thoughtfulness or reflection, merely the rote following of rule-governed procedures. Such methods have economic and bureaucratic value because they are predictable. They have little intellectual merit.

All of this has several implications for understanding method in human geography and landscape studies.

First of all, if one chooses to pursue geography as an art rather than as a science this still involves the use of rigorous methods, though these cannot be articulated with the same degree of formality as those of science.

Second, these methods are concerned with the representation of the truths of environment, landscape and place as they are mediated by our experiences, that is with being responsive to the world around us.

Third, the debate about whether geography is an art or a science has no great methodological significance and there are no firm grounds for maintaining that one is superior to the other; whether geography is approached artistically or scientifically Is largely a matter of personal inclination.

And finally, good geography is that which is based on direct and careful observation, which grasps relationships between personal experiences and larger patterns, which does not thoughtlessly use borrowed ideas and methods, and which does not contribute to violence, exploitation or environmental degradation. There are, of course, no exact criteria for any of these, and each one of them could be argued interminably. Perhaps what is really important is the attempt to draw a distinction between poor and worthwhile geographies, to think it through as clearly as possible, and then to err in one's own work always in the direction of what is considered to be good.

Geographical imagination

The artist must draw upon insight and feelings and literally imagine them into forms that will make an effective connection with the lives of others. The geographical imagination is a particular means of attempting this that is especially valuable for human geography and environmental understanding; it is a way of thinking that seeks to grasp the connections between one's own experiences of particular landscapes and the larger processes of society and environment, and then seeks to interpret these in a manner that makes sense for others.

Hugh Prince once wrote that the geographical imagination is aesthetic and poetic, it gives meaning and value to the facts of place. This is exactly so. It looks first at, and then through, individual experiences of places to broader environmental implications and then back to the experiences of others in order to appreciate the conditions of their lives.

The geographical imagination does not stand in isolation; there are also biological, historical, sociological and other forms of imagination which seek to capture the particular concerns of these fields of knowledge. Thus C. Wright Mills noted that each of us has worries about our financial security, our family, our health and so on, and we also have various enthusiasms and convictions; these always have social context, they are framed by institutions, are part of larger social movements and contribute, albeit in a small way, to the historical processes of social change.

The sociological imagination is, he suggested, the habit of mind which grasps these relationships between individual and social matters. From a geographical perspective these social matters also have a landscape and an environment; our lives are necessarily framed by landscapes, and our purchases and other actions contribute to the processes of environmental exploitation and sustainability.

The distinctive quality of the geographical imagination is that it aims to grasp personal, social and environmental processes in their interrelationship. For the person who has developed the geographical imagination no individual actions are without environmental and social consequences, and nowhere is remote, for the entire earth is implicated in each of its places.

The 19th-century French geographer Elisee Reclus once described humankind as 'the conscience of the earth'. This is an evocative phrase, a challenge in an age of potentially enormous environmental destruction. It implies that each one of us has a responsibility for the earth and for the environmental implications of human actions, both our own and those of others. To understand and accept this requires above all an act of geographical imagination.

Ways of practising response methods

Kimon Nicolaides wrote of drawing: 'To understand theories is not enough. Much practice is necessary'. What practices can there be for the geographical imagination and the responsive study of landscapes? All art requires perseverance and the patient acquisition of technical skills until they become almost second nature— learning scales, shading, grammar and punctuation. Similarly there are techniques that can be used to develop the skilful study of landscapes, whether in others through teaching, or in one's own practice.

Ways of seeing

Nicolaides claimed that 'There is only one way to draw, and that is the perfectly natural way. It has nothing to do with artifice or technique. It has nothing to do with aesthetics or conception. It has only to do with the act of correct observation, and by that we mean a physical contact with all sorts of objects through all the senses'.

It is not only through drawing that one's powers of observation can be developed. Raymond Williams has written that 'We learn to see a thing by learning to describe it', for description requires a kind of discovery. And Samuel Johnson, in an aphorism of remarkable relevance for geography, declared that 'The use of travel is to regulate imagination by reality, and instead of thinking how things may be, to see them as they really are'. Putting these ideas together it is apparent that describing landscapes, whether by drawing or writing about them, is a way of improving one's ability to see and to sense them clearly.

Written descriptions should be brief, for brevity demands the selection of significant details, and a long account easily degenerates into an ill-assorted list of bits and pieces. They should attempt to represent the landscape accurately and honestly without resorting to a trite inventory of features; borrowed knowledge, whether from books or other sources, should be weeded out because the aim is to see for yourself and other people's ideas will get in the way of this judgements should only be made on the basis of careful observation.

The overall aim, which sounds much easier than it is in practice, is to make a clear, concise account of somewhere so that this place would be recognizable to somebody else through your description. The only way to write a description like this, it turns out, is to look carefully for oneself, to think about what has been seen, and then to discover an effective way of conveying these observations and thoughts.

John Ruskin offered an especially useful piece of advice for doing this when he wrote that 'a curiously balanced condition of the powers of the mind is necessary to induce full admiration of any scene'. Too much observation leads to a confusion of unsorted details; too much thinking imposes inappropriate ideas and interpretations.

Ways of thinking

Thinking that is responsive rather than aggressive Heidegger called 'meditative'. Aggressive thinking involves poor habits of thought, such as using methods developed in other contexts, or imposing arbitrary judgements.

Meditative thinking offers no systems or remedies; instead it demands of us not to cling onesidedly to a single idea, nor to run down a one-track course of ideas' Heidegger wrote at considerable length about this way of thinking, indicating beyond doubt—that it cannot be summarized without serious misrepresentation. There are no technical tricks for learning meditative thinking; it is based in self-knowledge and requires a continuous effort of critical reflection that challenges any tendency to rely on second-hand techniques or habits of thought.

In teaching perhaps the most that can be done is to provide circumstances conducive to such thinking. Nicolaides offers some sense of what is involved in the preface to his book. The job of the teacher,' he wrote, 'is to teach students, not how to draw, but how to learn to draw. They must acquire some real method of finding out facts for themselves lest they be limited for the rest of their lives to facts the instructor relates'.

There is, he continues, no formula for doing this; his method is to enable students to have an experience, a deep insight, by planning for them things to do and wonder about, and then to point out what has resulted from it. After that it is up to individuals to maintain and develop this insight and their abilities to see and think for themselves.

Ways of describing

In methodological discussions, skill in writing is usually either ignored or assumed. There are, in fact, serious problems of obscure writing in all academic disciplines. Socspeak and economese are familiar forms of jargon-laden language being used to convey almost nothing verbosely. There is no equivalent term in geography, though Mark Billinge has recently identified in human geography a 'mandarin' dialect which involves a flowery appeal to sentimental ideas of uncertain substance.

C.W. Mills offers simple, sensible advice: 'Present your work in as clear and simple language as your subject and your thought about it permit'. He further suggests that to overcome academic prose you first have to overcome an academic pose by clarifying in your own mind answers to three questions.

(1) How difficult and complex is the subject matter? There are no set answers to this, except that the writing should be no more obscure than its subject.

(2) What status are we claiming for ourself as we write? The very act of writing assumes that one has

something worthwhile to say and it is therefore misleading to affect a neutral style. E.B. White suggested that 'Every writer, by the way he uses the language, reveals something of his spirit, his habits, his capacities, his bias'. So to write prose that is deeply contorted or so precisely structured that it could have been manufactured by a machine is a serious admission about one's personality defects.

(3) For whom are we trying to write? A strictly academic audience requires an attempt to clarify and inform - the aim must be to grasp and then to convey the salient features of some issue to an audience that is already committed; a certain level of specific knowledge can therefore be assumed and a relatively technical language used. For a more general audience the aim has to be to entertain as well as to inform; the interest of the readers cannot be assumed, it has to be claimed.

The value of responsive methods

An important consequence of seeing clearly and directly is that should you then try to change the world in some way, at least you will do it from knowledge which is based on your own experience. It is all too easy to follow intellectual fashions, or to work with abstract models, and then to impose these on to places and environments encountered only vicariously through a haze of words or statistics or formulae.

The uses of responsive methods as qualified by the geographical imagination are these: by teaching, to encourage and to direct others to experience landscapes and places for themselves, and so to arrive at a better self-understanding; by writing, to illuminate the places and environments of the world, and to interpret them, good or bad, so that others can appreciate their significance.

There are two related uses, perhaps less familiar in a field of geography widely considered impractical.

First, these methods have a role to play in the disclosure of obscured truths, in undoing environmental injustice and hardship, and ultimately in finding ways to restrain those human tendencies that would destroy the earth, any of its places or any of its peoples. This implies that geographers should act as advocates for the earth and its diverse environments, possibly by adopting a role as interpreters of landscapes and places, more actively by protesting against environmentally destructive behaviour, or even by saving to set an example of environmental nonviolence that others can follow.

Second, the geographical imagination can contribute to the design of places and landscapes, literally by imagining alternative possibilities and arrangements for settlements and-their arguing for changes according to one's convictions, and demonstrating how such changes can be effected.

Though they are enormously important there is nothing obscure about these aims. They amount simply to finding out about geographical matters through the direct study of landscapes and places, informing others of what has been discovered and then using this knowledge to argue for whatever social and environmental changes seem to be beneficial.

6
Constructing Knowledge

Investigating an image

Geography's major contribution to an understanding of urban imagery has been through the medium of perception studies. Such research is premissed on the ability of studied individuals to objectify what lies in their mind's eye and express it in a form suitable for measurement.

Generalizations about shared perceptions and group identities are subsequently inferred on the basis of the similarities amongst an aggregate of individuals' images. Such an approach has provided novel and illuminating insights concerning class- and race-related differences in the subjective availability of urban space, and, in drawing attention to the importance of the legibility of urban environments, it has significant implications for public policy. There is, however, another route into the world of public perceptions and behaviour.

It is based on the subjective understanding of a participating observer, rather than the formal schedule of a visiting interviewer. Such a route has found legitimacy hard to win, battling, as it has, with the conceptual imperialism of the quantitative revolution and with a conception of 'science' epitomized in the language of inferential statistics. Nevertheless, it can be argued that experiential research is quite as rigorous and demanding as the techniques of empirical-analytical science; and the logical consistency required to validate case analyses is just as scrupulous as the demands of statistical inference and experimental replication.

Amongst many arguments for and against the merits of qualitative research, there are two which speak overwhelmingly in favour of adopting such an approach to investigate urban imagery.

The first seeks to rectify a sustained imbalance in the kinds of knowledge pursued by social science. In the rush to produce immediately policy-relevant findings (from research ripe for cost-effective funding), we are in danger, especially with politically salient topics like 'race' and 'crime', of forgetting that an important aim of inquiry must be to capture something of the meaning of life in particular social settings. There are elements of this that simply cannot be grasped other than through the analyst's direct experience. Moreover, contrary to the opinion of some sceptics, the rationale for gaining such experience lies not simply in the thrill of the exotic or the fun of the unusual; it is grounded, rather, in a long philosophical tradition asserting the primacy of 'commonsense' understanding as the foundation of all more formal systems of knowledge.

Secondly, in the wake of what Pred terms a new consensus in social theory (which directs attention to the 'concrete situations of everyday life' where society is reproduced and individuals are socialized), it is disturbing that the empirical evidence needed to sustain the conceptual leaps associated with it remain very thin on the ground. There is stiff a conspicuous lack of information as to how the 'generation and consequences of Particular everyday individual practices at specific temporal and spatial locations fit into the continual workings an transformation of society'.

Although Giddens might be justified in claiming that the concept o routinization grounded in practical consciousness (the realm of tactic knowledge that is skilfully but uncritically applied) is vital to the theory of structuration, we know relatively little about how people construct and live their routines, let alone how they use them to challenge, sustain or mediate the structures of society in which they are embedded.

Experimental research is one (necessary but not, of course, sufficient) strategy required to satisfy these new demands of social theory. Subjective understanding will not conform to a priori categories, much less settle comfortably into the coding boxes of a questionnaire; but it is, the necessary means of divining (both through the experiential process itself, and by communicating it to others) a social understanding about-how societies work that is constructed from the 'bottom up' rather than from the 'top down'. Such a strategy will rarely appeal to policy-makers and it is unlikely to wed big business to the ideals of academia.

At a practical level, however, it allows local publics to define local-problems; and this, at a theoretical level, might begin to forge some much-needed links between the interpretative-hermeneutic sciences and critical theory. Emphasizing, therefore, the importance of what Habermas terms the 'practical' interests of the hermeneutic sciences, this chapter considers the contribution of qualitative research to the analysis of an urban image.

The argument draws on ethnographic fieldwork collated during two years' residence in north central Birmingham; it relies, therefore on 'data' subject to selective abstraction and subjective interpretation rather than to formal measurement, statistical manipulation and empirical generalization.

First, we follow Nisbet in regarding sociology as an art form. This is not to argue that such an art stands apart from, or in opposition to, scientific inquiry. It is, rather, to draw attention to the often neglected fact that both the physical and social sciences take their impetus from 'precisely the same kinds of creative imagination which are to be found in such areas as music, painting, poetry, the novel, and drama'.

Art and science are both concerned to illuminate reality and explore the unknown. Both are experimental, but whereas artists self consciously exploit their creative imagination to bring renown, intellectual convention places the imagination of the scientist at the margins o academic respectability. This established, a question arises concerning how to express the message of such an art form. Fortunately, anthropologists arid social psychologists have already given this some consideration. It is part of the 'reconfiguration of social thought', so cogently outlined by Geertz, that 'analogies drawn from the humanities are coming to play the kind of role in sociological understanding that analogies drawn from the crafts and technology have long played in physical understanding'.

The most prominent of such analogies are those which liken social life to a game, a drama or a text, so illuminating the strategies of face-to face encounter, the performance skills involved in collective behaviour, and the hidden meanings of social jokes or local gossip. These three analogies are used to structure the discussion which follows, and they affirm that it is in qualitative research that the analyst's role in constructing a studied 'reality' is most starkly exposed.

Research strategies

Any attempt on the part of an analyst to enter the life-world of others is, above all, strategic. However laudable the aims, such research begins with a deliberate and calculated decision to participate in someone else's daffy round. This raises important ethical questions and we hope that what follows will not be read without a sense of unease. At a personal level, it is easy to submerge the instrumental and exploitative elements of participant observation beneath a wave of altruistic intent.

Experiential research, as Giddens points out involves more than passively sifting information from a readily available pool of events. Access to the raw material of experiential research involves not detached observation but purposive entry into a stream of social encounters. At this level, the analyst is involved above all in a process of negotiation to gain access to established conventions and procedures in order to come to grips with the practical knowledge required to participate in local life.

The aim is not, however, simply to discover the 'rules' of the social game, but to become conversant with them to the extent that one feels safe angling for advantage and seeking privileged access to information.

The relationship to be monitored in this context is that between the observer and the observed. Such interaction is both risky and strategic, and the game analogy offers the most appropriate form in which to play out, and convey, the process.

The negotiations to be made in north central Birmingham concerned the entry of a white East Midlands woman into the culturally mixed milieu of a West Midlands inner city and into the male-dominated world of the local police.

Much of the initial part of the discussion can be illustrated with reference to a local 'community lunch' - a regular but informal lunch- time meeting of residents and workers, attracting 'gatekeepers' from all walks of local life. The attendance varied from month to month but would include community nurses and health visitors, members of residents' associations, people from pensioners' clubs, teachers, community liaison police, church-leaders, advice centre workers, and so on.

Stalking the odds

Gatherings like the community lunch encapsulate many of the 'rules of the game' so crucial to experimental research. By bringing together the different social worlds of a neighbourhood, such venues provide analysts with their greatest opportunities (both to meet a broad spectrum of local interests, and to see, in microcosmic form, the development and dissolution of the alliances and conflicts that give local life its dynamic), and also their greatest risks.

It is probably through the insights of Erving Goffman, master of the 'interaction ritual', that aspiring ethnographers can best come to grips with the strategies of face-to-face interaction required to manage such delicate encounters. Goffman draws attention to the importance in managing social interaction not just of conversation, but also of glances, gestures, positionings and verbal statements. His writing argues for the difference that even 'the fleeting facial move an individual can make in the game of expressing his alignment to what is happening'.

Vindicating this assertion, experimental and personality psychology has more recently developed an understanding of people's capacity to develop not only acute sensitivity to the social and interpersonal cues that signal appropriate behaviour in different settings, but also high degrees of self-monitoring to ensure personal compliance with these 'micronorms' of social interaction. When relying on the 'snowball effect' of heterogeneous venues like the community lunch it is crucial that the ethnographer develops these skills to the full. In Snyder and Cambel's terms, participant observers must develop an identity that aligns more with a model of the flexible 'pragmatic self' than with that of a dogmatic 'principled self'. In Goffman's terms, they must be good at 'face-work'.

It is face-work which, more than any other strategy, forms a basis for If monitoring required to win an entry to community life. 'Face' is an image of self delineated in terms of approved social attributes'.

Although face can usually be defined and presented in a manner finely tuned to the context in which an encounter takes place, in a setting like the community lunch, where a variety of group norms and expectations are brought together, one's confidence in face can easily be undermined.

This happened a number of times during our attempts to negotiate an introduction to the lives of the individuals and groups represented at the noon forum: when a police officer intervened in a conversation with a volunteer from the neighbourhood advice centre, our sympathies with the problems of law enforcement almost compromised our access to a rich world of locally-defined problems; when an evangelistic Christian confided his concerns about the 'threat' of the Muslim faith, the topic of religion had to be sacrificed altogether; when sustaining a conversation with an elderly white pensioner and a black representative of the local youth opportunities scheme our decision to 'sit on the fence' precluded a further appointment with either of them.

In such circumstances, the need for 'face-work'—the means of counteracting events and statements whose symbolic effect is a threat to face— is very high. Over time, such face-work will require the researcher to set up

- through attitude, gesture and demeanour— a reputation. Its nature, as the above examples suggest, will partly condition the outcome of the inquiry.

A number of strategies routinely employed to develop a reputation are outlined by Jones and Pittman, and some are more appropriate than others to the role of the participant observer. In opting for one rather than another, it is important to recognize that whatever impression one's more or less self-consciously constr-ucted reputation creates, it revolves around an interest in realizing, augmenting or maintaining the balance of power in a relationship.

It is for this reason that it is important for the participant observer to choose a strategy purposively, rather than to allow power to be abstracted and manipulated in ways that are unanticipated and unacknowledged. Jones and Pittman's first type of reputation—intimidation—is obviously inappropriate for the ethnographer if any kind of empathetic relationship is ever to be sustained. Ingratiation (the appearance of wanting to be liked), though inevitable to an extent, is equally to be avoided, in that it demands all kinds of compromises that could verge on the deceitful.

Resorting to self-promotion or exemplification (seeking to impress others with either professional competence or moral worthiness) are strategies that can be very successful in securing both data and prestige. They may, however, result in the kind of knowledge that lacks authenticity, in that appeal to professional or moral superiority begins to distance the observer, excluding him or her from the most intimate meetings and activities. The remaining option—supplication—is the impression that is at once the most risky in terms of one's reputation, but also most desirable because it leaves the bulk of the power of a relationship in the hands of those being studied.

As a strategy, supplication involves the exploitation of one's own weakness. It requires explicit acknowledgement of one's dependence for information and guidance on those (the studied public) with superior resources (in this case, knowledge about the commonsense wisdom surrounding the 'race and crime' debate).

Ideally, the strategies outlined above are the means to an end (that of gaining an insider's access to local life). They should not, in theory, become factors shaping that end. Face-work, for instance, should simply be a way of dealing with the lottery of unexpected and undesirable events punctuating daily routine.

However, the participant observer is more vulnerable than most to the unexpected because he or she is unable to assent to the half-truths, illusions and rationalizations that usually account for the smooth running of a social world. Though people generally cooperate to avoid confrontation and save face, 'finding that there is much to be gained from venturing nothing', this is not a luxury for the ethnographer whose very task is to probe the taken-for-granted and explore the undisturbed. This raises an important question concerning just what the consequences of self-conscious self-preservation and impression management are.

Playing the game

Experiential research is often criticized on the grounds that the analyst could—deliberately or unsuspectingly—'contaminate' or manipulate the social setting under study. Simply by being there, it is argued, the researcher is bound to influence the kinds of thing that people say and do. This is undoubtedly true, and there are two common responses. On the one hand, observers have sought to make themselves as unobtrusive as possible (minimizing 'participation' and maximizing 'observation'); on the other hand, analysts have viewed their role as an active one, shaping events, where possible, to further the interests of the researched population. Both responses have their pros and cons, but neither confront nor question the validity of the charge that the presence of an analyst can damage or distort the data.

Before the late nineteenth century, ideas about the self reflected theological conceptions of the separation of soul and mind: they assumed a distinction between persons and things; they stressed-the personal nature of identity; and they were founded on a set-of social mores which assigned responsibility for the social consequences - of action to the individual.

However, a major turning-point occurred with the publication of William James' Principles of Psychology, with George Herbert Mead's attempt to elaborate a theory of inter-subjectivity that would conceive of the self as socially originated, and with the airing of related work by Josiah Royce and Charles Peirce.

In the literature of symbolic interactionism which these early thinkers inspired, the self attained unprecedented significance, not as something innate to the individual, but as the socially constructed focus round which all other social processes revolve. So conceived, the concept found its way rapidly into the quantitative analyses of experimental and personality psychology, but curiously, it has rarely been a central concern of those involved in experiential sociology and humanistic geography.

The crucial significance of the pragmatists' redefinition of self for the oral ethnographic tradition of inquiry is apparent from Mead's class lectures in social psychology.

Accounts of the consequences of participatory research must be radically revised when it is recognised that the self (including that of the analyst) 'exists only in relationship with other selves and cannot be reached except through other selves'. The self is, moreover, 'continuously coming into existence, like the rest of experience; it shifts and changes with the social situation'. Indeed, 'one cannot exist as a self without the universal, the group, that makes the self possible'.

The self in the pragmatic sense is not originally given to actors: it is, rather, the product of a complex of social relationships, indeed, it can be conceived of as 'culture internalised'. From such a perspective, current conceptions of the self portray it as social and symbolic (i.e. not the sum of discrete and immutable attributes or traits), multidimensional, situational and transactional.

In fact, in so far as the pragmatic notion of the self is authentic, the issue for participant observers is not whether their presence contaminates a social setting, but rather the converse. The analyst must reflect on those elements of the social world that shape the self responsible for research.

For the analyst's self is not a coherent, static assemblage of personality traits that is able to observe without absorbing. Instead, it is continuously redefined in interaction with others to become 'a special mirroring and incorporation of the social processes in which it is embedded'. As analysts live local activity, they become part of local place. As much of what a study is to reveal will be etched into the self as will be written into a notebook, and by reflecting on self, to reveal something of the nature of culture and group identity, the participant observer can begin to analyse the social world in which he or she is immersed.

People's theories about themselves are important for their interpretations of social life, and the findings of experiential research are not fully analysed until the implications of this are acknowledged. This is an important touchstone for any attempt to negotiate an entry into different worlds of lived experience, but it is equally significant once the 'rules of the game' have been mastered and full participation in the drama of local social life begins.

Rehearsing the drama

The procedures outlined above draw attention to the importance of the self in all interpretations of social life. Subjecting the self to scrutiny, however, carries a further implication for the oral-ethnographic method. It emphasizes the extent to which public selves can be a variable reflection of private identities. There is a distinction between the inner 'I' and the public 'me' that suggests that, while self-scrutiny must give helpful clues about the nature of the social worlds under study, scrutiny of other selves is virtually impossible, in view of the layers of presentational strategy masking the private being of the individual. This is not, however, a disadvantage when experiential research turns for inspiration to the analogy of social life as drama.

This section is concerned with how to analyse relationships at the second conceptual level distinguished in the introduction, concerning socializing within a studied community. Addressing this task, Geertz has argued that 'accounts of other people's subjectivities can be built up without recourse to pretensions to more-than-normal capacities for ego effacement and fellow feeling.' His own studies in Java, Bali and Morocco show that, ideally, the observer's strategy is not so much that of entering another's self as that of 'grasping a proverb, catching an allusion, seeing a joke'. From this perspective, the analyst can glean much by entering local life in his or her own right rather than by attempting to emulate others, though the process still depends on techniques 'more like the skills of literary and dramatic criticism and of poetics than the skills of physical scientists'.

The social analogy perhaps best able to convey the symbolic meaning of the events and imagery of the world of lived experience is that depicting social life as drama or dramatic ritual. The dramaturgical perspective is part of a long anthropological tradition, tacitly drawn upon in masterpieces of interpretative understanding like that attained by Gluckman in his observations at the opening of a bridge in 'Zululand', and by Mitchell in his account of the Kalela dance.

Recently, however, the dramatic analogy has been applied much more systematically, and the line between drama as analogy and drama as reality—or at least as the only way of conceiving and living reality—has become blurred. The drama of social life can be appreciated most immediately in crowd behaviour: in the vibrance and colour of carnival; in the violent exchange of riot; in the ritual of institutionalized ceremony.

But the dramatic analogy is equally relevant for an appreciation of the minutiae of routine encounters that overlap and interlock during the everyday performances that form and reform group boundaries, and so sustain, dissolve or deny the lines of power and authority on which a social fabric hangs.

Erving Goffman excels in this arena, too, even though the dramaturgical perspective hinges more on the notion of performance than on that of suategic negotiation. By relating the concepts of performance, frontstage and backstage behaviour to social life, by showing how people variously present themselves in order to control both their own image and the overall theme of an episode of interaction, Goffman laid the groundwork of much that was to follow.

However, it is Hare who has pushed the analogy to its logical conclusion, formalizing a range of interpretative devices such as image, theme, plot, script, roles, protagonist, audience, and so on. Without labouring in quite the same way to achieve congruence with all things theatrical, we suggest that a focus on plot, script and performance is helpful in understanding the nature and consequences of the image linking crime and race in north central Birmingham.

The 'plot' has to be understood at the level of national ideology and politics. It revolves around tensions between the 'stick and carrot' of immigration control and race relations legislation; it reflects friction caused by the assignment of responsibility for illegal immigration and overstaying to the police; and it embraces the progressive marginal-ization and criminalization of the black population in political rhetoric, judicial opinion and police practice.

This 'plot', abstractly linking race relations issues with a moral panic over law and order, provides a pool of ideas around which the 'script' appropriate to a particular event or locality is constructed. Abelson argues that all public life is based on the scripts that people possess to guide their behaviour in different kinds of social interaction.

In an inner city neighbourhood where the crime rate is relatively high and fear of crime is widespread, the 'script' most frequently and routinely drawn upon is that relating to the management of danger and uncertainty. The skeleton of such a script is fleshed out as the mass media translate broad plots into a form more immediately accessible and utilizable by the general public. The process is particularly effective for sensational and newsworthy topics like crime and race relations, and the anxieties each generates are often conflated.

In north central Birmingham, the majority of public information about crime is gleaned from the mass media and from hearsay. Less than 5 per cent of the population claim to have any other source of knowledge about local crime rates, and as Piepe et al. have shown, it is the provincial rather than the national press that is the most effective source of such local wisdom.

Moreover, the 'script' put together by the provincial press in the West Midlands is one that fuses images of deviance with racial stereotypes, presenting black people in the inner city as a threat rather than as a cultural resource. These images are not, of course, received uncritically. The press does not dictate what people think and do; rather it indicates what they might think about and how they might ascribe moaning to events.

The news helps people work out what to expect as the consequence of their actions by providing a public record of what has happened, or what is thought to have happened, before. The script, then, is an unfinished checklist of cues providing the public with a basis from which to extemporize. In north central Birmingham, this basis is the image linking 'race' and crime. Such a script contains the necessary prompts to guide performance in times of uncertainty, but it also leaves much to the actors' imaginations: it is less a prescription for behaviour than a source of inspiration for the improvised drama of everyday life.

Plots and scripts may be deduced from surveys and secondary sources, but performance can only be assessed through observation and participation. To this end, participant observation and action research must be selective (socially, spatially and temporally). The consequence is that experiential data can only be reported in terms of some explicit or implicit theory.

At the broadest theoretical level, the Birmingham case study, like most observational research, was framed by the ontological presuppositions of interactionism—which assume that 'structure is animated by the everyday behaviour of people, not by an immanent and *sui generis* logic of its own'.

More specifically, the research was oriented around the (initially tacit) question concerning: How and why are the racial categories and stereotypes that arise as a contingency of national politics and international economy sustained and reproduced in a local structure of social relations? The 'raw data' of such a study are not, therefore, neutral. Rather, as Harre observes, they flow from the interaction of theory with experience 'in the course of which the matter under study is selectively perceived and interpreted'.

Fieldwork in north central Birmingham thus focused on those dramatic interludes that helped account for the salience of 'race' as a principle of social action. Had a different 'Plot' and 'script' been adopted as a starting-point, the focus could equally have been on the salience of age, class, gender or any other socially and politically recognizable attribute.

Having established a set of selective principles, it became apparent that the interludes with the most consistent bearing on the local salience of trace' in Birmingham related to the definition and subsequent avoidance of danger and uncertainty. Ideas about danger flowed both from public speech and social action, and the significance of each is considered in turn. Gossip and rumour about deviance in north central Birmingham tended to draw on, and thereby 'confirm', the association between criminality and racial stereotypes forged by the provincial press.

Such conversations helped people articulate their fears, enabling them to define danger easily and unambiguously (though not necessarily accurately). Analyses of forms of talk therefore proved important to the task of understanding the construction and utilization of urban images. Through talk, as Bourdieu points out, what begins as private speculation can, as discussion proceeds, assume hitherto unrealized legitimacy.

In Rock's terms, words objectify: they 'prise objects out of the stream of immediate experience and award them structure and enduring identity.' The act of speech makes people take sides and express an opinion to which they must adhere, if only fleetingly.

The consequences are well illustrated in the West Midlands case-study. There the analysis shows how, through gossip and rumour, uninformed speculation is articulated in terms of a prevailing wisdom linking race and crime. In north central Birmingham, with a plot and script that takes for granted the nature of deviance, little could be uttered on, the topic of crime without some allusion to the racial identity of criminals.

Constantly reaffirmed, such stereotypes shape attitudes and inform behaviour and so play their part in guaranteeing the salience of trace' in the structuring and restructuring of social relations.

Talking about danger, however, is only one way of defining it, and urban imagery penetrates far beyond the spoken word. One device useful in monitoring and analysing the infusion of danger in and out of particular social encounters is what Goffman terms 'frame analysis'. Its efficacy depends on detailed observations of how the mood of an encounter can change from one 'frame' to another as the terms of an episode of interaction are defined. For example, one quiet afternoon along the Lozells Road, the orientation towards 'fun' of an ebullient group of black youths eating the fares of 'Dolly's Takeaway' encountered the 'leisured' frame of two police officers approaching from the opposite direction.

A chain of subtle gestures was observed as the two parties became aware of each others' approach. An almost imperceptible sequence of exchanges provided enough impetus to transform the episode from one frame (fun and leisure) to another (danger and suspicion). The sequence was as follows:

The police officers seemed to stiffen their walk and move closer together. One twitched his hand towards what might have been a radio, and both fixed their eyes on the oncoming group with the consequence that their subsequent conversation spilled melodramatically from the sides of their mouths. The effect was to reframe a leisurely stroll into a display of professionalism. The youths, in turn, exaggerated their usual bounce into what could have been construed as a swagger. They talked more loudly and gesticulated more often. A frame oriented towards fun slipped into one characterized by ritual demonstration. At the same time, the reserved window-shopping of two elderly white pensioners became an expression of passive solidarity as they linked arms and drew their bags to their bodies. This became, too, an expression of deference, as they crossed the road to remove themselves from the path of the encounter. However, as the groups moved closer and one officer's request for a chip was laughingly answered with the flash of an empty packet, a friendly shrug of the shoulders was sufficient to dispel the atmosphere of confrontation and replace it with one of amiable sparring. Such switching of frames is achieved through what George Herbert Mead has termed a 'conversation of gestures', and this silent exchange is as significant for an, understanding of urban imagery as is the gossip and rumour described above.

Avoidance behaviour, however, entails more than simply defusing a situation defined as dangerous. It entails, too, the deliberate exclusion of potentially dangerous areas and people from one's daily round. In the Birmingham example, reliance on racial stereotypes to this end occurred primarily when some major adjustment of behaviour was required to minimize the high levels of fear that accompany acutely perceived threat. The salience of people's appearance or cultural symbols in the management of danger varied according to how dramatic a response was required to cope with the advance of the unexpected.

This brief sketch of how speech and action are directed towards the management of danger in Birmingham begins to indicate how, in the drama of daily life, the 'plot' and 'scripts' concerning 'race' and deviance that are nationally and ideologically constructed, tend to be locally accepted.

These terms of reference are not seized upon uncritically, and they are extensively reworked, redefined and improvised upon, according to the specific needs of a particular 'performance'. But for the most part, the effect of such reworking is to ensure that the local reproduction of social relations sustains the racial categories set up nationally and internationally. As far as the public are concerned, such a 'production' is acceptable because it works: plot and script offer a pragmatic basis on which to conduct everyday life in an uncertain environment. In this sense, the drama of social life in north central Birmingham is more than a metaphor: it is the way things are. The analyst, however, must retain the ability to leave the theatre.

The role of the analyst is to translate and interpret this image. Experiential research differs from the process of living as a non-researcher in that it requires not just participation, observation and description, but also abstraction, contemplation and selective communication to academic (and other) peers. This is the point at which research moves beyond the level of what Giddens terms discursive and practical consciousness, to gain access to information about the sources and consequences of social action that are not immediately apparent to other actors.

In drawing on such information, a third level of interaction requires analysis during qualitative research - that between researchers and their intellectual 'community of interest'. When this is incorporated, it is text interpretation rather than gaming or performance that provides the most appropriate analogy for the research process. In so far as the analyst's mandate includes interpretation and communication, one of the most underplayed advantages of participant observation is the very fact that researchers usually begin as outsiders, whose experiences and presuppositions differ from those possessed by the 'target' community.

Since knowledge is both historically and geographically specific, and because what people know is a constraint on what they can think and do, it is not arrogance but realism to suppose that the researcher will have access to some kinds of information not possessed by those under study and that this will have a bearing on subsequent analysis. In the same vein, as Bauman observes, since the meanings associated with other cultures can only be grasped in relation to the meanings of one's own culture, the latter might be thought of more as an asset than a liability. This reasoning suggests that a certain amount of detachment is necessary to achieve subjective understanding, and it follows that analysts' over-identification during participant observation can be as much of a problem as under-involvement and insensitivity.

The role of the analyst is finely balanced and the problem of understanding is that of how to 'produce an interpretation of the way a people lives which is neither imprisoned within their mental horizons, an ethnography of witchcraft as written by a witch, nor systematically deaf to the tonalities of their existence, an ethnography of witchcraft as written by a geometer' Geertz. One has to be close enough to grasp the significance of commonsense perceptions and behaviours - the cement of cultural systems that 'lies so artlessly before our eyes it is almost impossible to see'. One must move far enough away to provide a conceptual understanding of this world.

The 'race and crime' image can be described in terms of its role at the level of commonsense understanding (where it provides a pragmatic, if not necessarily rational, guide to the routine activities of daily life) but it can also be analysed in terms of its significance for an understanding of the distribution and manipulation of power. What must be stressed, however, is that in developing such an argument—that is, in sketching a conceptual understanding of the world of common sense, in presenting for academic scrutiny just one interpretation of a text rich in symbols and signs — the role of the analyst's creativity is central, though it is very rarely acknowledged.

One might not agree with Ricoeur that judgement concerning interpretation is guesswork, but one cannot deny the power of his argument that validation in this context is more indebted to the logic of probability than to the logic of empirical verification. For where meaning is concerned, the concept of accuracy of representation is redundant. The meanings associated with everyday life, like those associated with literary texts, are inherently unstable.

Thus as Menzel points out, meaning is never dictated unambiguously by what is observed, by the testimony of actors, or by any other data. No action or event has a meaning and 'in most instances, the determinants of the meaning of an act requires a heavy dose of researcher input'. People and events only seem coherent because we imagine them to be so, and because, in representing them, we find acceptable ways of smoothing over the incoherence, miscalculations and uncertainties that our inherently partial understanding of the world contains. This process is unavoidable. It does not so much contaminate the raw data of experience as render it understandable in the light of whatever set of presuppositions the communicator adopts.

Moreover, such 'smoothing over' is not just an academic exercise. It is an inevitable facet of the way in which life is lived and knowledge is constructed, and it requires analysis in just the same way as any other part of the process of experiential research. In view of this, most errors relating to the use of subjectively experienced data lies not in being 'creative' as a social analyst, but in failing to recognize the leaps of imagination required to apprehend the world and in insisting on excluding them from analysis. It is, then, the researcher who takes the initial responsibility for assigning meaning to the lives of those written about. However, the legitimacy of such assignations will be determined in large part by the vetting procedures invoked by the analyst's intellectual peers.

With a frankness rarely encountered in the literature, the manner in which the social scientist interprets behaviour, the manner in which data are employed for purposes of defending or criticizing a theory, and one's confidence in the validity of a theory are principally dependent on and limited by the social support systems operating within the sciences themselves.

The 'art' of qualitative research depends on a creativity sanctioned not only by what is given in the chaos of subjective encounter but also by what is assigned legitimacy by the social and professional worlds in which the analyst participates.

The authenticity of experiential research rests as much on the dictates of an intellectual 'interpretative community' as on direct encounter with a public; and interpretation, like experience, is a social and political act. The key methodological shortcoming of qualitative research is not, we contend, a consequence of dealing with the 'soft' data of experience but of appearing content to have discovered the rules of the game between researcher and researched, and feeling satisfied having reviewed the drama of local social life. The third level of interaction—that between analysts and academic peers, concerning the meaning and interpretation of observations—is crucial.

7
Dialectical Landscape

The process of landscape is very much like that of dance in dance, there is a long journey from the *barre* to centre stage. Along the way, the discrete *pliez* and *relevez* of the *classe* give way to undifferentiated movement. The dance cannot be reduced to its basic elements, but extends beyond itself as a totalization that includes its history and its potential. It releases time, space, form and movement, to bring dancers and audience into a common sphere of expression. And yet, we are fooled. For, the moment when the *pas de deux* reaches its exquisite climax, when the world seems to begin and end with a single subtle gesture, that moment, could never exist— or could never be the same—without each agonizing pliez that has gone before, without every dedicated encounter with the cold reality of the barre.

Landscape, too, is a process totalized, the extension and collection of human activity in a material setting. It is organized, choreographed, although seldom so expressively as in the dance; like the dance, it can produce profound emotional effects on the beholder whose senses are awakened to its presentation. Both landscape and the dance require a practised eye to appreciate their finer qualities. Both are irreducible to their constituent elements, both transcend their moments of expression, yet neither exceeds its physical features: buildings or props, movements, expressions in flux. Landscape too is a form of language, and it is necessary to know its history, its structures and its syntax if it is to be understood.

The study of landscape provides for geographers a means of analysing and organizing the surrounding material environment, confirming the major tenet that we look to that material environment for concrete expression of the facts of human existence.

Yet despite the well-established position of landscape study within the discipline there remain questions concerning how landscape is defined, and even greater questions concerning the relationship between landscapes and human beings. This issue has become more pressing in recent years in the general shift of interest from the study of landscape and culture (where culture was viewed as a phenomenon distinct from individual human beings) to humanistic studies of the process by which landscapes (and human beings) are socially created, within a context that views culture as a 'constitutive human process. Such studies require not only a rethinking of basic conceptual elements, but immersion in dialectical thinking.

The dance of the dialectic has caught geography within its flow in recent years, and we are now well rehearsed in its movements. The melody is polyphonic, voiced by self-professed humanists, pragmatists, realists, Marxists structuralists, post-Marxists, post-structuralists and the like, but there is none the less harmony in the common quest to overcome Cartesian dualism, and to interpret the world through synthetic understanding.

The concept of structuration, despite its flaws, has played a key role in bringing us to recognize the fundamental recursiveness of social conditions, and to transcend the simplistic dualisms that mark debates concerning 'structure and human agency' or 'individual and society'. Few attempts have been made by geographers to apply a dialectical methodology to studies of landscape. The meaning of landscape is, in fact, to a remarkable degree taken for granted given its privileged position within our discipline.

Geographical definitions of landscape abound, of course, but they are seldom critical, and an attempt to follow through upon the logic of these many definitions leads to many loose ends and contradictions.

The confusion is not an indictment of the profession, but rather reflects basic contradictions in philosophical approaches, as well as contradictions given by the term 'landscape' itself, which is variously interpreted as both idea and object, process and pattern, purpose and result. The challenge is to make landscape as all of these, as full dance production, but it may be necessary first to go back to the barre, to establish the foundations of the concept, and the possibilities for dialectical interpretation.

Philosophical directions in landscape geography

Despite the variety of definitions and philosophical perspectives represented, there seems to be general agreement that 'viewing' landscape is a selective process, that we 'must proceed in a sequence of "word packages" and can draw attention to only one aspect of the landscape view at a time'. A choice must be made. This choice is prescribed by epistemological limitations and ideological ordering. The epistemological problem is rooted in the fact that both the limitations of human perception and the parameters of organized logic preclude comprehension at once of total reality, which is in a continuous state of becoming. Geographers must therefore address the fundamental problem that there is an apparent gap between reality and reason.

Understanding does not grasp the whole, but requires some form of conceptual abstraction, or analysis, to be communicated. We therefore make analytical statements about a synthetic world.

The concept of landscape is a geographical tool used analytically to organize material reality perceptually and conceptually, denoting the total environment, but expressing it in a partial way. This partiality is the basis for some very difficult philosophical issues, because it follows that analysis must proceed on the basis of choices concerning what is to be abstracted from the total.

Such choices are informed by theories concerning how we account for the order that is imposed on the environment in creating landscape, theories based on fundamental assumptions concerning, *inter alia*, the existence of rules according to which material transformation (formation of landscape) occurs, the role of human or other agents in bringing about such transformation, the relationship between consciousness and praxis in the enactment of that human role, and the ontological status of the respective contents of the material environment and the human mind.

Geographers addressing the above issues with regard to landscape have tended to frame their arguments in terms of either idealist or materialist philosophies. Idealist perspectives have dominated humanistic studies that explicitly recognize the efficacy of individual human action in defining relationship with landscape.

Inspired by the statement that 'the most fascinating *terrae incognitae* of all are those that lie within the minds and hearts of men', a paper by Lowenthal pioneered the expansion of landscape studies to include epistemic phenomena. It was proposed that since 'the geography of the world is unified only by human logic and optics' account should be taken of 'personal' worlds of experience, learning, imagination and memory, the phenomena of which very image and idea about the world is compounded'.

This insight instigated the turning away by geographers from studies of holistic culture to studies of the qualities of existential conditions. The past two decades have seen emphasis on understanding human value, emotion and the quality of experience in general, and have produced a new sensitivity to the human condition.

Unresolved in such studies, however, where they have rested on subjective idealism, is the issue of how the partial world of individual experience is connected to the realm of social, political and material reality. To distinguish the subjective 'geography of the mind' from the world around is to assume a distinction between the 'real' and the 'perceived', or between nature and its mental image.

Beneath this assumption is a Cartesian separation of epistemic traits from ontological status, or being, and a concommitant isolation of action, experience and thought into distinct realms that are not synthesized in accounting for the material production of both landscape and social conditions. The resulting landscape as 'a centre of meaning constructed by experience' is an abstraction, and idealist humanism is thus open to the criticism that it falls to go beyond a critique of more mechanistic methods of explanation to provide a comprehensive philosophy of the world.

Paralleling the development of humanistic approaches over the past decade, Marxist approaches have responded to Harvey's appeal to pursue a theoretical interpretation of the world based on the exploitation of capitalism. Contained within that appeal was a gem of an idea that should have set studies of landscape at the heart of radical geography: 'One significant element in this general process of differentiation is that created space replaces effective space as the overriding principle of geographical organization'.

It is unfortunate both that Harvey chose to emphasize abstract space and thus set a generation of radical geographers on what now seems to be a logical wild goose chase; and that cultural geographers did not see fit to recognize in Harvey's suggestion the basis for a new interpretation of created landscapes.

Instead, cultural geographers remained for the most part trapped in idealism, and Marxist geographers who would claim to redress the shortcomings of humanism have done so at the expense of rejecting individual action and experience as the constituent elements of social history, and of rejecting the landscape as an essential element in the production of social reality.

Despite the emphasis in the works of Marx on a fundamental understanding of the material production of social conditions, Marxism in the structuralist form that has dominated geography, has failed to recognize the importance of the quality of landscape, concentrating instead on the relations of production and social classes, presented in aggregate terms and determined by structures that originate outside human consciousness.

For all that history depends, in structuralist Marxism, on the praxis of human beings to be produced, its terms are those of an external system that contains within itself the conditions of history. Rather than acting as a complement to the voluntarism of humanistic perspectives by releasing the potential to go beyond the individual in an incorporative way, therefore, Marxism has met humanism head on in a negation of the most appealing qualities of both philosophical systems.

The incorporative social philosophy

Two questions arise from the foregoing discussion. The first is, who sets the rules, human beings or some force or entity independent of human will? A broadly humanistic position asserts the anthropocentricity of human habitation of the earth, and the interdependence of the qualities of landscape and the qualities of human experience.

A more specific position is required in specifying the terms of human habitation, and in answering the second question, which is how is it possible to mediate between the aggregate of all human action in organizing and experiencing landscape and the immediacy of human action as it actually occurs, as individual experience at a unique temporal/spatial moment?

The aggregate is difficult to grasp because of its unspecifiable dimensions and thus is prone to reification; the immediate is impossible to grasp both because it is transcended in the contingent flow of experience, and because simple logistical problems preclude any but the most limited discussion of individuals.

The problem is an old philosophical issue. It is set out by Kant, who posits overcoming this contradiction between knowledge and object as the basis for truth, thus contributing to the ground rules for contemporary positive science.

Understanding does not grasp the whole, but requires some form of conceptual abstraction, or analysis, to be communicated. For Kant, this process required that knowledge be categorized prior to its application to sensory (empirical) data, making clear the distinction between the form and the content of knowledge. Kant's legacy has been to set for science the task of making analytic statements about a synthetic world.

The possibility of dialectical understanding (that is, where a distinction between the analytic and the synthetic is not only overcome, but also impossible) was for Kant merely the 'logic of illusion', a contemptible form of sophism. As geographers address this dualism, perhaps a phenomenology of mind is less effective a methodology than an encounter with landscape. For is it not in the common organization of landscape that the mediation of the individual and society occurs?

The terms of this organization are not self-evident, however, since it has no meaning until (a point which Lowenthal's proverbial hammer has so neatly hit on its head) it is unified through human action. Through logic and optics, we set out to achieve both an analytical selection of facts to be observed, and a synthetic integration of individual, society and material objects. This double-edged project provides the justification for Sartre's philosophical project. Sartre dedicated much of his career to the project of overcoming idealism of all forms, whether as the assignment of a non-material status to knowledge or ideas, or the separation of knowledge from the act of knowing.

Knowledge is depicted throughout his work only as praxis, engaged knowledge, a form (in fact the only form) of human relationship with the world. Knowledge and experience are synonymous. Sartre is most famous for his insistence on the freedom of knowledge, or consciousness, to define the quality of experience, as the projection of life toward the goal of life itself. A second aspect of Sartre's work, one that is often overlooked or discounted, is his adamant claim that human existence occurs only through material praxis within the concrete material world.

The fact that world includes others creates the inescapable situation that human beings are social beings, and precludes the possibility that relationship with the world can ever be understood as any single consciousness in relation to any specific set of physical objects, except as an analytical abstraction.

Sartre's major work, Critique of dialectical reason, is an unfinished attempt to overcome the duality of Cartesian reasoning, and the show the possibility, indeed the necessity, for a single, but dialectical, logic for thought and engagement with the world. The title of this work, derived from Kant's titles, is a statement of the impossibility of either pure or practical reason; there is only dialectical reason. The difference between internal (constituent) reason and external (constituted) reason occurs on a continuum, rather than as an abrupt switch of logical categories.

Within this logical framework, knowledge is always partial, necessarily contingent, purposive (if not purposeful), unbounded, and never separated from its concrete, material, historical circumstances. Knowledge and the world are not separate realities, but reality is the knowledge relationship. Knowledge is always thought, never a thought.

Furthermore, a combination of the necessity of plurality of consciousness with the necessity of dialectical transcendence leads to the rejection of the possibility of absolute truth occurring at any level of analysis. In this respect, Sartre is in complete agreement with Marx, Within most Marxist interpretations, however, the quality of experience is determined not by the conscious appropriation of a necessary material world, but by the conditions imposed on consciousness by that world at the point''' that its physical properties become manifest in the process of production.

This difference defines the critical point at which Sartre departs from historical materialism. It amounts to a rejection of a 'dialectic of nature', and denial of all forms of historical determinism, or of any intrinsic logic, such as the 'logic of capitalism', independent of human consciousness. In thus refuting both idealism and materialism, the logic of Sartre's argument proceeds according to the principle of 'dialectical reason'. To render an extremely complex discussion in a few words, dialectical reason refers to what Sartre terms the 'intelligibility of praxis'.

At the most fundamental level, human existence is also the intelligibility of praxis, in that all action is social, and constitutes a form of language, and is therefore at least potentially intellible. Because history is nothing but the totalization of praxis (occurring within a material world that is continually transcended by praxis) historical process can be understood as the condition of intelligibility of praxis.

Praxis imposes on knowledge the synthetic engagement with the world (existence), as well as the possibility /necessity to transcend existence (becoming) through distantiation, in the mode of knowledge we refer to as analysis, by which particular moments of thought are thought through.

Dialectical reason originates in individual consciousness, as the form of relationship between individual and environment, but it sets the conditions for all forms of social relationship. This continuum proceeds from the interior of individual thought to the exterior of social structure. At each 'Point' is imposed the need for critical interpretation of the world, and of ideas about the world.

The practical result of the principle of dialectical reason is that it allows a contextual interpretation of the world as relationship. This can occur at two scales, as a phenomenological description of human consciousness, or as an examination of history as social relations, but there is no absolute boundary between the two, and they are based on an identical logic.

Dialectical reason thus encompasses the constituent terms of existence, that is, the possibility for human existence and its exigent conditions, as well as the constituted terms of history, where material conditions, and as we shall see structures, emerge. Put another way, the dialectic between individual and society, or between consciousness and the world, is expressed as a trajectory from 'the possible as infinite totality' (individual consciousness) to 'the possible as conditioned and limited field.' Not only does this dialectic mediate the theoretical and the empirical, and the analytic and the synthetic, it also defines the contradictions of individual and society, past and future, regressive and progressive thought.

This programme not only destroys the spurious association of humanism and historical materialism with the study of agency and structure respectively, but it allows an understanding of relationship that expresses not a duality but an inter-connectivity. Far from lapsing into subjectivism or positing an individualist perspective, this is a truly incorporative approach to social science. Furthermore, it is a critical perspective that allows exposure of the terms of reference of the analyst according to the same terms as those of society as a whole.

How do structures operate within this system? Sartre was a strong critic of structuralism, on the basis that it is non-dialectical. Relationships independent of consciousness may be necessary, but they must be dialectically related to consciousness. He criticizes Levi-Strauss for applying his analysis only to systems that were already constituted, thus divorcing them from immediate consciousness of them and discrediting history. Foucault, he claimed, failed to interpose praxis, which would mean to consider society as the passage from one structure to another, rather than simply to uncover successive structures.

Structuralist approaches are a reversion to a form of positivism wherein,thought is only language, as if language itself were not spoken'. If Sartre rejects structuralism for its inability to comprehend the synthetic totalization of history, he does not reject analysis of structures as a legitimate mode of historical investigation: an analytical mode in which the heuristic abstraction of structure makes understanding possible.

Structures are real, to the extent that we experience a diachronic progression wherein structure comes about through the praxis of its agents, but then gains the power to condition subsequent praxis.

Structure, simply put, consists of rules by which human actions are guided. We set the rules, change them, but also submit to them. They are materially real and exist as signification, through linguistic action, which includes both the production of formal language, and the production of landscapes, the physical setting for life.

In being material manifestations, however, they are not inert. They are charged with meaning and heavy with ideology; their power lies in the knowledge of the consequences should they be broken, and their power is wielded in exact proportion to the cumulative praxis invested in them, and to the extent that praxis was itself structured. Sartre also claimed that 'superstructures' constitute regions of relative autonomy above the relations of production and praxis. Their autonomy derives not from an external dialectic, however, but from the fact that human beings have created them and, through prax's, given them the power of relative autonomy. This is how the condition of alienation occurs.

Structures thus construed can be interpreted on two levels, first as: the moment of structure, where totality appears as the thing without man (sic), a network of oppositions in which each element defines itself by another one where there is no term, but only relations of difference. But analysis of structure as a momentary manifestation must be followed by a second level of analysis where:

> ... it can no longer be a question of structures already there which will exist without us... Structures impose themselves oil us only to the extent that they are made by others. Thus, to understand how a structure is made, it is necessary to introduce praxis as that totalizing process. Structural analysis must pass over to a dialectical comprehension.

A dialectic of nature is then refuted:

> In nature you will not find oppositions such as those described by the linguist. Nature knows only the independence of forces. Material elements are placed one next to the other and act one over the other. But the lines of force are always external.

The human system, on the other hand, is one that originates in internal relationship, and Is sustained only through the active engagement (exteriorization) of human will. If we accept that all engagement of the environment (action) is simultaneously a linguistic statement, then language becomes the fundamental mode of socialization.

As social, structured beings, we are never independent of our history and our history only functions as it is linguistically acknowledged in each moment of praxis. The importance of analysing structure comes in knowing the role that it plays at the moment that it maintains order in history, for a structure's efficacy occurs in direct relation to its ability to maintain order. A structure is nonexistent if unacknowledged, even if acknowledgement consists of denial or misunderstanding. A structure must be known although this prerequisite does not give it the status of pure thought. In being known, or incorporated within the sphere of human action, it gains historical presence; however, at that very moment, 'history is already on the way to undoing it'. To put it another way, human beings are somehow developed by the development of structure, 'in all moments totalizer and totalized'.

The real problem, then, is not in simply uncovering (knowing) structures, but in going beyond structures to understand what Sartre terms 'depassement', the perpetual integration and reintegration by which structures are created, transcended, and given conditioning power, and by which their consequences become subject to rational enquiry.

To stop at structures would be to create an 'intermission' in the realization of the depassement. That is what has occurred in the modern Marxist project, and that, Sartre claims, is a 'logical scandal'. Sartre's Search for a method was an attempt to rectify this scandal. An important concept in this dialectical method is that of 'process'.

A process is an abstraction, an analytical device, by which synthetic, totalized history is organized for the purpose of analysis, and structural conditions are uncovered. It is the assignment of pseudo-organic character to a particular range of moments whose existence cannot, of course, be made absolute linguistically, but can be depicted. This is why we must deny absolute truth, but affirm concrete understanding.

In everyday life, we unreflectively engage in process creation continually. For example, we claim to 'go for a walk' and in doing so acknowledge and communicate the pseudo-organic character of the walking process.

Linguistically, we turn the walk into a thing, without thereby reducing the walk to each of the steps required in completing the circuit, or each of the muscle contractions required to produce the walk, and so on.

At the same time, we engage an entire historical context in which going for a walk holds a specific set of structured meanings. We walk to obtain exercise, to ponder a problem, to vent frustrations, and so on. We can therefore understand walking as a process, but only by understanding the context for a particular walk can we uncover the degree and manner in which that walk is structured.

The designation of process in this way is more than a simple statement of the constraints of language. It illustrates the condition of life as a constant dialectical interplay between the analytic and the synthetic, where, in projecting ourselves between past and future, we also move between the totality that threatens to engulf, and the organization that makes rationality possible.

In so doing, we cast ourselves into the 'flow" of experience, where language, being and action are synonymous, adelphous, but not undifferentiated, for they are organized through the mechanisms of process and structure. The constitution of process (like structure) is therefore a necessary aspect of engaging the world, the means by which we recognize, give meaning to, our actions. The researcher utilizes process in a similar, but more critical, manner to denote, or make into a thing, that which is analysed.

We speak of the 'process of change', the 'process of modernization', or the 'process of urbanization', and we recognize that these are abstractions. None the less, they are legitimate abstractions if we wish to convey history as pseudo-organic phases in order to provide a basis for communication.

We cannot convey totality, but we can convey a pseudo-totality through the concept of process. This does not change the fundamental material character of all language as praxis, but it does illuminate the dilemma we face that time and space, as the qualitative conditions of material development, cannot themselves be made objects. The best we can achieve is then a homogeneity of comprehension and development, but it is important in doing so not to confuse analytical organization with empirical totality, in either a practical or a critical sense.

In depicting structures in this way, Sartre provides a logical justification to overcome not only dualism, wherein structures are viewed as either determinate of or determined by human agency, but also duality, wherein an ameliorative, or recursive, relationship is posited between structure and human agency.

The 'duality' of agency and structure is mis-specified if the relationship between the two is seen as merely recursive, each constituting the other, for such a depiction provides a basis only for understanding the constituted terms of contingent history, not the constituent terms according to which history is possible.

Whereas Giddens, therefore, provides a framework for analysis of emerging social conditions, he does not provide the basis for understanding how human beings possess the potential to be part of social conditions. He begins with a theoretical, rather than a philosophical perspective. Sartre's work allows us to connect the two, by creating a link between the possible and the empirical. This link gives access to history and geography, as well as the spatial/temporal organizations of the social.

Geographers concern themselves with a certain range of structures that define the quality of the human being/environment relationship. One of the major concepts that allows us to do this is landscape. The methodological logic outlined above can be applied to the concept of landscape to achieve two tasks. The first is the conceptual clarification, and by corollary philosophical justification, of the term within the geographical lexicon. The second is the confirmation of landscape as one of the central methodological entries to an understanding of human habitation of place. To achieve the first purpose, landscape can be understood in exactly the same way as the concept of process just described. It is the assignment of pseudo-organic quality to the ongoing dialectical relationship among a set of material elements.

Landscape is a process. Its quality is pseudo-organic, because unlike simple nature, something that is historically transcended cannot also be organic in itself. It carries with it an irreducible context. It is therefore a totalization at any historical moment. Its qualities are limited, however, by the power of human perception, and landscape is not therefore 'everything', but a choice of interconnected elements within a totality. Its status is analytic.

Landscape is a process organized, as Lowenthal noted, logically and optimally, while at the same time it is always a concrete, material transformation of nature. We can then speak of the 'urban landscape', the 'agricultural landscape', 'landscapes of despair', or 'fear', or the 'physical landscape', as particular organizations of the environment by geographers.

In doing so, it is not necessary to idealize landscape as so many generations of cultural geographers have done. It is quite possible to avoid idealism simply by specifying that we refer to moments of organization that are immediately transcended, but that none the less can be expressed linguistically. At the same time, it is not possible to reduce landscape to its constituent elements, or to a set of structures, since the dialectical quality of existence makes such a reduction a logical impossibility. What is important, however, is to achieve an analysis of landscape as homogeneity: of comprehension and development, praxis and process, form and meaning, structure and human agency.

To achieve homogeneity, or integration, is to uncover rationality, on which analytical understanding is based, and from which synthetic understanding can proceed. Rationality can be defined after Sartre's discussion in Critique of dialectical reason, as a form of congruence between understanding and language. To make something rational is to reveal its structures,, as they are expressed in its physical manifestation. The way in which landscape is most useful to the geographer is as a form of language that structures and is structured by the production of social relations. This applies not only to the geographer, but to all those who inhabit the landscape. Habitation becomes expression. An aspect of landscape as language that is of especial importance to geographers is its relative durability.

We need to recognize not only the theoretical principle that life is a continuous process of landscape formation, but also that the process according to which landscape emerges includes the very forceful imposition of physical conditions that structure the actions of human beings over long periods of time. In this sense, a historical understanding of landscape formation is necessary to link the qualities of particular landscapes to both their social meanings and the technological means by which they are controlled at particular times and places.

The creation of landscape comes about through human labour in its broadest sense, the process by which human beings produce and reproduce their lives. Labour expresses the dialectical relationship with the natural environment:

> its possibility and its permanent necessity rest upon the relation of interiority which unites the organism with the environment and upon the deep contradiction between the inorganic and organic orders, both of which are present in everyone. Its primary movement and its essential character are defined by a twofold contradictory transformation: the unity of the project endows the practical field with a quasi-synthetic unity, and the crucial moment of labour is that in which the organism makes itself inert (the man applies his weight to the lever, etc.) in order to transform the surrounding inertia.

Thus materiality is the bond, forged by labour, by which the relationship between the individual and nature is constituted. The relationship is reciprocal, a vast symbiosis, wherein humans are "'mediated" by things to the same extent as things are mediated"' by them. The relationship, however, is always both social and univocal. That is, people share the landscape they create through their labour, and only humans are capable of initiating the act of totalization by which the environment is organized in a purposeful manner. They have projects. In the absence of human labour, the world would be a meaningless and mechanical collection of energy.

The concept used by Sartre to indicate the surrounding world of material possibility is the 'practico-inert':

> ... every object, in so far as it exists within a given economic, technical and social complex, will in its turn become exigency through the mode and relations of production, and give rise to other exigencies in other objects.

This is the world, created by and embodying human praxis in fulfilment of its projects, a world of objects that surpass their objective quality because they possess a history, and therefore human significance. They have been imbued with the power to act upon both human beings and other objects through praxis. Every human action is constituted as 'primarily an instrumentalisation of material reality'. It is a totalization undertaken with specific tools and technology and, as such, a statement of an entire ensemble of social relations. The statement occurs in the landscape as signification:

> ... precisely because signification takes on the character of materiality, it enters into relation with the entire Universe. This means that infinitely many unforeseeable relations are established, through the mediation of social practice, between the matter which absorbs praxis and other materialised significations.

In nearly all situations, the exigency of the surrounding landscape is diffuse and complex. Sartre gives the example of deforestation in China. The Chinese peasants removed the forest cover over large sections of the country in the positive project of producing greater agricultural yields. In so doing, they humanized their landscape, inscribing It with the significance of their actions, embodying a cultural tradition.

At the same time, they created the unforeseeable effect of massive flooding, and the peasants' positive actions became the means of their own destruction,, which nothing in their set of cultural structures could circumvent. This set of events was possible only within the historical material ensemble that produced a society in which certain tools, certain methods of labour and certain projects occurred as the cumulative result of preterit action that was also more than it was intended to be.

Human action was united in the material environment, inverted and turned into an exigency that set new conditions and alienated the peasants from the land that was their means of survival. In this sense, the landscape is capable of usurping the human attributes of those who sustain it and give it power. It is in understanding the diffusion of power within the landscape that geographers face their greatest methodological challenge. In discussing method, we wish to focus on only two aspects of the linguistic expression of landscape, as crystallized praxis and as ideology.

To term landscape 'crystallized praxis' is nothing more or less than to recognize that it is the totalized appearance of all praxis at a particular moment. It has a history, or as Samuels calls it, a biography. Since the depassement of its biography occurs only as actual physical manifestation, it is open to investigation. It can be read, or interpreted. There are practical constraints to interpretation, but these do not prevent legibility in principle.

We may therefore recognize that:

> Given the fact that... landscapes are typically the product of design... i.e. the result of many decisions by many people over long periods of time, it is very striking indeed that they 'add up'. They develop coherence, they are instantaneously recognizable; If one knows the cues, a single slide can be enough to identify a place.

This intelligibility is an intrinsic aspect of all praxis as human beings engage their surrounding materiality, organizing it to produce meaning. The organized landscape 'adds up' in the literal sense that it is composed of every praxis that has been initiated toward it, nothing more. Every prax's, however, has meaning, draws upon former meanings, and transcends its own moment. Through this process, structure is engaged to maintain order.

The clarity of the landscape message, however, is problematic. The landscape is fraught with contradiction and new contradictions are created each moment, and interposed at three levels. First, human consciousness may be defined as the synthesis of contradiction, not in the Marxist sense of an imposed alienation, but in the sense that it involves a mediation of internal and external reality.

Consciousness becomes itself as the constant mediation of this contradiction. Second, as the above example shows, in the production of the material object, praxis is alienated from itself. Its power is usurped, made inert by the material world, thence to be returned in a transformed state.

The world acts back on the univocal relationship established by human praxis. Third and most importantly, praxis refers not to the single act of an individual, but to the totality of all those who inhabit landscape. Individual intentions are seldom expressed intact, but are countered by the actions of others and by the unintended results of former actions.

In the interpretation of landscapes, therefore, geographers are faced with the task of trying to ascertain, among other things, the levels of ambiguity according to which it was created, the degree of contradiction that is manifest, and the efficacy of the linguistic statement in putting forth intelligible messages.

All of these qualities rest on the structure of landscape, as the rules by which actions are guided. Efficacy of structure depends on its clarity, and the amount of power that it wields. Clarity of structure, as in any form of language, is best achieved when a high level of formality exists. The Japanese formal garden, for example, is created according to a set of rules that is well established in historical tradition, and relatively inflexible in form despite infinite capacity for expression. These rules have been created in such a way that their strength lies in their aesthetic appeal. The Japanese garden is thus a poetic form of language, and as such plays a powerful but limited cultural role.

If the power of structure is measured by the degree to which it is commonly understood and expressed within the landscape, then it is ideology, as the form of structuring and sharing value, that underlies the power, or effectiveness, of landscape as a linguistic statement. Landscape as ideology takes as many forms as human beings are able to construct in exerting power over others.

A totalitarian landscape, for example, is an expression of alienation, where ideology is made to be an autonomous superstructure with relative control over the agency of social individuals. We may envision another form of landscape in which ideology is expressed as common project, shared concern, the fusion of praxis to create congruence of structure and the agency of individuals.

Geographers have Identified particular landscapes that emerge when an organized ideology is imposed to create specific political goals as in 'Mao's China' or where particular groups effect a common ideology at the local level in opposition to the imposition of institutionalized structure.

Historical processes such as 'post-industrialism' may provide the basis for structuring of landscape as a way of life. In each case the landscape is the depassement of ideology, a statement of the social relations of its production and the ground for further development of geographical landscape studies.

The geographical challenge of modernity is to recognize ways in which particular landscapes emerge, and are organized, as expression of the conditions of the world at this time.

Technological advances in communication, for example, allow dominant ideological systems to gain hegenionic influence over landscapes in far-flung corners of the world. At the same time, never before have human beings been better equipped to use global communication as a means of addressing common concerns.

Technological organization, with all that it implies, is therefore one of the most important aspects of contemporary landscape analysis, and must be taken into account in addressing the environmental expressions of contemporary world issues, sonic of which have been addressed in this volume, such as hunger, the restructuring of the labour force and the livability of cities; all issues which will influence the character of future landscapes.

8
Feminism as Geographic Analysis

Feminist geography, is about the social and environmental processes whereby the two genders—women and men—which make up the category 'human' are constituted, reproduced and changed. Feminist geography is about the way in which gender is constituted and how this relates to the constitution of the environment. The development of a basis for feminist geography—concerned with the relations between gender and environment—had two initial components. First it was necessary to disaggregate the category 'human' and to reconstitute it as a category which included the activities of both genders. Second, it was necessary to disaggregate the category 'environment' and to reconstitute it as a category which was sensitive to alterations in gender.

Feminist exploration in geography, as elsewhere, began by breaking down the a historical category 'woman' and asking —what kinds of social relations structured and changed gender categories? This social conceptualization of gender depends oil seeing gender—those socially constructed activities and attributes ascribed to women or men—as historically mutable. Gender categories are socially and politically constructed, socially and politically contested and socially and politically changed.

A good deal of feminist analysis is concerned to understand the nature and process of these changes. For example, the gender category 'women' in North American and Western European society has altered significantly within the last 50 years, largely through changes in what women are doing.

A generation ago, a woman was someone imbued with an overwhelming maternal instinct who confined her person to the home and her activities to nurturing an unrestricted number of children and a breadwinner husband. A 'woman' is now an energetic actor, capable of reconciling two demanding jobs—one at home and one in the wage labour force— and doing so rationally and cheerfully. Some of this alteration was media stereotyping. But it was and is also a reflection of very real and substantial changes in the activity patterns and expectations of women and men. These altered activity patterns were themselves reflections of general social changes, which included relatively safe and reliable female-controlled contraception, access to better domestic working conditions, and a rise in female wage labour force participation.

Although the women who organized for better fertility control, better housing and access to education and jobs did not, on the whole, consciously see the implications of their actions as leading to changes in the definition of 'woman', this was the necessary outcome of their new activities, as well as the precondition of further campaigns in these areas. This constant change of gender categories proceeds in a reciprocal manner. Changes in the activities and attributes which make up 'woman' imply, result in and respond to changes in the activities and attributes of 'man'.

The change from 'total mother' to 'superwoman' was accompanied by a concomitant change in 'man':

from the sole breadwinner with his mind on the market rid the sports page to a family companion and partner. The historical constitution and change of the two gender categories 'woman' and 'man' in combination, constitute and change 'human'. For feminists, therefore, to be human is not a static thing. It is a hangeful and active process, altering through alterations in the activities and attributes which constitute 'woman' and 'man'. Just boundaries of gender categories are not static, so the sum total of human activities and attributes is not static.

Alteration of gender categories does not proceed through the transfer back and forth of a fixed set of a historical human characteristics from one gender to another. Change of the androgynous human is a creative process. Like all creative processes, it involves, at times, the destruction of some attributes in the creation of new ones. For example, men did not take on the roles of instinctively guided social maternalism as women failed to reproduce these, although fathering did become a more central and qualitatively different social institution.

A feminist geography suggests first that we look at 'human' as a category constantly changing as women and men alter gender attributes through altering their activities. It suggests we see that constitution of 'human' as an active and often conscious process. But the constitution of 'human' is only one half of human environmental relations which forms the basis of geographic enquiry. The second requirement of a feminist geography is that we develop a concept of environment which allows us to see the change of gender relations relative to environmental relations. This involves breaking down the category 'environment' and seeing environments as changing sets of resources appropriated in historically variable ways, these modes of appropriation altering through alterations in space and time patterns.

A feminist geography therefore suggests that we see the environment, too, as an active, frequently political and sometimes conscious creation. And it suggests that we see the constitution and change of an androgynous human and the constitution of environment proceeding simultaneously, in a process of interaction. In analytic terms, gender becomes a space-structuring force; -environment becomes a component of gender constitution. The link between 'human' and 'environment' is the active use of time and space which simultaneously alters gender and alters the social environment.

Over the past century, people's space and time have become increasingly separated into work for wages and life been a function of, and has reinforced, a growing separation between wage workplace and home, on a continuum which runs from the pre-industrial home-workshop to the suburban home distant from centralized industrial-commercial firms.

This spatial separation has been correlated with an increasing differentiation between the gender categories woman and man. Yet this separation and the form of this differentiation are in the process of fundamental alteration and potential convergence in the current period of economic restructuring.

Work and life

The 19th-century 'woman question' was resolved by confining most women's persons and defining all women's natures in terms of the home and community. The newly separated residential suburb had collected together all requisites of social reproduction and areally distanced them and the women who carried out domestic work from production. Throughout the 20th century, women lived and worked within the bounds of the gender-typed, separated city, invisibly organizing to improve their working conditions. The bounds extended spatially into more extensive and ever more far-flung suburbs. The suburbs 'worked' for that brief historical period between the 1930s and 1950s when some men had secure, remunerative jobs, and most women could devote all their time to planning around and caring for the home and family. And their working assumed and reinforced this gender-typed separation.

Male wages were sufficient to purchase a home and most of the raw materials to run it. Full-time female labour was required to actually shop for these materials and to turn them into the components of family life. Neither alone was sufficient. The social definition of 'woman' and 'man' became strongly imbued with connotations of natural differences which led to social reciprocity and consensus.

By the 1960s, however, the maintenance of this form of home came to rely increasingly on two incomes. Growing numbers of women took on dual roles, and the bundle of spatially reinforced gender differentiation began to unravel. The activities appropriate to women came to include earning money as well as providing goods and services in the home.

Just as the suburban solution depended on and reinforced one set of gender roles —the full-time domestic worker-mother and the full-time breadwinner— so the maintenance of temporally and spatially separated homes and workplaces depends on another set, primarily women's dual roles. But women's dual roles are themselves problematic. Whereas the 19th-century 'urban question' had been primarily focused around inadequate conditions for reproduction in the central cities, the solution to these problems—the extensive, distant and expensive suburb separated from wage workplaces -becomes the mid-20th-century 'urban problem', a problem which is especially acute for that growing proportion of the labour force who are also domestic community workers. Work in the home, the place associated with leisure, is not seen as real work, nor are the home and neighbourhood designed as workplaces. What women do in these places is invisible in the public sector, as it was meant to be.

Employers make few concessions to the fact that women have other jobs. As it is assumed that someone is looking after the children in the private home, child care is not a public priority. And at the end of a long day, having got her family off to school, to child care, to work, travelled to a wage job herself, to shop, to see a child's doctor or teacher, the woman comes home again to a domestic workplace which requires hours of hard work and complex planning to keep running. In response to the fact that women are working at the intersection of home and work, providing not only resources in kind in the home and community but also monetary resources, they are creating services at the intersection of home and work, services which bridge the two spheres and fill the formerly invisible gaps in the separated city.

As employment opportunities and flexibility decrease with economic restructuring and as government restraint programmes cut back the already inadequate social services available to families, especially to wage-earning mothers, these small and socially unacknowledged services at the intersection are becoming increasingly important to the economic and social survival of households. A growing number of women, or at least an increasingly obvious group of women, begin to extend their home roles to earning money at home.

Homeworkers are a heterogeneous group. They are doing a wide variety of things; a recent study identified over 200 types of home-based businesses. These range from international import-export businesses and internationally renowned artists working from home studios to the woman down the street who crochets dolls for sale at local craft shows or minds her friend's children a few hours a day. But whatever their differences, all these women have two things in common. They have all adjusted their organization of time to include work in the home for pay as well as providing goods and services to their families. And they are all attempting to use the resources available in the 'private space' of the home and community to carry out a new set of activities.

The rigid, spatially reinforced separation between wage workplace and home—the concomitant basis of clearly demarcated gender roles—was severely weakened by women's dual roles. It is being further dissolved by the adaptation strategy homeworkers are developing in response to economic restructuring and to the problems of maintaining dual roles. Homeworkers' adjustment of their space and time has implications which arc potentially significant for restructuring the relation between home and work and between women and men.

Homeworkers

In an attempt to ascertain some of these implications, we inter-viewed independent homeworkers in the Trail-Nelson area of the interior of British Columbia and in the Kingston area of Eastern Ontario. Weasked them not only what they did-and how, but also about how their homework affected their relations to the resource base of the home and community, including their networks of family and friends. These homeworkers—were utilizing existing local resources, primarily their homes and communities, and their given networks and skills. They were doing so in the context of specific environmental constraints. Many lacked viable employment alternatives, either because of their domestic responsibilities or lack of available jobs. And while most earned relatively little from their homework, the job often provide a substantial part of family income.

Within these constraints, however, the social relations involved in attempts to utilize a limited set of resources designed for one purpose—private family life and individual consumption—in order to carry out a related but different purpose—the provision of a public service and the gaining of a livelihood—are causing homeworkers to alter the environments in which they work. They are using their given, limited environments and skills in new ways, principally by converting or redesignating resources formerly seen as private into public or collective productive resources. In the process, they are extending these resources, and often creating new resources.

This process of extending and creating resources at the interface of home and work has three implications for women's activities and for domestic community life.

First, these women are developing new sources of employment, providing new social areas for 'work' and thus contributing to redefining the nature of work. Women—caring for each other's children, sewing each other's drapes—are creating their own jobs. In the process, they are redefining and extending the sets of skills which are 'considered worthy of payment.

These women are taking their 'natural' parenting skills, their homemaking skills or their experiences in home manufacture and crafts and redefining them as marketable skills. The private experience they have gained as mothers and housewives has been converted into a set of defined and valued skills with which to make a living. And the majority are attempting to extend their personal skills.

Most have had some outside training to enhance these skills immediately prior or subsequent to starting homework. This training varies from professional qualifications to informal drop-in or self-organised collective work sessions.

Most of these homeworkers have also redesignated networks among friends and neighbours as 'working' networks. This takes a variety of forms, based around formal or self-created organizations, or around informal ad hoc meetings of homeworkers with similar interests. Such networks were not only sources of contact, advice and assistance, but also often acted as referral and in some cases monitoring agencies. These networks acted to self-regulate and to disseminate information about the quality of goods or services provided by the homeworkers.

In developing and utilizing these networks, homeworkers are providing themselves with some of the protection and services of a combined trade union and professional association. They are also attempting to increase the social recognition of their skills through involvement in professional associations ranging from nationally organized groups to ad hoc neighbourhood networks.

Homeworkers have also altered and extended preexisting networks with family. Most indicated that family members often helped with their work, either through directly working on the money-earning activities or in taking over other domestic tasks.

Second, they are providing services to other members of the community, thus contributing to restructuring domestic community working conditions, and to altering the nature of reproductive activities which go on there. Homeworkers are providing direct 'public' services to other members of the community, services which, are becoming increasingly central to domestic community life, and are often the only alternative available. And this has the effect of altering the conditions, and the environment in which domestic community work goes on.

For homeworkers, both the household and the neighbourhood become workplace as well as living space, simultaneously public and private space. In fact, the division into public and private becomes an increasingly meaningless one.

For homeworkers, the formerly 'separate' activities involved in maintaining the household become increasingly incorporated into the activities involved in earning money, 'and their content merges. A childminder cooking lunch for her own children as well as those she is paid to care for is simultaneously doing a 'labour of love' and wage-earning labour. In many cases, the places where these two sets of activities go on are the same, or parts of the home are set aside primarily or exclusively for money-earning work.

Homeworkers are redesignating their neighbourhoods as workplaces, assessing the local and wider communities in terms of demand for their product or service and in terms of facilities to assist their work. Women using their homes and neighbourhoods as workplaces are also actively redesigning these environments. Not only do the houses of many homeworkers include spaces set aside for the activities of homework, but these women are creating, in concrete terms, new public spaces; milieux where both 'private' domestic-community work and homework go on collectively. Such spaces include the sites of playgroups and drop in centres, attended by both mothers and homeworkers, the crafts guilds which include both 'hobbyists' and homeworkers, cooperative craft shows, stores and networks which purchase materials and equipment for both homeworkers and 'private' domestic workers.

Therefore, these networks and spaces not only provide services to homeworkers, they are also restructuring the conditions under which women with dual roles or no paid jobs are carrying out their 'private' domestic community work.

A regular part of parenting increasingly includes attendance and some organizational work at a co-operative playgroup. A regular part of maintaining the home may include attending informal classes on craft manufacture and the purchase of materials from co-operative networks.

Third, they are altering the balance of resources in kind and monetary resources which households need to survive, and thus changing the relations between home and wage workplace. Women earning money at home are restructuring the balance between domestic work—producing free services and goods in kind—and wage work - producing money for the purchase of services and goods. This alters both the value of labour power and the conditions of its reproduction. Wages have never been sufficient for most people's subsistence.

Subsistence has always required some form of domestic work, and for most, some form of family and community-based mutual aid. Women in the community have a long tradition of organizing community mutual aid, based on attempts to compensate for the quantitative and qualitative differences between the male wage and the needs of the family. But such organization has necessarily become more dense and more formal in increasing number of women, especially mothers, entered the wage labour force.

A loose network of extended family and friends could meet the needs of a community of full-time housewives-mothers on an ad hoc basis. However, more regular assistance, more often coordinated by exchange value relations rather than use value relations, became necessary to meet the needs of a community of dual role women. The forms of mutual aid provided in the community thus become more central to the exchange process between labour power and capital as a growing percentage of the labour force define themselves as domestic workers as well as wage workers. Wage work patterns are also influenced by the homework sector.

A socio-economy where the maintenance of family life requires both adults to be economically active tends to break down the barriers, real and analytic, between wage work and consumption on a number of levels. And this breaking down is extended as the services necessary to maintain the labour force include more and more aspects of the 'social wage', and issues such as child care become workplace issues.

Formerly 'private' activities like child care become workplace issues not only in a formal sense of being union bargaining matters or incentives to attract labour, but also in the sense that the availability, affordability and accessibility of child care help determine the availability of parents for wage work.

The location and accessibility of child care influences the range of places parents are able and willing to work. And as the majority of child care is provided by home caregivers, the size, location, cost and quality of this sector becomes intimately bound up with both the availability and the satisfaction of the wage]about force, especially the participation of mothers in the labour force. 18 The homework sector, as a community source, also influences the amount of money a family needs in order to reproduce itself, that is, it influences the balance between use values and exchange values in the household budget.

The homework sector often provides alternatives to formal market services, not only in the case of services like child care, typing or household maintenance, but also in the form of alternative sources of household goods. Not only do homeworkers manufacture goods for sale, the networks of all homeworkers are supplemented by lively barter relations. This includes both barter in kind (e.g. pottery for clothing), and also services for goods (e.g. baby-sitting for paintings, craft lessons for garden produce). In addition, the cooperative networks set up to purchase materials for craft manufacture, utilized by both hobbyists and professionals, also provide alternative sources of raw materials for household manufacture.

Homeworkers are thus involved in altering the nature and content of exchange relations, sometimes on a small scale, as with most craft manufacture, sometimes, as in the case of the home child care sector, dominating the field. In some respects this takes the form of an alternative economy. In most respects, however, it is an alternative intimately bound up with and changing the nature of the mainstream socio-economy.

A feminist geography is based on the understanding that gender and environment alter simultaneously, in a process of interaction, and that the link between an androgynous human and the environment is the active use of space and time by women and men. Women's dual roles can thus take a multitude of forms. Women can work in two separate and functionally disparate places, attempting to bridge constant discontinuity in their daily lives, largely through individual effort and the use of a range of use and exchange values available in their communities.

Alternatively, they can obtain a variety of resources in a variety of ways within the home and community, and thus alter not their location, but the social meaning and function of home and work. However they carry them out, women's dual roles are not a radical break with the past, but another adjustment of their use of space and time in order to maximize access to resources.

In their daily activities, women make multitudes of small, daily decisions and choices attempting to adjust the time and space for care of children, for domestic community work, for moneyearning work. All of these arrangements must take into account the fluid constraints imposed by the specific balance of resources and family needs.

Women's allocation of space and time must attempt to balance the resources the family needs - the amount of money, the number of commodities and services, the amount of time from the mother, the wife, the cook, the wage earner which is required to achieve a desired family lifestyle. All of these adjustments have had specific effects on the nature of capitalist society, and more immediately but less obviously, on the nature of both the home and community and of gender relations within this society.

Homeworkers, in creating a new social space at the intersection of home and wage workplace, are thus part of a radical, rooted continuity. This is a continuity which stretches both across time into the social history of pre-industrial society and across space into the economies of contemporary third world, countries. But saying it is not new does not imply that its implications cannot be new, nor that the social milieu it creates cannot be the source of new and potentially consciously creative social and gender relations. The implications can be both exciting and horrific; they are certainly worthy of serious analysis. Carrying out such analysis requires not only that we recognize the reciprocal alteration of gender and environment, but also that we define the 'necessary relations' or the essential, definitive parameters of gender constitution and change, which in the case of feminist geography are simultaneously the parameters of environmental constitution and change.

Restructuring space and gender

Both socialist and radical feminists have defined, albeit in very different ways, the essential parameters of gender constitution as the relations between the production of society's goods and services and the reproduction of people as biological and social beings.

While radical feminists concentrated on the politics of reproduction, socialist feminists attempted to articulate this understanding to broader theories of social change, primarily, although not exclusively, historical materialism. In so doing, socialist feminists have not just adopted, but also adapted, historical materialism. Including,gender is not just a matter of an empirical addition at the historical level. It involves, or more accurately makes evident the need for, a shift in our analytic focal point.

Women in capitalist society are defined from, live and work in, and analyse themselves from an inherently contradictory material position. Women are defined as responsible for essential social work—mothering and caring for adults—what is commonly called reproductive work, in a society where power and analytic categories derive primarily from the productive sphere.

Like class relations, but in a more obvious way, gender relations are constituted not only by relations of production, but also by the dialectically related relations involved in the reproduction of people. Seeing the articulation of gender relations with environmental relations means focusing on the activities involved in the production of goods and services, with reference to or simultaneously with those involved in the biological and social reproduction of people.

As a consequence, socialist feminist analysis focuses not primarily on production, not primarily on reproduction, but on the relations between the two. The nature of this intersection is seen to define gender relations. These are the essential social parameters which analytically encompass women's activities, those activities which constitute and change gender and environment.

The relations between production and reproduction are thus the 'necessary' parameters in defining gender and its interaction with environment. But the proposed articulation of gender and environment implies even more than a change in the initial focal point from which our categories are formulated. It implies a new political focus, one concentrating on understanding the content of categories and the human activities which make up this content.

We cannot focus long on the relation between production and reproduction without moving a long way from both the bad old days of economic determinism and from the seductive Althusserian moment—the theoretically comfortable but politically irresponsible view of people as bearers of relations. In part this is because such a focus breaks down the neat conceptual divisions between production and reproduction; between work and non-work or life; between productive and nonproductive, even between class and gender, or structure and agency. It forces us instead to see people's activities anew, conceptually unclad and undisguised, so to speak. In part, looking at reproduction as analytically important, as politically pertinent, makes a focus on content unavoidable. There is little else to see apart from the small, 'insignificant', 'common-sense' details of keeping people alive and socially integrated in a capitalist society. And as these become evident, they mingle with or even crowd out the abstract questions of tendencies and structures which formed the basis of positivist geography and which still linger on in some contemporary work

So a focus on the intersection of productive and reproductive activities tends to create an analysis which is full of content, which is concerned with the kinds of interpersonal relations through which we get by day by day, and which is concerned with how we can change these.

It suggests that we recentre our attention on the taken-for-granted details, the small human actions which constitute and change our categories, our tendencies, our structures, that we look for social changes at the level where they are created, in human lives, as well as at the higher levels of abstraction with which many of us have become so expert at conjuring. In short, this focus is one of the major analytic bases for the emphasis, in feminist political actions, on prefigurative politics, on building a new society from the bottom up, so to speak.

Socialist feminism remains profoundly committed to historical materialist analysis—seeing life ill capitalist society as structured by our relations to the means and processes whereby we produce goods and services and reproduce ourselves as biological and social beings. It is also profoundly humanist in being centred on human agency, concerned with daily actions as the basis of social change. The preceding discussion therefore suggests that the development of feminist geography has implications both for the theoretical methodological basis of the discipline, and for the nature of our empirical work.

Feminist geography was initially defined as a study concerned to understand how changes in environmental relations—changes in the way people use and create space and time —interact with, help structure, reflect and reinforce the social definition of the gender categories 'woman' and 'man', and the relations between women and men.

It is concerned to understand the ways in which the activities involved in being a man or a woman in society relate to appropriation of and activity in time and space. It implies an interactive and creative relation between gender and environment, and much current research is devoted to understanding the nature of this reaction

The extension of this perspective to the discipline as a whole and its contribution to current debates oil human environmental relations directed our attention to two areas.

First it implied a disaggregation and reintegration of the 'human' half of the human-environmental equation to include the diverse and often oppositional creativity of the two genders.

Second it implied a focus oil environ-ment as actively constituted and changed simultaneously with gender, through alterations in the activities of women and men. This latter was seen to involve a focus on the interrelated activities of production and reproduction.

Empirical discussion of the historical nature of this relation revealed not only its variability but an emerging tendency toward breaking down the spatial and functional separation between productive and reproductive activities. Although the activities of homeworkers in creating this breakdown were in one sense reproducing women's domestic community skills, they were simultaneously altering the basis of gender constitution.

A geography which asks us to study the reciprocal relations between the constitution of an androgynous human and the constitution of environment asks a great deal, nothing less than the disaggregation and reintegration of the most fundamental concepts in the discipline. Within the last generation, women have seen tremendous alterations in their daily lives and in the conditions under which resources for these lives are provided. They have also seen the image of woman change radically, and seen and experienced feminism redefine 'woman' from a state of being to a political force.

9
Participant Observation

In approaching the study of social and community life, of which we as researchers and individuals are a part, we cannot ignore the competing tensions active in the array of social research methods. Broadly, these tensions result from two diametrically opposed approaches to social research—positivism and naturalism. For some considerable time positivism, the endeavour to construct a science of society modelled on the logic of experimentalism in the natural sciences, has been dominant in empirical method.

The positivist method operates by the categorization of directly observable social phenomena into variables which are tested in their causal relationship to certain independent variables in an attempt to produce testable laws and theories. The logic of the model relies upon quantitative manipulation. Thus in community study-a positivist would approach social phenomena by the use of questionnaires and attitude surveys, which test the incidence of certain responses to attitudes or questions against independent variables such as social class.

The shortcomings of such an approach lie in the preoccupation with social phenomena which are directly observable. Such a preoccupation is evidenced in the positivist obsession with sampling and standardizing techniques in an attempt to create categories of data generalizable across all situations and research circumstances. By restricting the extent of social phenomena to that which is directly observable there is a tendency to extract the phenomena from the social context in which they are observed and measurable. This in turn leads to a tendency to omit consideration of the largely nonobservable values, meanings and intentions which may be present in such situations.

Finally, there is an inclination to presume a neutrality of observation and to ignore a cultural perspective on the part of the observer. As Charles Darwin once said, 'How odd it is that anyone should not see that observation must be for or against some view, if it is to be of any service'.

In following the imported logic of the model of the natural sciences, positivism strives to create a neutral observation language and artificial experimental settings in an endeavour to counter the real possibilities of researcher bias which exist in social research. However, to consider, as positivism taken to its logical extremity must do, that observation can be carried out in a value-free vacuum, is unrealistic.

Naturalism, on the other hand, differentiates the social disciplines from natural science on the basis that social phenomena are different in character from natural phenomena. Furthermore the naturalist stance proposes that the social realm should be approached in its natural state, and its first requirement is that the integrity of phenomena should remain unimpaired. Thus whilst the naturalist accepts that social phenomena do appear as directly observable, that characteristic alone is insufficient to understand and explain their existence.

All variations of naturalism place emphasis on the social meanings, intentions and attitudes which are the underlying basis of the appearance of social phenomena.

To understand appearances we must therefore employ a method which gives us access to the underlying meanings, etc. The point of access which naturalism identifies is that we are all, as members of society, able to participate in the social phenomena we observe and thereby learn the underlying meanings which produce them. One such approach is termed participant observation.

However, the tendency with most forms of naturalism is to place such a high premium on the retention of the integrity of phenomena as to isolate the researcher to an extent that participation becomes largely meaningless. For example, Kurt-Wolff's method of 'surrender to' relies upon the manipulation of the researcher by the phenomena to such an extent that the focus is upon the contortions of the transcendental acts of the researcher rather than the community being studied.

The ultimate effect of naturalism is that because 'the naturalist resists schemes or models which oversimplify the complexity of everyday life', we are left with what amounts to descriptions rather than explanations of social phenomena. The appearances of social phenomena become so highly valued as 'reality' that they become conflated with 'truth' to the extent that to delve beneath the surfaces of observed phenomena in order to seek the meanings and intentions which produce it becomes sacrosanct on the grounds that it would somehow distort 'truth'.

Thus naturalism leaves us with little more than positivism; an emphasis upon the directly observable and a divorce between the researcher and the researched which ultimately amounts to an artificial separation of theory from method. Yet the essential advantage of participant observation remains that the researcher as a member of society has access to participation in social phenomena which in itself constitutes a method: the use of the researcher as methodological tool. Traditionally such an approach has developed from Dilthey and Weber's use of the concept of Verstehen as an endeavour by the researcher to achieve an empathic knowledge of the state of mind of the actor in order to reconstruct social phenomena. In recent years Verstehen has been developed as the principle of reflexive explanation; that each of us as members of society are able to participate via certain roles and come to reflect on the products of that participation. But this in itself is insufficient to develop the objective interest that researchers have as participants.

To rely on reflexivity alone is to divorce the researcher from the researched. Self-interrogation to calculate the extent to which we change during the research procedure is a measure of the reaction of the subjective realm upon oneself and would depend ultimately upon this in relation to what we were like prior to entering the research setting.

Furthermore, just because we as researchers have made explicit by a process of reflexivity our, meanings and intentions, and gained a knowledge of the way that they translate into actions, does not necessarily entail us understanding that same process in others; all we see in fact are appearances, the results of the process. For this reason interpretation becomes necessary, and in that we do not accept social phenomena at face value (i.e. are interested in underlying processes) such interpretation is of a critical persuasion.

Thus as opposed to the phenomenological dictum of the suspension of received notions, participant observers we must suspend belief in the reality of appearances. In fact, in contradistinction to the suspension of received notions, participant observers become informed and employ theories and hypotheses in the very act of research; an experimentalist attitude is adopted in the sense of 'trying things out'.

By introducing theorization to the research situation we are, of course, conjoining theory and method. But it should be borne in mind that theory is after all, like any knowledge, produced by social practices and reflection on those practices. Knowledge is in turn transformed by practice, just as practice is altered by knowledge.

The suspension of judgement as to the reality of appearances, the adoption by the participant observer of a critical, interpretative stance, necessitates an evaluation of the relation of the researcher to the researched. This is perhaps best considered in the context of Simmel's formulation of the role of the stranger. The researcher may in fact be a stranger to the social phenomena in question by virtue of not being a recognized participating member within it. But more importantly the researcher as a marginal individual, by the suspension of belief in the reality of appearances, is also adopting the role of the stranger and achieves a level of objectivity by it.

Because he is not bound by roots to the particular constituents and partisan dispositions of the group, he confronts all of these with a distinctly 'objective' attitude, an attitude that does not signify mere detachment and non-participation, but is a distinct structure composed of remoteness and nearness, indifference and involvement. In adopting such a reflexive, critically interpretative stance as participant observers and thereby conjoining theory and method, there would appear to be problems of both validating and verifying research.

A research method achieves a level of validity when the knowledge which it constructs is considered to be an adequate articulation of the social phenomena which it purports to understand and explain. The verification of the method thereby becomes the extent to which it is able to achieve a level of adequacy in other research situations, i.e. is repeatable. Participation is in essence really only a refinement on the methods used to reflexively understand and interpret in everyday life. To this end, the measure of adequacy of the articulation of the social phenomena researched is the success of the participation by the researcher in the collective contract of the everyday life being studied.

As George Herbert Mead points out, participation is the very essence of meanings which form a collective contract; indeed he identifies two characteristics of what we term meanings:

> One is participation and the other is communicability. Meaning can arise only insofar as some phase of the act which the individual is arousing in the other can be aroused in himself. There is always to this extent participation. And the result of this participation is communicability, i. e. the individual can indicate to himself what he indicates to others.

Validation is, therefore, by the very act of participation, internal to the research in that whilst interpretations must be justifiable in terms of the cited evidence, they are still the product of the ability of the observer to participate meaningfully. In terms of verification,

> What is necessary is that the participating observer be able to provide other potential participating observers with a set of explicit instructions (which are at present taken for granted) on how to put themselves in the same situation so as to have the same or similar experience.

If the aim of repeatability is to assist potential participant observers to put themselves in similar situations, then heed must be paid to the considerations of methodological framework we have thus far made in this section. Other researchers should be made aware of the hurdles which the dominance of positivism and the challenge of naturalism present, the relation that they as individuals have to what they research and the reflexive and critical character of the interpretative process.

The manner in which research problems come to be identified is a matter which is rarely given consideration. In the natural sciences there is still a widely-held belief (although less common today) that the agenda is established externally by the logic inherent in natural phenomena. But social influences, and in particular the imperatives of technological change (e.g. the influence of the Cold War on the development of nuclear science) cannot be ignored. In so far as social research has been modelled along the lines of natural science by the influence of positivism an emphasis has been placed upon the rigour of an imported logic to the detriment of the subtler qualities of social processes.

Positivism produces a concentration upon observable phenomena and its categorization at the expense of ignoring the underlying motives and intentions guiding human action. Furthermore in trying to create a neutral observation language positivism attempts to discount the fact that the researcher is a participant in society, and therefore a tool of research, in his or her own right.

Yet it has for sometimes been recognized that social scientists as interacting communities have endeavoured to establish paradigms of problems and methods of investigation, but it is only recently that a recognition of the researcher's place in a wider community of everyday life, and its influence upon the researcher, has come to be recognized. The problem which our research addressed was influenced by an academic community in which neo-Marxist and structural theories of the city were in the ascendant. In particular, however, the absence of an ability in this framework to account for human motivation and action in anything other than a mechanistic way, directed our attention towards the Marxist conception of ideology.

Nevertheless, it seemed to us that the prevailing accounts of how ideology operated placed an overemphasis on the power of institutions (e.g. factory, school, church and media) and in the last analysis, the economic base, to determine consciousness. The word 'seemed' is important here; what was the source of our dissatisfaction? Although the structuralist contortions of Althusser (the major influence on neo-Marxist conceptions of the city) were receiving a severe mauling at the hands of E. P. Thompson and other humanist Marxist representatives, the academic community was not the sole source of our scepticism. Perhaps more influential was our participation in the everyday life of the area where we resided.

Socializing and listening to people there revealed concoctions of fragmented values, beliefs, stereotypes, cliche myth, superstition, prejudice, humour, pathos and drivel, little of which could be directly attributed to the supposed institutional bearers of ideology. Even if elements of such dialogue could in some way be seen as determinations of power structure, it was usually juxtaposed with other contradictory elements. The concrete basis upon which the assertion of ideology as functional to the maintenance of social order was founded therefore began to interest me.

The identified theoretical problem then became a problem of how to research it. The positivist paradigm of social scientific research offered the possibility of survey techniques including questionnaire and attitude sampling. Whilst this offered the attraction of data which was accessible, verifiable and quantitatively testable, such an approach was rejected on two grounds. First, the items which we would have had to choose for subjects to respond to in attitude surveys would necessarily involve us in a priori assumptions of what ideological values were. The research would take the form of a self-fulfilling prophecy. Secondly, and more importantly, the interview situation necessary to attitude testing takes respondents out of an everyday, concrete setting and places them in an abstract situation where their responses are likely to be different.

Although an interview situation is still a social situation it is a world apart from everyday life. From our own experience of everyday life it was obvious that the ideological, as identifiable in values, beliefs, etc., was not necessarily a directly observable phenomena but operated on a largely unconscious plane.To place so-called ideological items in an attitude survey and present them to respondents would elicit attitudes towards them not typical in everyday circumstances. Having said that, however, an attempt at an attitude survey was made at the end of our research, although never to be used in the written-up form. The items used were derived from data from participant observation, and therefore constituted a representation of items to the community.

The reason why this attitude survey never became part of the final research are those of the second ground given above. Why the survey was carried out in the first place says more about the standing of and attitude towards qualitative techniques as a supposed poor relative of positivist social science than anything else. The method of study finally chosen was that of participant observation of a community for an eventual period of twenty months. This appeared the most appropriate method with which to tackle the study of the workings of what were not essentially considered a directly observable phenomenon. Because the method of participant observation relies heavily upon the 'social skills' of the researcher, it is also a method which requires a considerable amount of introspection, questioning and (sometimes) self-doubt.

The very fact of participation means that there is little in the way of objective techniques that the researcher can employ to assess the consistent quality of data. Subsequently data are apt to vary throughout the process of the research. Nevertheless there are initial considerations that all participant observers make to some extent prior to entering and during fieldwork.

The practice of participant observation

There are basically six areas of consideration to which the -researcher should pay some attention. These are research design, access to the unity, field relationships, questioning and listening, recording data, and analysis and presentation. The final area will, of course, mainly come under consideration upon the completion of fieldwork, but it should be stressed that the remaining five are also likely to alter in substance during the course of research. Participant observation by its very nature is a fluid process involving changes in the researcher and his or her relation to the subject community in the course of the research.

Research design

Considerations of research design include the setting of the research and its time span. The setting of this particular research was that of a local community. This setting was chosen largely on the grounds of theoretical concern. If it was claimed that ideology maintained social order, surely it did so in an all embracing way, encompassing all aspects of everyday existence. The local community where many different social interactions and practices occur, it was thought, would reflect such a holism at a microscopic level and enable such a focus as we desired. Furthermore, such holism would be reflected in the context of interaction, whereas a factory or a hospital would under-represent certain segments of experience in favour of others.

We were not interested in the possibility of the local community as an ideological structure per se, but as a localized basis of interaction; a setting in which to examine the workings of ideology in a concrete manner. We were therefore particularly keen not to choose a locality in which a community spirit was celebrated or where particular forms of solidarity were of notoriety.

An account of the background of the researcher is important in any participant observation research, if only that it may be indicative of any biases contained within the researcher's world-view (e.g. class bias). A possible failing of such a 'personal' choice of setting could be that the researcher is over-familiar with the community; too much participation at the expense of observation. However, as noted earlier, the advocated stance of the participant observer is very much that of the stranger.

This is not necessarily characterized by one who is 'not of the locality' but more by one who is 'marginal to the locality', a description of a quality that the individual bears in relation to the community. In our particular case the researcher's background as somebody of the locality who is 'differently marked' by virtue of a higher education, developed such a marginality; a natural observer as well as participant. This comes across in the biographical section of the research, but it should be borne in mind that membership of an academic community as well as of a local community inevitably leads to such a marginality.

There was also a theoretical reason for the choice of our own community for study; and this lies in the very type of community which the research problem required. The relationship of ideology to the local community was not posited in such a manner that the community was considered to be an ideological structure in itself, but rather a setting for ideological processes.

It was the local quality of interaction that was to be examined, and not anything particular to the community itself. This is not to suggest that the social history of any community is unimportant, but rather that ideological processes would manifest social order wherever there existed the necessary local social interaction.

Access

The participant observer also has to surmount the problem of gaining entry to the field setting chosen. This largely amounts to the problems involved in making contact with people with whom to participate, and these may be considerable depending upon the setting. One of the commonest ways in which the participant observer approaches the problem is by identifying significant individuals and attaching themselves to them. These individuals become 'gatekeepers' to the research setting for the participant observer, as for "ample 'Doc' was for William Whyte. An attempt at this was initially made in our research, however data derived in this manner did not form a significant part of the final written form of the research.

Although important for checking out certain qualitative impressions of the local community, we found that such gatekeepers were often by their role and its power content also marginal to the community and their values reflected such power however minimal. Association with such gatekeepers also seemed to affect the field relationship with other community members, in that we were seen as part of 'that crowd'.

More important to us was that as a participating member of our own community we had as it were, 'natural access' by virtue of our own local social network which acted as the basis for the development of participant observation. The settings of the research reflected aspects of the social network of the researcher (i.e. pubs, clubs, friends' houses, socials, doctors' waiting-rooms, and meetings, etc.). For participant observers generally, attachment to gatekeepers may be necessary depending upon their status as community members; the problem then becomes one of not over-identifying with such gatekeepers and carefully monitoring the degree of this.

Field relationships

Allied to the problems of access are those of the field relationship that the participant observer establishes once within the setting. The role that the researcher plays (and the extent of choice in adopting that role, and whether indeed it is the role of reparcher) will define the character of field relations. In particular the researcher must be aware of the definitions made by 'others' of 'self'.

Much of the parameters of roles are ultimately beyond the direct control of the researcher and concern the physical, biological and existential characteristics of the researcher (e.g. gender, age, race, education, religion, etc.). However within such parameters the researcher is able to 'manage' his or her impression to others (e.g. in terms of dress, speech, mannerisms, affability, etc.).

Generally however, the management of impressions on the part of the researcher is guided by the type of community under study (e.g. a three-piece suit, briefcase and clipboard will appear incongruous and suspicious in a working men's club). This raises a wider issue in respect of participant observation in that it is often claimed that this technique is most often used in the study of working-class communities because it is much easier to operate there as researchers are dealing with people less powerful than themselves.

> Access to society's underdogs generally proves relatively simple, partly because it involves the sociologist in intrusions upon people who are less prestigious and powerful than himself... it is somewhat simpler to infiltrate a working men's club than it is to gain entry to the Masonic Lodge, and the difficulties of participant observation on the factory floor are likely to pale into insignificance when the sociologist moves into the boardroom. This is obviously both a valid criticism and limitation of participant observation and one which should be borne in mind by potential users of the technique, both in its practical and ethical overtones.

A further consideration which has bearing on field relationships is the extent of participation on the part of the researcher. Much discussion has ranged around degrees of participation or observation along a continuum extending to either extreme, from total observer to total participant. It is clear, however, that both extremes do not reflect the spirit of the method of participant observation, and each leads to problems of objectivity on the part of the researcher. The advantage of the method lies in the use that researchers make of their access to meaning systems, and the success of reflexive understanding in observation. Both involvement and detachment are necessary components, and the dynamics of changes in the research process which may arise should not be resisted.

An important aspect of considering total observation or participation as ideal types is the overtness and covertness of the researcher implicit in each. Covertness is a matter for the conscience of the researcher, but it is one that will have bearing on how data are recorded and will ultimately depend upon the nature of the research design. In most cases involving participant observation it is the case that 'if the researcher is completely honest with people about his activities, they will try to hide actions and attitudes they consider undesirable, and so will be dishonest. Consequently the researcher must be dishonest to get honest data.'

The ethical kernel of this stance is stated by which as the researchers' maxim: deceiving the society so as to study it and wooing the society to live in it. Such a position has led the method to be levelled with the charge of voyeurism by the critics of covert participant observation.

However, it should be remembered that the researcher is responsible in large measure for the situations in which he or she records data in so far as the method involves the very act of participation. To such an extent researchers are no different from writers who doubtlessly draw upon their experience and contacts for material, and as long as identities remain well concealed there should be no real cause for pangs of conscience.

Questioning and listening

The practices of questioning and listening are central to obtaining data in participant observation; they are the routes of access to subjective meanings. By their use we obtain data and in this respect they have an informative function. However we are also able to use questions and our ability to listen to accounts as a means of acquiring the perspectives of respondents, at which point we tap the underlying processes of social phenomena—the essence of empathy.

At all times, nevertheless, the researcher is a methodological tool; it is the fact of participation, of being part of a collective contract, which cartes the data.

Much has been made of the benefits of listening as opposed to questioning: 'The central paradox of the participant observation method is to seek information by not asking questions'. Whilst this may well give researchers answers to questions that they may not have considered asking, it is at the same time a step towards complete observation and the method suffers by the loss of its essential impetus; participation.

One suspects that listening is favoured amongst some researchers since questioning can be considered manipulative. For example, a leading question may take the respondent outside the bounds of the context of everyday life. Yet by their very use leading questions illustrate the benefits of the participant observation method; the researcher as methodological tool testing hypotheses and theories acquired by reflecting on fieldwork so far.

Having said that, however, the major use of questions in the context of participant observation are largely of the qualification variety in order to prompt the respondent to proffer further information. This was the case in our own research; however as community member and participant we were aware of the need to maintain our normal role in the community and was able to use that to good effect in questioning.

Recording data

The major considerations behind what to record, how to record it and when to record it depend upon research design (the problems being researched) and whether the research is carried out covertly or overtly. Even if the research is being carried out overtly the nature of participation is such that it is not often done with one party constantly using a pencil and notebook; this would be disruptive, to say the least.Therefore most data are retrieved on reflection as soon after the situation as possible, and thus are very dependent upon memory. It is in the best interests of research that the data be concrete in nature, with the researcher making every effort to record speech and accounts as verbatim as possible. This has led to some use of mechanized assistance in the form of recording equipment, and whether this is used overtly or covertly again becomes an ethical issue.

In our own research, some covert use was made of a Micro-recorder and tapes were later transcribed. Its use was the subject of much conscience-seeking on our part. We eventually reasoned that as the machine was in fact an *aide-memoiroe*, the burden of the ethical problem lay in the fact of the covertness of the research. If we were possessed with a perfect memory, the problem would have remained. The ethical issue therefore reduces to that dealt with above. In the end the use of the micro-recorder was abandoned since the quality of the recording was poor and in most cases the memory of the researcher had to be relied upon.

Two further considerations need to be made in respect of recording data. First, it is important to record background information about respondents (if known), the place the situation occurred, others present, what people were doing and anything else which may be relevant, as this may not be apparent in the speech. It is seemingly incidental factors such as these which are important in defining the situations which people are in and they will have a bearing on the meanings and attitudes offered. Secondly, the storage of data should be given some prior to this as this is often overlooked. Having said that, it is likely that categorizations under which data are stored are likely to change as themes and research directions fade and emerge. In our research a major reclassification occurred when the typifications referred to in the developed model emerged. Prior to this, data were stored according to subject-matter of responses (e.g. politics, education, family, health, etc.); that is, what people were referring to in their speech. This was cross-referenced for access purposes. Reclassification and final storage form of the data ultimately depends upon how theory develops in the course of application of the method.

Analysis and presentation

Participant observation presents at least one great advantage to the social researcher. In pursuing the universal validity of reflexive interpretation (that is, its applicability to both 'lay' and 'scientific' explanations of social phenomena), it avoids an artificial divorce between theory and, method. The positivist will test the validity of a theory by the application of research methods, and will only return to examine the components of the theory if the theory fails to prove its applicability to the particular situation researched.

Theory and method have essentially separate existences according to positivism. A follower of the naturalistic school of methodology claims that the integrities of the appearances of social phenomena are sacrosanct. Theories can be made of them but never about how they came to appear that way.

In placing such an imbalanced weight upon the integrity of phenomena we are only left with subjective accounts: descriptions of phenomena. We cannot go objectively beyond them as such, which makes both our theory and method subservient to them. The participant observer in such a naturalistic framework really only observes.

On the other hand, if the participant observer accepts the universality of reflexive explanation, and applies it critically within the research, theory and method develop in a dialectic. The process is one of trying out hypotheses in the research situation. In this way the patterns and interpretations of the data develop due to the introspection and critical reflexivity of the researcher.

Ultimately the manner in which the researcher chooses both to analyse and present the data will depend upon the features of it which highlight the hypotheses and research problems investigated. That a basic grounding in relevant theory is important is borne out by the extent to which every possible theoretical avenue is explored in analysis, and the success of endeavours to explain phenomena which do not fit such theories by the development of new theory, models or typologies. Likewise presentation will vary according to the research problems.

The model developed out of the dialectical process which exists between theory and method, and with particular regard to two theoretical problems which our research identified. These were, first, what human psychic needs does a sense of community arise to satisfy? Secondly, how could ideology be said to function as a social process, or, how does it operate in everyday life? Drawing on the work of Robert Ardrey and Frank Fraser-Darling on the social psychological needs met by territory, and applying them to the conception of local community as a symbolic construction, the major needs identified were those for security and identity. Our reasoning ran that as these were fundamental human needs they would require to be met in some way, if not by a sense of community. The notion of ideology as a social process serving to interpellate subjectivity seemed most appropriate to explain how individuals make sense of the world, create social order and satisfy their needs for security and identity-therein.

According to Therborn, the three fundamental modes of interpellation are: (1) what exists and what does not exist; (2) what is good, beautiful, etc. and what is not these things; (3) what is possible and impossible. The underlying rationale of the process by which ideological interpellation emerges to meet needs in the absence of their satisfaction by local community was derived from Marx's early work on the notion of alienation, and more especially from his concepts of real and illusory community, whereby illusory community is the alienated, represented ideological form of community.

—

10

Social Interaction

With the increase of theoretical discourse in social geography in recent years discussion of interaction has been relatively eclipsed. It is noteworthy in this respect that relatively few recent reviews of social geography refer directly to interaction as a discrete topic. One clear exception to this, however, is Jackson and Smith in which interaction and community identity are touched on in a -consideration of the legacy of the Chicago school and the reinterpretation of its contribution in a non-positivist light. That the development of the subject should owe so much to yet another revival of a one-time discredited area of study is perhaps paradoxical, but nevertheless the tradition stemming not so much from the ecological aspects of Park's work but rather his pragmatism or 'moral order' and subsequently social interactionism is viewed here as forming one part of an understanding of qualitative research. The other one stems from Giddens' exposition of structuration in the explanation of social phenomena.

Social interaction and social thought

Park's pragmatism, which included recognizing the importance of everyday experience in the formulation of interaction and group relations, has been much more clearly carried forward in sociological as opposed to geographical research. Perhaps best known in social geography in Suttles' work on inner city territoriality, although as the subject has widened other work in this strongly anthropological bent is being appreciated.

These illustrations are more than inter-subjective recon-structions of the life-worlds of particular social groups and the interaction that bonds them, however. The hermeneutical importance of such studies has never been lost on the Chicago school, even if only implicitly, in the sense that all action has a particular context or frame of reference in which it takes place. The content of this is much more problematical, however, in the work of Chicago sociologists.

Park's original studies were undertaken in an atmosphere of humanism and qualified optimism for the future of capitalism—this indeed was the main facet of pragmatism, although Ley does not accept this interpretation. It is not surprising, therefore, that recent radical geography has dismissed their contribution as naive and even justifying the *status quo*.

Symbolic interactionism, on the other hand, includes a perspective which views reality as socially produced through the meanings given to objects by individual and group action—inherently then dealing with communication. It has, however, been criticized as falling uneasily between individual and society, even though this should be its strength in overcoming the antinomy between the two.

In an environment where structuralist thought derived primarily from Marxism has tended to straight jacket social groups into rigid and generally unproblematical divisions along class lines, it might seem that there can be no meeting of interactionist theory and questions thought of as belonging to 'society in general'.

This is a flawed assumption, for whilst a too narrowly defined radicalism cannot accommodate status as opposed to class, there is no reason why interactionist theory cannot make a substantial contribution to radical debate. Indeed this makes strong sense since problems have occurred within Marxism over translating structural categories to actual active class actions.

Central to this assertion is the view that the theory of structuration epistemologically links questions of the objective basis of society with the ways in which its members construct and then reproduce their everyday reality within this. The crucial link between these two lines of thought is meaning and its hermeneutical basis. As outlined above, symbolic interactionism posits that all objects carry meaning which is socially constructed through group reference—these meanings may be shared within a small or large group but set definite parameters within which norms operate therein.

Within social geography these constructs have been used to examine landscape identity. Duncan in particular has investigated different social landscapes to see how these are maintained and frequently threatened by other symbols of identity. Stable groups require these symbols less overtly because other rules are utilized, through peer group action for example. From these analyses whole social group divisions can be examined and their landscape identities explained.

Change is not easily dealt with in this framework, as readily admitted by symbolic interactionists, and therefore some other theoretical approach is required to supplement this. Structuration can this difficulty because hermeneutically its framework of reference is wider. Giddens shows that post-positivist social theory became too subjectivist in its search to stress human construction of reality because it feared relapsing into structural thought which was itself too deterministic of action. Much 1970s social geography examining the life-world can be faulted for this overreaction.

Ley offers a good overview of the problem but concludes by rejecting a balanced perspective. As a result no explanation of human action is forwarded. On the other hand, structuralist theories of community have simply viewed them as 'bearers' of the wishes of finance capital, for example in creating suburbs, reducing them to the level of contingent relations only.

In structuration, however, 'structure is not a constraint or a barrier to action but is instead essentially involved in its reproduction' and 'neither human agent nor society or social institutions should be regarded as having primacy. Each is constituted in and through recurrent practices'.

By this Giddens; means that actors as 'agents', in drawing on the norms and interpretative schemes provided by previously defined rules ('structure'), must reproduce this same set of governing guidelines to action. But in doing so they display an understanding of the practicality of everyday life revealed in those 'structures' which essentially removes from them the element of constraint or barrier. These rules are communicated through a common body of knowledge.

Hence action and structure in the sense defined are recursive—each constitutes and guides the other. This does not make for a static social structure (recurrent practices), however, because all action involves both unanticipated or unacknowledged conditions and unintended consequences. The former deals largely with the ideology or taken-for-granted assumptions behind action, the latter the unforeseen outcomes of it, which may of course challenge the nature of recurrent practices and modify them.

As Giddens points out, there is actually a double hermeneutic within this approach—the meaning given by the social actor (observed) and that of the researcher. Cultural anthropologists would no doubt claim that this has long been accepted within their research, but this reflexiveness is somewhat more novel in qualitative research in sociology and geography.

Macro-theory as posited by Giddens needs to be made more specific when examining social interaction. There is no logical difficulty in reducing the scale to particular cultures and groups provided that the reference is both meaningful to actor and researcher alike. In practical examples this will be shown to be equivalent to much interactionist work but permitting change to be examined in the wider context of society, without reifying that term.

It is also possible to create divisions in Giddens' framework for methodological purposes, distinguishing structural issues from those of action; this is important in applying the theory through qualitative research and this is undertaken in the case-study. It must be made clear, however, that these divisions are contingent, and that other, equally satisfactory, methods of making Giddens' theory operative might be found. This claim may rest uneasily with those more attuned to positivist method, but it must be appreciated that in this new form of qualitative research, theory and method cannot be easily divorced, nor indeed should they be.

Some criticism has been levelled at Giddens' theory, particularly in the definitions and terminology used. Dallmayr considers that the ideas of systems and structure of society are used with too Much ambiguity, although in the same volume Giddens is at pains to define terms such as 'action' and 'recurrent practices' very precisely. Another type of problem could lie with the assumption that the wider structures of society are understood by actors as they reproduce them, although again Giddens is aware of this and notes that unconscious action is being considered as well. However the original impetus for the theory of structuration does owe much to studies of relatively closed cultures where change is slow.

Probably the most serious criticism yet brought against Giddens is that structuration is too abstract to be translated to empirical research. For Gregson, structuration is a second-order theory and no way can be found to use rational abstraction to translate its constructs to meaningful empirical contexts.

Now all this is fine in the world of realist philosophy where very specific and limiting rules are followed to judge theory, but it seems to be rather bad sociology and anthropology. Why should theory be constrained to these narrow bases of judgement in a reality where irrationality is present, where some practices appear to be a historical whereas others are extremely specific to time and place? Gregson appears to fear relativism, but this is necessary to understand the historically specific.

After all, to take a simple example, the Trobriand Islander might use a table as a shelter whereas we write papers on it, but this does not mean that cultures switch arbitrarily from one meaning of the object to the other.

In the final analysis Gregson wants more of structuration than it can offer: it can never directly generate substantive issues, for it is a theory of action and its consequences. Even though Giddens has further refined the detail of the theory, this basic aspect has not changed. Although we agree with Gregson that structuration offers an ontology of society, fundamentally it is epistemological, dealing with communication and ways of knowing ground rules of action. A more balanced interpretation is offered by Duncan, who explores the social-psychological link between action and structure through Giddens, bringing to bear the importance of ideology and unequal power of actors - an aspect of structuration which is weak in Giddens, even though he is acutely aware of power relations in his writings generally. There have, of course, been a number of other attempts to use structuration as an empirical referent, but most of these fail to return to the core of Giddens' paying initial lip-service.

Social interaction and localism

More recently there has been an attempt to link ideas of localism or locale with the wider structures of society and this has become most evident in the work which is being actively pursued in the United Kingdom through the ESRC urban and regional systems study. This has led to differences in interpretation of localities research. Smith is wary of 'the empirical turn', fearing a relapse to ideographic place studies with an abstracted theory bearing little relevance to this.

Notwithstanding the taunts of realism that a meeting of abstract theory necessary relations and empirical reality founded on contingent relations is impossible, we think that Cooke's answer is essentially correct. Research involves fundamentally exploration and the discovery of new knowledge in the field; this is as true now by becoming a consultant at the sharp end of economic restructuring as it was when Engels ran his cotton factory. This is part of the 'clinical inference' to which Cooke alludes. Structuration is not simply 'dynamic structuralism', nor a theory to be tested in some positivistic way. It must find empirical referents, and a single case-study will not throw up all aspects of the substantive research issue under investigation.

Within social geography more specifically there have been some studies examining locale which have not simply used the term as an organizing or typological tool but have sought to explain social interaction and identity through it; that is, the content of the group and its coherence is defined.

General definitions of localism are outlined, some examples detailed, and a wider interpretation of the term given which can be applied to the case-study.

Localism has often assumed that there are 'limited horizons', a belief that in terms of identity no interest in or commitment to places far from one's own is held. More crucially the social, economic and political issues that dominate those spaces are also viewed as irrelevant, a most crucial point, since it can be seen that in reality this is unlikely to be the case and the strategic conduct of capitalist institutions will affect these locales.

Localism as a generic term has been used widely in political studies and associated with metropolitan fragmentation. In more fundamental terms it is also essential to the definition of property. More specific links again to the development of capitalist institutions have been made by Bell and Newby who see localism as a guide to social control itself.

The local spheres of influence found in pre-capitalist society were broken down by the expanding market. Locally-oriented interests subsequently reappeared, however, through an ideology of community, particularly neighbourhood units which were to guide local loyalties and social control.

Inter-war planned neighbourhood units are given as one example of these; others could be added from unplanned suburban 'defensive' spaces to inner-city enclaves, depending on the identity so defined.

Landscape identity is used to communicate cues as to the socially-shared meaning of tastes and identities, which both define the extent and content of social interaction. Duncan which sought to expand this idea further in an intriguing set of papers which examine the meaning of the objects within the home in market society. This aims to balance earlier work which has shown that to middle-class social groups the local landscape matters more than it does to other groups, hence a symbolic defence of the community results particular when unacceptable symbols threaten to intrude.

Duncan and Duncan have also compared upper-class group landscapes in North American cities, arguing that their control derives from the social status invested into these, itself part of market society norms. There is however, a far less clearly stated theoretical position in this later world which may devalue its contribution to a better appreciation of social interactionism.

The concept of localism can in fact be taken further. With particular reference to 'turf' defence, protecting our own or 'defensive' space, social group identity is very much linked to fear of symbolic presence. This symbolic avoidance behaviour, so-called because money can be used temporarily as wealth to buy the desired exclusion of undesirable objects and persons, can be outlined as follows. Social groups who maintain a certain consensus of status identity through shared landscape cues will aim to preserve that identity via landscape control, and exclude objects threatening to their esteem. These same objects mediate between the social group, other status groups and institutions representing the wider external world, so that particular symbols are associated with them.

For example, cluster homes may be associated with lower-income groups and the developers and planners who have given institutional backing to their intrusion. Wider societal change is important, since the landscape identity can seemingly be preserved by the apparent substitution of space for time. For example, as long as locales are available in which to implement ideologies, then other communities can resist change, but only up to a point, as will be seen in the case study. These aspects of identity construction both define and are in part created through social interaction in locales.

The foregoing review and explanation of localism is now developed further by reference to a case-study. Primary emphasis is placed on a community within the Greater Vancouver Regional District of Canada where no-growth policies and sentiment impinged considerably on local groups and their interaction.

The nature of qualitative research undertaken is discussed both in terms of Giddens' framework—the grounding of structuration in an empirical context—and in demonstrating its general value in the study of social interaction. The selected municipality, the District of West Vancouver, is a well-established community of over 36,000, lying in the northwest corner of the Greater Vancouver Region under the range of mountains which form a backcloth to Vancouver itself. Figure 7.2 shows the setting of West Vancouver and details of the sites referred to below. Research was conducted during a six-month period during 1977, and then selectively until 1984 on the response of the community to growth pressures, in particular for new tracts of middle and upper-market housing on the mountain slopes.

A mixture of conventional and more novel qualitative methods were employed including semi-structured interviews with planning officers, newspaper content analysis and absorption into the community through contacts and attendance at key meetings, involving some participant observation. Such analyses were not, however, aimed solely at describing or classifying actions, but involved searching for wider consequences.

The process of synthesis could not be undertaken at the time of research investigation—indeed, the large majority of the work was research investigation —indeed, the large majority of the work was completed before Giddens' theory was published. weI make no-apology for this timetable, nor is it critical, for the application of structuration depends on a detailed 'taking-apart' of findings and their reconstruction into the wider context in which these actions have taken place. In an earlier paper this was referred to as descending the ladder to the least chaotic conceptions and then reclimbing it to build in the implications of those localist actions. From this 'suburb' could be seen to take on a wide set of meanings, but neither arbitrary nor based on a subjective typology as had been apparent in much previous research.

It was during this research that an awareness grew of the locality as a 'defensible space', both in the more commonly known sense of exclusionary social practices aimed at ethnic and lower-income groups, and in a newer sense of anti-growth sentiment opposing the entry of any social group into new housing landscapes. This led to a definite view of localism in the sense discussed generally in the previous section, which as a force in social interaction can be interpreted in terms of the structuration thesis. The municipality developed as a series of largely disconnected villages, always hemmed between mountain and water, which over time became linked through urbanization. The District Council had a reputation for excluding industrial development from these early days and until the 1960s large-scale commercial activity as well.

The general residential development since the Second World War had at the start of the research resulted in the community being viewed as middle to upper class, popular with in-migrants of the nouveaux riches, which earned it the label of 'Martini Mountain', an image in keeping with an exclusive suburb. Excluding the commercial core and contiguous blocks along the waterfront, where high-rise development is dominant, virtually all residential areas are single-family with densities as low as one to the acre.

Exclusionary practices of the more conventional kind were found in West Vancouver through 'restricted covenants' acting against ethnic groups. As in the United States, these were declared illegal by the 1970s, but zero-growth sentiment was becoming more generally apparent in the community.

Although the District Council was required under a regional plan to investigate seriously growth possibilities, developer pressure as early as 1975 was resulting in proposals to construct higher-density, but still exclusive, cluster homes and town houses in a belt above the limit of existing residential development. Broadly, with the exception of certain canyons and steep slopes, these would ultimately occupy all remaining land up to the 1200 foot line, moving westwards from the existing sub-community of the British Properties to the Caulfeild Plateau. The two social groups involved here form the main strand of the analysis, and their response will be examined in terms of the interactionist framework which is outlined after a review of the evolution of anti-growth sentiment. Various land developers were encouraged by the Greater Vancouver Regional District's policy to expand in West Vancouver by some 500 persons per annum from the late 1970s up to 1986 — not an excessive target set against the proposals for Vancouver as a whole.

The District Council undertook a public relations exercise to monitor developers' proposals which came in a series of stages. Major concern was voiced at environmental damage from increased runoff if housing were constructed on higher slopes, in turn affecting properties lower down.

Social impact such as household mix and increased net densities also resulted in strong hostility. In the east and central sections of the municipality local ratepayers' groups opposed any development beyond existing sites, whilst in the west new groups sprang up where none had existed before on sites proposed for town houses in single-family areas. In the east the principal ratepayers' group to be studied was the British Properties and Area Homeowners Association, a body that found itself opposed to a developer group with a similar name owning more than 80 per cent of the developable land above the existing limit.

In Canadian terms the British Pacific Properties formed a very striking landscape with a 'gate' entrance and curvilinear structure. Referring to Giddens' framework the unacknowledged conditions of action of the group mirrored those of the community as a whole and were based on an assumption, rarely stated, that West Vancouver was in some way 'outside' the norms of advanced capitalist society and hence not subject to speculative development or indeed any kind of overt business ethic. Nevertheless links could not be denied - the chief director of the Association was a vice-president of a major industrial group, and its policy and planning officer the former editor of one of the city's newspapers. The views of the Association were largely expressed through an annual news-sheet, insidiously titled Tally Ho!, which acted as a medium for uniting this group in its attempts to prevent new housing development.

Socially the homeowners of British Pacific Properties were largely seen as nouveaux riches by the other groups in West Vancouver. Furthermore no established resident of the sub-community would ever publicly accept that he or she resided there - only those at the very bottom of the social ladder, and of recent arrival, made public expression of their status.

This view was ratified during a public meeting at which a resident opposing new growth was later reported in the local press as a 'newcomer' to British Pacific Properties. Other investigations through council officials suggested that the external stereotype of British Properties was that it had the only strong Homeowners' Association in the municipality. This was backed up by an exaggeration of the nouveaux riches image in the city-wide press, with typifications of avid status expression.

Examples included the ownership of large single-family homes, but no income to furnish them whilst keeping garden meticulously in order. In practice, however, the Association was viewed as politically weak by older established elite groups in the west of the community such as the Caulfeild Property Owners Association. This and other central area social groups took the attitude that the British Properties should be given 'first chance' to oppose new housing and having failed would let the established groups take over. This was a paradoxical development given that the Caulfeild sub-community only formed any sort of a claim to represent community feeling when conflict over landscape control became rampant throughout West Vancouver.

Differences between the two main social groups in the community were most evident in the question of landscape control and identity. This became a central issue in opposition to new housing since population growth as such was something of a red-herring. From 1971 to 1976 West Vancouver experienced zero population growth but considerable household formation, the total remaining close to 36,400. This was connected to most of the opposition to new growth which focused on provision for smaller families including younger professionals and executives in up-market town houses and condominiums often fetching higher prices than existing single-family properties.

At public meetings it was generally argued, however, that these types of home would lead to the in-migration of lower-income families and it was here that symbolic contamination. This reaction was not quite the same in the two main social groups, however. In the case of the British Properties and Homeowners' Association great play was made on overt features of the landscape itself.

A letter stated: 'Why should we be subjected to a 3000 town-house development in a fine residential area such as this... [the road] should be untouched and a 600 foot green-belt retained at the end of [it]. This type of comment was backed up by a small pressure group which acted independently of the main Association at public meetings. In keeping with the image of the British Properties it called itself 'The Group of Seven' after a famous set of Canadian artists of the same name, and which included landscape painting in its work. Social degeneration of the area was associated with higher densities than previously agreed under zoning ordinances which the Association believed were going to be imposed on them by the municipal council.

Central ratepayers' groups, who did not have to sustain the nouveaux riches image, tended to focus closely on environmental damage caused by increased run-off on the higher slopes. This more considered opposition was also evident in the Caulfeild part of the community. One petition from the Association here well represents the use of symbolic landscape stereotyping, in addition to the other tactics used that were similar to the British Properties Association, such as zoning alterations. This accepted that some new housing development was inevitable to satisfy the Greater Vancouver Regional District's demands and to spread the burden of costs associated with drainage improvements on the mountain side. All in all this was a more realistic attitude than that expressed by the British Properties Association. The petition then suggested adding only one new access road with the town house development, which it was claimed 'would not pass a single existing home'.

More closely questioned on the explanation for this view one petitioner responded: 'Well, town houses and access roads go together, don't they? If these people will be living in town houses then they should put up with busy roads.' This is an excellent example of symbolic typification, illustrating the reification of a group who are deemed to be of a different status. It is argued that there is a type of household right for a town-house and which must 'suffer' access roads with that identity. In this way the social group was able to preserve some of its own identity whilst controlling access to the landscape.

Of course, the overall group representation within West Vancouver as a whole was considerably more unified in the face of growth proposals. Previous positivist research on social interaction has tended to throw up red herrings here by attempting to measure linkages and structures in the context of a defined network.

Yet the real distinction is between the subtle but real differences across a social group and what Suttles calls the 'representative image' or 'average differences' that are used to give identity to one group or landscape over another. Even if there are variations in perspective individuals will nevertheless attempt to live up to these representative images and often let them guide their social and political norms. These are part of the recursive agency-structure link which has become imbued in the group.

So far little mention has been made of the unintended consequences of action, which themselves can aid in building a wider perspective than might at first appear. These can be seen to have effects both on the locale itself and in the wider structural setting: as suggested above these should not be seen as epistemological distinctions—they serve methodologically to demonstrate how the use of a structuration thesis adds to previous approaches. Both affect the form and the content of the social interaction examined.

In the case of West Vancouver the internal consequences of the anti-growth sentiment defined by political localism were largely expressed through socio-demographic changes. As a result of higher house prices the possibility of an increasingly ageing population arose, due to the reduction of in-migration of younger families with children, a position directly contradictory to the 'average image' held up of the community.

In turn this was viewed as having undesirable consequences on community life, making it 'unbalanced' with falling school enrolment and reduced use of facilities. Such a conclusion is fairly consistent with findings in more conventional community studies. But the wider consequences of such sentiment, if successful, could be seen to lead to a major contradiction for the social groups of West Vancouver, in that ultimately anti-growth would challenge the very foundations of the business ethic upon which these groups claimed their lifestyles and source of employment, even though this was denied as applicable to 'their' community. Several developers and many businessmen were living in the community and active in ratepayers' groups, as has been seen; on these contradictions they were remarkably quiet. Their former belief that West Vancouver could some-how exist 'outside' capitalism only survived whilst the land development industry had elsewhere to go; when this ended due to city policies of growth restriction, the myth was shattered. This is consistent with structuration as suggested above spatial expansion is used in an attempt to avoid in situ temporal change.

Through the institutional procedures that in turn affected the unacknowledged conditions of action the reality of the local groups was seen to be untenable without major disruption. The attempt by residents to develop in their own eyes a post-industrial ethic was not realizable without consequences and contradictions.

The avoidance of change through spatial expansion which had worked so well in the development of the community image long before stronger preservationist attitudes grew up could not continue when other groups in the metropolitan region began to achieve their own slow-growth aims, described by Ley as the creation of a 'Liveable Region'. The response of particular social groups in West Vancouver was varied. Those in Caulfeild tended to accept reluctantly the inevitable loss of open space, which was completely developed by 1984, but considered leaving the sub-community.

11
Social and Economic Imperatives of Restructuring

The term 'restructuring' is used here to describe the empirical experiences during a crisis event or a phase of adaptation and change in a whole system of production, be it at the local, regional or national level. As we use it here it embraces the modifications in the production system itself which have repercussions on the location and distribution of work and industry and on the viability of the whole process of capital accumulation. More specifically the term suggests both positive and negative processes: positive restructuring when new production relations are generated and negative during a phase of deindustrialization.

Spatially these differences have some obvious repercussions, to wit: decline in one region's industrial base may be matched by an equivalent growth in an adjacent zone or even in another country. The theoretical concepts explored here are derived from observations of empirical events in the recession of the late 1970s and early 1980s. In this period it became clear that a new perspective was needed to see the processes of restructuring both in terms of their context holistically and globally while retaining an important sense of the internal complexities (concretely and regionally) and the implications for capital, workers and the state.

The recession pointed out quite clearly that swift

movements by firms in the developed, developing and underdeveloped worlds were in response to declines in profitability in some locations and the growth and relocation of investment in others. These movements resulted in the decline of industry in some settlements and regions and its growth in others.

The changes in locations of firms were matched by some equally significant reformulations of the work people do, especially the mix of skills, the introduction of new technology to replace labour, the search for pools of cheap and pliant labour in 'greenfield sites' and the extended deployment of youth and female workers in factory sites and other 'places of work around the world. All these changes took place at an increasing rate during the recession as capital, generally with the compliance of the state, embarked on a period of intensive restructuring. The theoretical parameters and the social and economic consequences of these changes are the subject of discussion here.

The chapter is divided into four parts. In the -first section we outline the framework of analysis and discuss some of the causes of the current round of geographical and economic restructuring. In the next section we address a specifically materialist view of restructuring drawing on current literature and observations of empirical trends. In the following section we focus on what happens to labour in a: restructuring event; and in the final part we look at a comparison of first and third world restructuring events.

Causes of geographical and economic restructuring

In capitalist-based societies the fundamental determinant of the restructuring of geographic space and of the social and economic relations of production is the arena of production itself. The pattern of motion of investment or disinvestment of capital imparts its own particular features on a regional economy. The spatial component is important because the production system itself, having become increasingly internationalized, operates within and between regions and across national boundaries. As such, the process of restructuring has taken on an international character with regions, towns and firms vying for favourable conditions and policies. Indeed, as Palloix has argued, the successful large-scale expansion of multinational firms can no longer be accomplished within a single region or nation state and must be based on an ever-widening circle of industrial investments and locations. This too makes the restructuring imperative increasingly complex as large firms are able to expand and contract their systems of production and sets of production relations in accordance with differential spatial rates of profit.

The restructuring process embraces investment as well as disinvestment which in turn presupposes crises -and crises demand solutions. It has been argued that the two processes must be applied simultaneously in order to maintain viable conditions for capital accumulation. In the international crisis of the late 1970s and early 1980s, however, the opportunities for switching investment from one industry to another or even between sectors were limited. These limits embraced energy costs, technological traps, high relocation costs, the increasing pace of technological change and the immobility of fixed capital, especially in some of the traditional 'sunset industry' regions such as in the northeastern United States and in the north-east of England. Thus the changes in the amount of capital required to be invested in machines, technology and fixed capital in general increased exponentially, placing considerable stress on investments and on investing institutions. The result was a phase of increased disinvestment in certain sectors and areas and the growth of new industries in other locations. We must caution against seeking the causes of restructuring entirely within a local area, region or even within the nation state. Actual changes are most likely to be the result of interaction between internal and external components of the international division of labour. This is particularly so within relations between production units such as factories, branch plants or foreign-owned firms. Clearly the developments in the productive forces embracing capital and ownership are dominant. But they exist in a conflictual and often contradictory relationship, that between the workforce and the social and technical division of labour.

The dynamics of restructuring must therefore embrace an understanding of the rate at which these relationships develop and change; conflict is an integral part of the relationship especially in the workplace, but as has become obvious in a number of instances, some of the immediate conflict has been removed by the employment of nonunion workers.

We do not subscribe to a linear framework of explanation of restructuring, but rather to a cyclical and crisis-oriented form of change within different modes of production. Linear models suggest that restructuring and modernization are directly associated with the process of growth. Needless to say this view is not always valid, because evolutionary change is not a matter of steady moves from one stage to the next.

Although there is some evidence to suggest that plateaux of development do actually exist it is difficult to provide supporting evidence of the causes of entrance or exit from each 'stage' of development. Nor do such models allow for ready analysis of the processes of stagnation, decline, restructuring or uneven development which are an integral part of the process of development, at least within the capitalist mode of production. To this general schema of events we must add the comments made by Holloway & Picciotto. They suggest that the process of restructuring involves three main areas: an increase in the rate of exploitation; devaluation and destruction of constant and outmoded fixed capital; and the redistribution of total surplus value through state policy from less productive state expenditures and inefficient capital. It is also apparent that the tendency towards a falling rate of profit and the struggle between capital and labour and between different classes of competing capitalists provides another arena in which conflict and restructuring merge.

The conflict evident in these situations appears during periods involving job change, the redivision of labour and the restructuring of skills. We can also turn to a framework which permits the analysis of the internal and external conditions of restructuring, within a mode of production at specific times. In this manner, it is possible to analyse both the dialectics of change and the apparent contradictions which exist within the different levels of development. Furthermore, the impetus for change is evident within cyclical patterns of upswing and downswing, although the occurrence of cyclical behaviour in and of itself is not an adequate explanation of economic change and restructuring. Indeed, the engine of change and the motive force of the mode of production hold the reasons for the occurrence of uneven development and the need for constant restructuring.

Although there is some general recognition of the problems of linear and cyclical development, there is one internal debate which encompasses all these issues: that the processes leading to uneven development are a necessary prerequisite to continued capital accumulation; or that the spatial and sectoral manifestations of unevenness are the logical outcome of different phases in the overall restructuring process.

The answer to this question lies not in following one or the other, for both in their own ways are inappropriate. What may be more profitably pursued are the actual premises of restructuring and the underlying logic of the mode of production being examined. What will become clear in the course of this chapter is that changes in the mode of production, at the level of mine, null and factory, induce and effect the restructuring of capital and the social and economic relations, of people within and outside the workplace.

Materialist view of restructuring

A materialist view of restructuring embraces those conditions within the mode of production which either impinge on each other or interact within the constant ebb and flow of investment, industrial production, employment and cyclical behaviour. Much of this type of change can be understood under the rubric of a crisis theory of economic behaviour in which restructuring is both an end and a means to continued capital accumulation.

The crises themselves may be derived from any number of sources, including fluctuations in both supply and demand of inputs and outputs. For the most part these events embrace interruptions in the smooth running of a production system, whether they be from the state, capital or labour. These 'trigger events' are followed by 'general process changes' embracing the reformulation of the production relations in a plant or a community. These events in turn have a 'structural outcome' which has been summarized by Massey & Meegan as technical change, rationalization and intensification.

The final geographical impact is a result of the combined effects of trigger mechanisms, general process changes and structural outcomes. For without capital the production system itself is unable to continue. Furthermore, as is notable in the crisis of the early 1980s, there is an urgent search for new technology which will replace labour. This technology is being produced and reproduced by companies involved in the production of technology per se and in the overall production system itself. In some instances old machinery in 'sunset' industries wears out and is replaced entirely by new technology; in other cases, new parts and new machines replace the older machines at the same, or perhaps a slightly more sophisticated, level of technology.

Technological change per se is one way in which restructuring can take place. We must be careful, however, to distinguish between technology which 'leads' a major phase of restructuring, and technology which is implemented by lagging firms to catch up or to maintain levels of productivity and competitiveness. In both cases the technology may be considered as an innovation in that it adds to or substitutes for an older form of technology; and whatever its status it will probably have an impact on the numbers of employees and their skills and job tenure.

Technological change has a number of effects whether it is in a leader or laggard status. The new technology may introduce plant-saving techniques making it more efficient, at least in the short term ' which will mean that job levels may be retained., The longer-term incremental substitution of labour with capital (workers with machines and nowadays 'hi-tech') can result in a slowing down of new employment and ultimately in the absolute replacement of labour. New technology is part of the system of, machines in a production process. Given the ultimate aim of capital to substitute for labour wherever it is financially possible, the place of technology is very important. Technology is therefore a major variant in the restructuring agenda both during normal phases of production and during periods of unusual growth or crises and downswings. This is one good reason why technological innovation is constantly sought, by firms -who can afford it, in order to improve the efficiency of existing fixed capital.

The addition of sometimes simple devices may mean that machines can be speeded up or permitted to adapt to other or additional tasks. This type of innovation can occur constantly, and in some instances it is required in order to maintain the integrity of older or 'mature' production machines. The competition for innovations and the speed at which they can be commanded and brought into production bears on the relative success of an industry's restructuring profile.

Competition and secrecy within the field of innovations are often high, as is the cost of maintaining a constant vigilance in the 'technology race'. Those firms and even whole sectors which do not maintain spending in replacements of machines and in new technology may not maintain access to new technology and therefore may not survive a restructuring crisis. Occasionally, they may survive by 'Heath-Robinson' or 'wire and string' modifications to existing plant, but for the most part their access to industry-wide technology is limited by their lack of capital or by a lack of ,modern management' at the plant.

Competitive behaviour both within and between sectors also provides the impetus for restructuring. The level of competition *per se is* dependent on the success of the production system and the capacity of firms to create a production unit and a set of labour/capital relationships which can match or overcome those set up by other firms. We must also note, however, that not all firms compete at all times; there is plenty of evidence to suggest that different levels of co-operation do exist at the level of sharing information, joint ventures and interlocking directorships.

The crisis of the 1980s demonstrated a number of significant strategies in management and labour relationships in restructuring. In many instances the firms under stress opted for a reduction and 'rationalization' of their workforce. In most cases, this meant that labour was substituted for by machines of increasing sophistication and productive capacity. Where no technology was introduced, firms endeavoured to cope by reducing the numbers of workers on the job, increasing the hours worked and the intensity of the work process. Restructuring of this nature was notable in many large-and small-scale industries in Canada and elsewhere.

Some firms chose to conduct their restructuring as a series of combined events during the recession, suggesting that the weakened position of labour and the need for technical innovations in a downswing were sufficient to trigger a series of labour rationalizations and the introduction of new and sophisticated machinery. What became clear in the restructuring of the 1980s was that many workers would no longer be employed in the industry they received training in and perhaps had worked in for many years. Furthermore, many of these workers would be required to migrate to other communities ill search of work.

Lastly, many more would not be employed again, especially those of a particular age group approaching retirement and even those in middle-and late-middle-aged categories. In some industries workers with long-term standing were retained instead of short-term workers; such was the case in a number of plants in the Canadian steel industry in the 1980s. The prevailing condition, however, is one of crisis behaviour and modification both within and between economic sectors. In the event of apparently traumatic events, the state is generally called on to intervene or to promote or modify the direction of change in the restructuring process.

The state is an integral element of the system itself and therefore of the restructuring events which occur. The state may become involved at the level of policy, ideology, action in the market place and in the production system itself In all events it has become apparent that the role of the, state is changing constantly, depending on the direction of the needs of the restructuring process invoked by capital and on the ideology and degree of involvement of the state in the production process. Whichever position is adopted by the state it is also evident that it responds to the call of the private sector in times of need either selectively to apply state resources and finances or to shape policy and control and protect markets and production relations. In the event of the rupture and closure of a plant or indeed of a whole production system, as was evident in the mining industry in northern Quebec and Labrador in Canada, the state may also be called on to supply financial support for the companies and the communities which were closed down.

What causes the mode of production to change? Answers to this lie within a multi-causal set of relationships surrounding the drive toward constant capital accumulation. To this we must add the profit imperative and the constant climate of competition within the overall centralization and concentration of capital. Similarly our analysis must embrace consideration of the effects of contractions as well as expansions in the system of production. For no system expands at an obvious or continuous rate, and all are fraught with problems of slow growth, recessions and downswings. Furthermore we must also allow for the effects of changes in the rate of profit within each sector and even within each enterprise; all of which will dramatically influence the capacity of each unit of production to continue investments in both fixed and variable capital, in machines, labour, people and social infrastructure. It is apparent in the real world of economic and social geography that there are many factors which militate against a simple linear growth pattern and are rather faced with a pattern of continuous expansion and contraction processes. Indeed, as we shall see, these are built into the very logic of the system of production.

The dialectics of expansion and decline, renewal and deindustrialization, employment and unemployment, all under the rubric of restructuring processes, are the logical outcome and consequences of the imperative of capitalist growth. That this takes place unevenly over space, time and by sector is not an unusual or unpredictable phenomenon. Indeed it is becoming increasingly obvious that the cumulative effects on people and places are evident in the waves and cycles of upswing and downswing.

The internal dynamics of these waves, while they do not deploy a driving mechanism of their own, are evidently influential on the rate, location and sectoral behaviour of upswing and downswing. Thus the dynamics of the production system itself provide both the medium, cause and need for restructuring. And, although the need for restructuring is constant, it occurs at different levels and sectors in different locations. We must therefore caution against viewing the current phase of regional and industrial restructuring as something new or unique. Rather, it is the acting out, albeit unevenly, of the cyclical, dynamics of the system of production itself.

There is some evidence to support the 'mode and submode' construct, but the scale of change required to invoke this type of explanation may sometimes exclude non-conforming or non-fit restructuring which is implemented to iron out or ease small fluctuations in the production system.

Gibson & Horvath's case of transition between submodes is illustrated by major alterations in technology, the social division of labour, changes in the work process, confrontation between the banking sector, industry and commerce; and the reshaping of relations between the state and productive capital. They also point out that major forms of change in a mode of production result in institutional and ideological changes which support the general direction in which the restructuring is moving . In their framework, economic and cyclical crises, originally outlined by Wright in 1978, form the trigger mechanisms, and the medium for restructuring. According to Massey, firms involved in a crisis situation must escape the outcome by restructuring.

Massey argues that several options are opened up during the crisis phase and the subsequent shakedown which takes place in restructuring. She summarizes the overall process into three summary types, to wit: rationalization, intensification, investment in technical change. Massey & Meegan provide evidence of this form of change in the United Kingdom, but we must be sure of the evidence for such changes elsewhere. It is clear that research and case studies of restructuring and its social and economic impacts are needed in other countries, both in the first and third worlds to complement this work.

The general processes of restructuring can be researched at the level of the plant, sector and region. At the first level, in the workplace, we must observe changes in the labour component of production. Are there changes in numbers, gender of the workers, levels of skills and hours worked? It is apparent that within separate workplaces and work processes the shaping and texture of restructuring takes different forms. What took place in the 1980s' recession was a reshuffling of the balance of capital and labour within the specific format of fixed and variable capital.

The strategies deployed in the drive toward restructuring suggest that separate firms are placed in a position of revamping their production methods or lines *per se*, or of decreasing the labour content of the commodities they produce: The reduction in the number of workers is the most commonly deployed method and first step in rationalizing a labour force at the level of the plant.

The second step is to rationalize the numbers of hours worked with fewer workers. Changes of job hours and the revamping of shift structures can reward industry with similar production rates and lower labour costs. At the same time as these labour reductions occur firms have been known to replace machinery and to reorganize the speed and output of machinery in the plant. Firms may also 'furlough' parts of their operations, especially where there are duplicates of machines and processes or multiple assembly lines. In such cases the reduction of labour can go hand in hand with partial plant closures.

All of these methods go under the general name of rationalization of both plant and labour in the restructuring process. The absolute reduction of labour *per se*, however is only one of a number of such strategies. Workers may be moved from place to place, from city to city and across regional boundaries. Workers may be reallocated to different work stations or to different plants in an attempt to mobilize a lower number of workers around a reduced number of work stations. There is also evidence to suggest that computerization of the spatial allocation of workers within plants and work stations has led to a higher rate of movements within a plant and to a redifferentiation of skill structures and job types.

Instead of workers becoming specialized within one particular area of a plant or some other work area such as a hospital we see an increase in the number of tasks expected of a worker and a consequent reduction in the area of specialization. It seems we are now entering an era of 'reverse-Taylorism' in which the workforce will be required to have multiple skills of perhaps a limited type but nevertheless expected to cover a wider range of jobs. Labour reallocation in both a spatial and technical sense is, however, somewhat more difficult in some sectors, especially those which over the years have built specific skill structures and work stations into the fixed capital of a plant.

Similarly the adaptations are limited in circumstances where workers cannot move to new stations and use new skills without expensive retraining. For the most part the major moves toward labour restructuring in the recession of the 1980s resulted in absolute job loss in some sectors and gains in others, although there is no evidence to suggest that these changes were equivalent or mutual. Though some have argued that absolute numbers are likely to be replaced after a job loss it is rare that such claims can be verified and even more difficult to find jobs in the same area, sector or with the same skills.

Most movements require costly retraining to absorb workers into the same plant or industry; debates ensue about whether the state or the private sector should pay. Similarly the job skills are seldom equivalent in different sectors and the job loss and job gain statistics used to date cannot differentiate between the types of skills that are mobile and those that are incompatible. It is, for instance, difficult to imagine or to persuade miners and steel workers to become shopkeepers or nurses. There are some job types, it seems, that do not match the technical, social or cultural dispositions of workers in some localities.

Nevertheless in some countries such transfers are touted as the answer to the wave of displacements created by disinvestment and restructuring in the 1980s. It is argued that the fabled 'post-industrial society, will enable this form of mobility and in fact will demand It. At present, however, there is no foreseeable guarantee that jobs in the service sector have their equivalent in terms of locations, numbers, salaries, benefits and skill profiles. Smooth movements or transfers of labour in a cross-sectoral restructuring activity are thus very difficult to achieve satisfactorily. If moves do occur after a plant closure then workers tend to orientate toward lower-skilled areas, the service sector or to periods of unemployment.

What Harvey has referred to as a 'spatial fix' in terms of fixed capital in machines and factories, has its equivalent in communities and workers too, especially in zones of older industries where several generations of families attached to industrial communities predominate. Movements of firms away from such areas or the revamping of job places, skill requirements and work stations can act with equivalent trauma on the labour force. What is most common in such areas is the restructuring of capital followed by revamping of both conditions, location and remuneration of work. This is most noticeable in regions and sectors attached to sunset industries where firms become detached from older sites and in this footloose state either relocate, revalorize their capital into new forms of production or lose the absolute value of investments through bankruptcy. In such regions labour is forced to become mobile, if this is possible, or it becomes dependent on the state or on some new form of diversified economic activity, often based on the service, sector, or on new industries which may locate in order to obtain access to a cheap, by then cheaper, labour force.

Increasingly, labour-management relations and class conflict in the community and-the workplace are seen as factors which must be considered in the process of geographical- restructuring. Evidence drawn from the Canadian experience in the 1980s would suggest that the major restructuring to come out of free trade with the United States may bring about job losses in some areas and job gains in others; the balance of such moves will depend on the types and locations of industries affected in Canada. Trade unions are concerned about the protection of jobs and the maintenance of wage levels and standards of living. In periods of upswing, wages are increased through bargaining, but in downswings negotiations are marked by intense bargaining and the withdrawal of labour as well as the denial of the right to work in the factory or plant.

The conflict inherent in such situations becomes focused on control of the work process and control over the workplace. Firms may parallel this conflictual activity with a period of contracting out of certain parts of a production process which may exacerbate the conflict or remove parts of the local labour force entirely. Conflict also arises when layoffs and dismissals occur in a plant and in a community. These bring about displacements and destruction of community linkages and structures. There is evidence in North America and Great Britain that the recession of the 1980s induced considerable restructuring of this form in some of the older 'sunset' regions embracing -older industrial systems and primary production plants such as steel mills, mining towns, textiles and clothing mills. Such was the intensity of this conflict that tensions focused entirely on the attempts to retain jobs and maintain the integrity of local operations, communities and working-class life and culture.

- Attempts were made to negotiate with factory owners to keep jobs or to trade off with community facilities or state compensation. Workers in some areas, especially in mill towns related to steel or textiles, even went so far as to attempt to purchase their local plants and production facilities. A number of strikes took place before and during the closures in an attempt to pre-empt or prevent the closures of the plant. The restructuring which takes place in the economic arena has direct repercussions in the workforce and on the social relations which exist among workers in the workplace and in the community.

The workforce which is 'released' through 'rationalization' and restructuring and the subsequent relocation of jobs and workers has been increased not only by the proletarianization of workers *per se* but also by increasing the numbers of women and youths in the labour market. This particular restructuring strategy enables business to lower the average wage and change the location of work both within the city and from region to region; it can also increase the intensification rate and increase the number of workers per household. This 'new' labour, consisting of women and less politically powerful groups such as immigrants located in 'ethnic' areas of the city, is often paid very low wages. Married women, for instance, are paid low wages because it is sometimes argued that they are either second earners or primarily dependent on some other wage earner.

The same strategy is also deployed in third world countries where women are paid at significantly lower rates and employed for very long hours. The oft-quoted example of female electronic component assembly workers working long hours at eye-taxing and stressful work and then fired after four to five years because their eyesight has failed, is an indication of the kinds of redeployment of industry and about which came out of the international restructuring of capital and labour in the post-1970 period. We must also note that the low-wage female-dominated workforce is also likely to be non-unionized and credited with low levels of political awareness and strength. Furthermore, they are located within regional labour markets which give ready access to a constant supply of migrants and an ever-changing cohort of compliant and youthful workers.

In the next section we discuss aspects of the movements of capital to the third world and point out the linkages between the systems of industrialization. We note that the 'global process' is indeed a result of the continuing industrialization of capital and an extension of a network of production units, albeit into different cultural milieux at widely dispersed locations. The overall linkage, however, courses through the network of finances, ownership and control of international capital, and the search for new pools of labour as well as new markets.

Restructuring in the third world

Although much of the literature on restructuring has been written with a first world perspective, there is still a great deal of restructuring in the third world, especially as a result of the long-term internationalization of capital and ·the latter day movements of some specialized manufacturing and assembly firms to so-called ,off-shore platforms' and 'labour havens'. The concept of the 'global factory' means that we must organize our framework of analysis to include both the moves of first world firms to the third world to engage cheaper labour, and the subsequent impact oil workers everywhere of these moves. The form of multinational intervention in developing countries has changed significantly in response to a new-relationship between national and international capital, with the latter preferring to leave the total ownership of all production stages in favour of different forms of joint-ownership and concentration on the most profitable arenas. By means of the multiplication of joint-ventures, production licences, subcontracting and the moving of entire production units to developing countries, multinational firms have embraced both deepening and broadening of capital. The choice of restructuring strategies in the developing countries depends on the particular nature of the labour market.

However, the persistence of non-capitalist or 'traditional' social formations mediates the subordination of labour, even where the labour form is present (but not universal). Thus third world proletarianization is not reduced to the availability of the workforce recently excluded from agriculture. There is as well a persistent form of subsistence economy which embraces a 'domestic community' or 'family household' in the modern capitalist sector in which there is no 'free labour'.

The persistence of this subsistence economy in both the informal and the formal sectors affects the supply of labour and the nature of the proletarianization taking place. The result may be found in the various forms of semi-proletarianization which exist in many developing countries. Here we note that the presence of this noncapitalist sector allows restructuring to reduce wages by increasing the supply of labour of 'willing workers', through the increased participation of women and youths, or by including workers displaced from a previous mode of production. Much of this workforce may be made available only through the changing commitment of the family division of labour. It allows industry to lower wages while permitting the intensification of activities and increasing the numbers of workers per household. In developing countries the moves of high-technology firms In the 1970s and 1980s are the most obvious and dramatic wave of a transfer of productive investment to off-shore labour havens and to special economic zones and free-trade zones. For here the wages are low, benefits to workers few and taxation breaks favour those firms most suited to using the 'long and nimble fingers' of workers.

Many cases have been documented of the moves of electronics and other factories to the third world labour havens and, while these form part of the concept of the global factory, they must be distinguished from the forms of labour restructuring evident in local industries adjacent to these enclave industries. Here the evidence differs on the impact of indigenous industrial growth versus that derived from 'off-shore' foreign investment. Sonic argue that the spin-off effect of these foreign investments is high whereas others argue the opposite, suggesting in fact that they operate as foreign enclaves.

On the other hand it has also been argued that job creation rates in local areas of industrialization in some parts of the third world are much higher than first thought. Between 1960 and 1979, for instance, industrial employment in less developed countries grew at a rate twice that of some Western countries between 1900 and

1920. The effects of this relative growth in the present conjuncture have, however, been masked by expansion of the overall growth of population.

The most powerful tool of restructuring in the third world in the post-1973 period was the move to 'labour havens' which occurred in conjunction with the start of a global downswing. This was the start of a long-term trend toward switching the location and the sectoral operations of numerous multinational corporations whose traditional arena was the first world. In this phase a spatial movement of capital took place in response to the downswing crisis of international capital; this was precipitated by a 'switching crisis' which involved the movement of capital as one response to the problem of falling rates of profit. In developing countries extensive use has been made of new male and female skilled and unskilled labour.

More has occurred since multinational companies have become involved in the transfer of production systems into the formal industrial system of some third world cities. In terms of gender differences in the labour force it is clear that the contribution of women, be it in the formal or the 'informal' sector, has become increasingly important. Within the phases of general restructuring, however, as in each local region, women face a host of obstacles, including: inappropriate education and training; lack of capital; resistance by institutions to grant loans and credit; and limited employment and income opportunities. In those cases where jobs have been created in the enclave sectors, say in electronics, the work periods are long and hard and as a result the burnout rate and turnover are very high.

Although the number of women working in Asian industry has more than doubled over the last two decades, they are mostly concentrated in a narrow range of low income occupations, with inferior terms and conditions of work and little opportunity for advancement. Furthermore, their cultural status and position limit their access to jobs in the first instance and predispose them to quicker exit from the workplace during restructuring crises which include reductions in the-numbers of workers.

Similarly the demand for their cheap labour has been accompanied by sexual discrimination and damage to health in unprotected situations. Nowadays there is widespread concern at the conditions in workplaces where jobs are boring, repetitive, dehumanizing and in some cases dangerous to physical and mental health. Similarly, in a number of developing countries there are strong cultural prejudices which influence the manner in which women are incorporated into the labour process in the current phase of international industrial restructuring. They have fixed and subordinate roles in the labour market, which means they are designated positions within the international division of labour-on the very bottom rung.

Women's status is traditionally low and this simply reinforces their position in the social division of labour in the new industries. At the same time, however, many urban dwellers, and now some rural women, have found jobs in large-scale assembly and components factories, but mostly under unfavourable working conditions and incomes.

12
Geographical Fixations

Human geography was not discovered; it was created - in particular places, at particular times, strongly influenced by one or a few leading individuals, to perform tasks acceptable to (or at least not unacceptable to) those with power in the relevant society, as Peter Taylor has made clear. Once created, it—through its powerful leaders—developed its own *raison d'etre.* It was not free of constraints, of course, either of patronage or of state sponsorship, but it was able to develop relatively independently within society. This involved individuals and institutions (such as the Royal Geographical Society and the Geographical Association in the UK) promoting the discipline, and fashioning a niche for it in the educational structure; implicitly, if not explicitly, their promotion of geography involved campaigning against the interests of other disciplines, a tactic described by Goodson.

These campaigns were set in particular contexts, or 'contingently related conditions and so were responses to perceived opportunities and constraints. It is this contextual approach to understanding a discipline that justifies what many see as the trite definition that 'geography is what geographers do' (though not in conditions that are necessarily of their own choosing). There is no *need* for a discipline of geography, though there is certainly a need for at least some of the work currently done by geographers. But there is a discipline called geography, historically constituted, embedded within academic, institutional and educational structures, and continually being reconstituted. It exists, and will continue to; what, then, is its rationale?

The existence of geography as an academic discipline in many places should not bolster the belief in the 'naturalness' of geography, for definitions and practice vary substantially from place to place. Here attention is focused almost entirely on the British context: this, of course, is closely linked to the North American, but there are important differences (not least in the role of geography in school curricula) and we must not forget those between the situations in the United States and in Canada.

Discussion of an individual discipline can take place only within a framework provided by the constellation of other disciplines. All of these are human creations too (though some may claim that a few—for example, mathematics—are 'natural') and so the nature of geography in any place has developed out of conflict (however polite, subdued, implicit) with other such creations.

Some argue against any academic division of labour, certainly any division within the social sciences. Proposals have been advanced for unidisciplinary (i.e. the dominance of one social science, usually economics), multidisciplinary, interdisciplinary and transdisciplinary reconstructions of social science, but Eliot Hurst has argued against them all, and propounded a new structure based on historical materialism and thereby involving a de-definition of geography. As he puts it, we need a position:

> that de-defines the disciplines as we know them... it is not a matter of rearranging the fragmentation of

> epistemological space, but of transcending all such boundaries as we know them to emphasize the' unity of scientific practice. Historical materialism as the science of human society ranks alongside mathematical and natural sciences as the only tenable scientific practices.

Alongside this idealistic position is the more pragmatic one, which defends the division of labour, not in any absolute sense but, for geography, with regard to two features.

1 The division provides a necessary subdivision of knowledge, without which progress is very difficult in the advancement of understanding. This immediately raises the problem of the chaotic conception, and also that of reductionism. Clearly, the first problem is a crucial one, for fragmentation into unrealistic parts provides for counter-productive scholarship. The second is only crucial if a given academic division of labour is ossified. The recent history of science, at least, shows this not to have been the case, with new disciplines being invented to follow promising research lines and to promote certain interests.

2. The division provides niches for scholars and researchers to work in. Each discipline is internally structured, and individual careers within it are largely governed by discipline-defined peer review; it is a society that practitioners join and which, through its (written and unwritten) rules, provides them with a comfortable environment. It can, and sometimes does, encourage self-satisfied isolation, untrammelled by external contact and evaluation, and the role models that it provides may be stultifying. (As the recent history of human geography shows, however, external contact is not negligible and the discipline has been redirected by people dissatisfied with its current practice—though not always, without

difficulty.) But again, this is a question of practice rather than principle.

It is the pragmatic position that's adopted here. Human geography exists, so how should it be practised? That question is explored by looking at four geographical fixations of recent decades.

Environmental fix

The inter-relationships of human and physical geography have been the source of considerable debate over a very substantial period. The grounds of that debate have shifted very substantially, however, as the following brief categorization suggests.

1 *The quasi-deterministic approach,* including much traditional regional geography, presented the discipline as very much the study of environmental stimulus and human response. Its extreme forms were some variants of both environmental determinism and possibilism, but most occupied a 'middle-of-the-road' position. All were holistic, because they stressed the interactions between peoples and environments (frequently termed the 'man-land' approach to geography).

2 *The holistic/synthetic approach,* also linked to some forms of regional geography and based on the case - put, for example, by Wooldridge and East and widely accepted among British geographers at the time - that a discipline (geography) was needed which took the findings of separate systematic studies (inside and beyond the discipline) and put them together to create a description of the whole phenomenon complex. This, it was argued, needed both human and physical geography because without either the whole could not be appreciated. Hence, it was contended, geography straddles the arts and the sciences (the social sciences were rarely considered) and was the bridging discipline between the two.

3 *The technical approach,* linked to spatial analysis and certain forms of applied geography. In this, the main focus was on methods. The so-called quantitative revolution of the 1950s/1960s led to considerable, valuable, methodological cross-fertilization between natural and social scientists: in Britain, because of the presence of both physical and human geography, the links were within geography, as in the works of Haggett and Chorley; in the United States, the almost complete absence of physical geography led to extra-disciplinary links with sympathetic natural scientists, such as the geologist W. C. Krumbein.

The links were almost all forged through common interests in technical issues and —apart from a few odd attempts at developing homologies, many in the context of general systems theory—there was very little substantive linking of the two fields.

4 *The environmentalism approach,* which stressed the interactions among people, societies and the physical environment. On the one hand, the physical environment is identified as a resource to which people respond and on which they act, both aesthetically and economically. On the other hand, society is one of the agents controlling the rates of environmental processes. Thus, it is argued, physical and human geography need each other: without the--former, the latter is ignoring the fundamental resource base for a materialist society; without the latter, the former is ignoring the forces that accelerate, retard, and catalyse environmental processes.

Of these four, the last has the strongest rationale. The determinism underpinning the first has been discarded; the arrogance of the second has been repudiated; and the weak intellectual base of the third has led to exposure of the poverty of links founded in shared techniques (what price a University department of chi-square analysis?) but epistemological incompatibilities. It is therefore, with the environmentalism approach that the rest of this section is concerned.

Environmentalism

The need for physical geographers to be aware of human use of the earth's surface and for human geographers to appreciate the nature of societies' physical resource bases have led some authors to claim the necessity of a discipline of geography which not only brings the two together, but integrates them.

In particular, several authors have argued that this integrative activity should focus on the topics of resource analysis and management. The rationale for this focus was clearly put by Goudie, when invited to answer the question 'Should Human and Physical Geography go their separate ways?'

> ... not only are the pressures posed on the environment by man becoming greater rather than less as time goes on, but the pressures posed for man by the environment are also not necessarily diminishing... who is the more dependent on his environment: the Kalahari bushman who can find food and water in an hostile environment, or the city dweller who could only last for a few days if his supplies of food and water were to be disrupted? The world is still a hazardous place, man is affected by his climatic environment..., human health is related to' environmental conditions, climatic change is a threat to human welfare, environmental influences *cannot* be denied.

None of this will be gainsaid here. Nor is an argument raised against Balchin's claim—except the sexism—that:

> Man interferes with the natural ecosystems at his peril and, until he learns to harmonize his activities with those of Nature, he can expect only a problem-ridden existence.

All that is debated here is whether this requires the integration of human and physical geography. Human and physical geography involve two separate groups of scholars, each seeking to understand their subject matter. They share a common history of being wedded to evolutionary forms of thought, and a recent history of associations with empiricism and positivism. Among human geographers, positivism has been relegated and replaced by various other approaches, such as the realist advanced here.

Among physical geographers, positivism still has a strong hold, despite the development elsewhere of a realist physical science. Nevertheless, even if both were to adopt a realist position, the two would remain very different research pursuits, for reasons set out above. The physical, chemical and biological processes that are the foundations for the production of landforms, weather and vegetation complexes are givens; the structures of society are human creations, forever changing.

What, then, of the resource analysis and management research which supposedly bridges this divide between human and physical geography? An examination of the literature has identified four types of work:

1 *Resource appreciation* covering (a) work by physical geographers presenting their subject matter (e.g. climates, water) as resources which societies exploit; (b) work by human geographers on that exploitation (e.g. the use of water resources); (c) work by human geographers on 'popular' conceptions of nature and how the physical environment works; and (d) work by physical geographers promoting the understanding of environmental processes before they are altered through, for example, land use changes.

2 *People in the physical environment,* covering the human impact on physical ecosystems and processes, and application of the understanding gained through environmental impact studies.
3 *Conflict over the environment,* focusing on conflicts within society over the conservation, preservation and use of environmental resources.
4 *Human demands on the environment,* with particular reference to possible environmental constraints on social trends (both long-term, as in 'The limits to growth' debate, and short-term as with the Sahelian drought and famine).

In virtually none of this work is there any integration of the separate research by human and physical geographers into the processes involved in either the creation of demands on the environment or the processes that create the environmental resource.

Work in resource management is conducted either from the environmental process perspective of the physical geographer or from the social demand perspective of the human geographer (whether positivist and based on neo-classical economics or realist and based on class conflict). The two groups meet in common subject matter, but do not combine their research skills. Nor do they need to.

Everyday life is acted out in terms of stereotypes of individuals and societies, models which structure our thinking. We have similar stereotypes of the physical environment, conceptions of nature which direct our interpretations of the physical environment. In terms of understanding how we live, it is necessary to understand those conceptions, as the work of Gilbert White and others on various natural hazards made very clear. In order to improve the quality of life, it is desirable to improve those conceptions, with regard to environmental outcomes; resource managers need valid models of the resources they are managing. But there is no need to understand the actual way in which floods are produced, any more than the practising demographer needs to know how the birth control pill works. It is the probability of the outcome that matters and no more—which is why you find no physical geography in White's work.

Ron Cooke has recently disagreed with this position, arguing against the exemplar contention:

> that physical geographers interested in the impact of farming on soil erosion do not need to understand why it is that farmers are intensifying their demands on the land.

But his example of slope failure in Los Angeles does not support his case. He shows that the greatest volume of failure occurred away from the areas of highest potential, and matched the distribution of 'newer affluent communities, often of young, articulate professionals, who can effectively command local influence'.

But this tells us nothing of the reasons why such communities exist, and although knowledge of their attitudes to public help and the availability of insurance allows us to understand their activities Cooke's work in no way brings together the separate modes of analysis of contemporary physical and human geography. He is right in arguing that:

> the natural processes that fashion slopes impose themselves intimately on the patterns of human behaviour, and the complex network of action and reaction demands that they, too, are understood.

This cannot be gainsaid, for appreciating the links between society and environment is a crucial task that geographers undertake. Cooke places such appreciation at the centre of geography, which he presents as a web of relationships between human activity and environmental contexts. He then mildly castigates:

> some extremists on the fringes of the web [who] will probably see little of interest in the centre of it. In writing the post-war history of geography, they will be tempted to ignore or underplay, for example, those geographers who have contributed most influentially to studies of the relations between communities, cultures and the physical environment. The names of Carl Sauer and Gilbert White, and their numerous students, will not figure prominently in their reviews.

The term geography has two major usages. The first - the vernacular - refers to the features of places: physical geography is about landscapes; human geography is about what is done where. The second - the academic - refers to the content of the discipline: physical geography is about understanding environmental processes; human geography is about understanding why things are done by people where they are done. Unfortunately, few physical geographers know much about academic human geography, and vice versa. Thus when physical geographers are arguing for their integration with human geography they are using the latter in the vernacular sense. As so often happens, our meanings are distorted by the words we use, both by us, and more importantly, by those who read them and interpret them according to their dictionaries, not ours.

As an educational discipline, geography does much to promote awareness - of the nature of the physical environment among human geographers; of the nature of society among physical geographers; and of the various conceptions of nature among all. (It could well be argued that in universities the student's awareness is much greater than that of the specialized staff, for the physical:human divide is a major one with regard, for example, to seminar attendance.) Dave Pepper's discussion of the problems of stimulating such awareness provides valuable insights to this, and his book on *The Roots of Modern Environmentalism* develops the sorts of theme that are valid for both physical and human geographers. We need to be aware of the social construction of environmental images, and the sorts of behaviour that this results in, and we need to be aware of the structural bases for our attitudes towards the environment. As Sayer reminds us, nature is something appropriated for human use under capitalism; it is the focus of human labour, so that:

> Human labour, as distinct from animal labour, requires understanding of Nature's mechanisms, and this knowledge is not innate but socially acquired. Knowledge of Nature is never produced through an unmediated reflection of the subject upon Nature but always uses means of production' in the form of the existing social knowledge.

Part of the emancipatory task of geography, therefore, is to unmask the ideological presentations of nature as something that we control totally (recall the debates about nuclear power). We need to demonstrate, with Lukacs, that:

> Nature is a societal category. That is to say, whatever is held to be natural at any given stage of social development, however this nature is related to man and whatever form his involvement with it takes, i.e. nature's form, its content, its range and its objectivity are all socially conditioned.

An academic discipline which does that is, to me, a viable one, even if it does it in two separate parts.

Spatial fix

From the mid-1950s on, a movement promoting geography (basically human geography) as spatial science - alternative terms were locational analysis and spatial analysis - spread outwards from its major foci at four centres in the USA. It drew on a variety of roots, some in geography (including work by Scandinavian and German pioneers) and some in other social sciences. As has been pointed out, there has always been a geometrical tradition within geography. But this movement—rapidly dubbed the quantitative and theoretical revolution—took a new approach, and was hardly a continuation of that tradition, which is now mainly in surveying and mapmaking. It was presented either as a replacement for, or as a logical development of (by introducing precision and rigour), the then dominant regional approach, which Peter Gould described as:

> bumbling amateurism and antiquarianism that had spent nearly half a century of opportunity in the university piling up a tipheap of unstructured factual accounts . . . it was practically impossible to find a book in the field that one could put in the hands of a scholar in another discipline without feeling ashamed.

Alongside the criticisms of current approaches to human geography, spatial science was rationalized (retrospectively) as a necessary move given shifts in the nature of society. As Kevin Cox expressed it:

> In a world of spatial interdependence... locally experienced environmental dependencies lose their rationale: men relate less and less to the land on which they stand and more and more to socially-created geographical patterns over a much wider area.

In a locally oriented society, environment is crucial: in a globally organized society, spatial relations are crucial, and the 'new geography' thus had to stress the latter. It comprised two elements. The first was *the focus on spatial distributions - initially* via deductive models but later, as their axioms were found wanting, through more inductive searches—with the aim of identifying what Schaefer termed morphological laws and laws of coincidence, generalizations about the spatial arrangements of individual phenomena and their correlations with those of other phenomena; human geography was to become a science, within the (implicitly positivist) general conception of that term. The second was the use of mathematical languages for modelling and statistical procedures for hypothesis-testing. Put the two together, and you get the orientation to human geography defined by Berry and Marble as:

> building generalizations with predictive power by precise quantitative description of spatial distributions, spatial structure and organization and spatial relationships.

Various approaches to the structuring of human geography as spatial science were adopted. Dick Morrill, for example, focused on the location of all activity as a reaction to the frictions of distance: location decisions were taken so as to minimize the consequent transport costs, as were movement decisions (e.g. journeys to shop).

Peter Haggett focused on the outcomes, identifying five (later six) main components of a spatial system, each subject to the operation of basic spatial laws. Others sought to specify the fundamentals of spatial science more precisely. In a pioneering, but largely disregarded, paper, Allen Philbrick identified what he termed the 'principles of area functional organization'; they hinged around the basic postulate that:

> Human occupance is focal in character,

with the patterns of nodal organization which reflected this displaying hierarchical spatial structures. John Nystuen followed this with a search for the concepts necessary and sufficient to a 'geographical point of view'. He identified three: direction (or orientation), distance, and connection (or relative position). And Gerard Rushton used inductive procedures to identify patterns of 'spatial behaviour', the general rules that:

> exist independently of the environment where the decision is made,

and can be derived from studying particular patterns of

'behaviour in space'. What these approaches shared was a desire to show that human geography is as rigorous as the other social sciences, most of which were then in a purple patch of quantification, and also that it had a particular perspective to contribute to the social sciences. That perspective was the focus on space - on the spatial variable. It was very largely a restricted view of space, however, for it focused almost entirely on relative (and relational) space, on distance as the determinant variable in location and movement decisions; what happened in a place depended on its relative location.

In terms of the Haggett system, the earth was a surface. Absolute—spaces were identified—through the equation of regionalization with classification—but only as simplifications of that surface for didactic and analytical purposes. (According to Haggett, like the NAS/NRC committee quoted above, regions were the 'test beds' for systematic ideas.)

This approach has been interpreted since as based on a spatial fetishism. Space and/or distance were reified; inanimate things were given an existence of their own and a power to influence, if not determine, people's actions. Distance is, of course, an important influence—as is made very apparent in Geoffrey Blainey's portrayal of Australia's development as a consequence of *The Tyranny of Distance.* But it is really only a constraint to the extent that we let it be, because we have built societies that use distance as a barrier, as a form of cocoon.

The tyranny of distance has been incorporated into society, and used by it, so that relative space is really what we make it and has no independent existence; and of course, societies have also been concerned to annihilate space by time, to get rid of the tyranny and so foster the process of capital accumulation. The argument against the fetishism involved in spatial science, because of its focus on relative distance and its naive belief that a separate social science can be built on that reification of space, is important; even more important is the relative absence of consideration by spatial scientists of absolute space. This is surprising because our daily lives are lived out in absolute spaces, and our societies are organized similarly. We live in nested, partially overlapping containers, some of which have more porous walls than others.

For most individuals, there are four such containers—home, workplace, local government and state —each of which has clearly defined boundaries, most of which are in some way 'policed'. None of these is 'natural'; each is created, defined by us, in our local context. (Places matter in the interpretation of places.) We live out our lives, in large part, in a system of absolute spaces. These are created, at least in part, to manipulate relative space and the frictions of distance. We have separate homes, with walls, to provide us with privacy and separate us from contact with others.

Some of us have gardens, too, to provide a cocoon and a further layer of insulation, especially effective if they are surrounded by hedges/fences. We have states to protect us from others. Many of our institutions are organized in terms of absolute spaces as well, as David Harvey illustrated for the Baltimore housing market. We have ghettos, into which we confine our 'undesirables', and we have asylums and prisons to contain those we perceive as threats; nowhere is this clearer than in South Africa, where the apartheid system involves the careful manipulation and policing of absolute spaces to achieve control by a racial minority.

Many of these absolute spaces are legally defined and have demarcated boundaries. They are part, as Bob Sack has told us, of a territoriality that is basic to the organization of societies. To some, this territoriality is innate—one of the essences that phenomenologists seek to humans, as to other animal species. Sack does not take this view, but rather just notes that:

> social organisations are often territorial... the assertion by an organisation, or an individual in the name of an organisation, that an area of geographic space is under its influence or control. Whereas all members of social organisations occupy space, not all social organisations make such territorial assertions. The social enforcement (and institutionalisation) of such assertions... provide the context necessary for social facts to exhibit the first type of spatial properties. The forms such territorial structures take and the functions they provide depend on the nature of particular political economies.

Thus absolute spaces are not natural; they are human creations, produced in a particular context, to serve a particular purpose, and once produced are an element of the milieux within which socialization occurs. The systems of territorial containers—both de jure and de facto (e.g. the 'turfs' of neighbourhood gangs)—are in no way fixed; they are continually changing.

The state system is in constant flux, for example, as those in power seek to extend the territory over which they have some power: to advance accumulation (colonialism, for example, and the creation of the EEC) to promote legitimation (the Argentinian invasion of the Falklands/ Malvinas?); and to create social cohesion (Israeli expansion?). Others both other states and would-be states (e.g. nationalist movements) -compete with them, occasionally producing armed conflict over the possession of certain areas.

Some of the contests are culturally-based, some have very vague roots in the visions of grandeur of certain individuals; but many have economic roots (colonization is the basis of Ulster's problem, for example) or goals. Relative space, or distance, is a hindrance and has to be overcome, the process of annihilating space by time involves restructuring the" pattern of relative locations in order to promote individual and group gains.

In the development of telecommunications and the delivery of weapons, space has now been virtually annihilated; messages can be relayed almost instantaneously to any major settlement, and nuclear weapons can be delivered anywhere in a matter of minutes. These twin 'developments' have been crucial to the extension of capitalist hegemony. Power has been sustained by transforming the map of the world. It has also been sustained by the creation of absolute spaces, whose maintenance and restructuring is similarly crucial to the exercise of economic and political power.

Space is central to the organization of societies, but there is much more to its influence than the friction of distance that has been the focus of spatial scientists. By concentrating on relative space as a fixed variable they have both (a) ignored its creation and modification as a resource by societies and individuals and (b) paid insufficient attention to its manipulation into absolute spaces. Given the broader focus implied by the previous paragraph, is the spatial fix a viable focus for a separate social science of human geography?

Sack has provided a series of authoritative statements arguing against a separate discipline that feeds in the spatial variable as an autonomous influence. Geometry cannot provide an explanation, only a description; to explain you must appreciate the context of that description, for you cannot separate space from substance, any more than an historian can separate time from substance and create a discipline with time as the independent variable. Space has no independent existence outside its construction by society, any more than nature (or vernacular physical geography) has.

Neither is irrelevant, and because of either one or both a human project may fail, with the failure leading to a rethinking of the nature of the constraint.

Spatial components characterize most human projects. In many, they are so trivial as to be virtually irrelevant. In others they are crucial, and thus non-trivial. In the social sciences in general, therefore, it is necessary for, proper attention to be paid to those non-trivial spatial components. To separate out the spatial - whether relative or absolute - and study it and it alone is undoubtedly to commit the sin of studying a chaotic conception., But to ensure that the spatial is neither overlooked nor torn out of context is to make a valid contribution.

A human geography that makes such a contribution is viable, therefore, so long as its practitioners are providing a perspective from *within* the social sciences rather than for them. In this way the general understanding of society will be promoted, as the study of a whole not a set of disparate parts.

Regional fix

The regional fix preceded the spatial fix as the geographer's major fetishism. There were many interpretations, but fundamental to most was the belief that the earth's surface is divided into a mosaic of different regions each of which had a particular character as a consequence of the symbiosis between the physical environment and the society occupying it. Hence they were organic wholes, 'natural regions' which were not to be confused with the artificial regions imposed on the earth's surface by the drawing of political boundaries. This approach was imbued with a strong, if implicit, environmental determinism.

The term region was not discarded when the regional fix was replaced by the spatial. Instead it was modified, and used by some spatial scientists to legitimate their quantitative work; they could define regions 'objectively' and could model them as systems. This 'regional science' replaced humanistic appreciation by quantitative, pragmatic description; the study of places all but disappeared. For a while—perhaps 25 years—regions were little more than heuristic devices for most human geographers.

A few continued to argue for the understanding of place as an important geographical contribution, particularly places other than one's own. But the preaching was rarely satisfied in the practice, and regional geography went into abeyance. And then, in the late 1970s, people started to ask if they could have it back. Derek Gregory ended his expose of the ideological bases of the many varieties of human geography by noting that:

> Ever since regional geography was declared to be dead -.most fervently by those who had never been much good at it anyway -geographers, to their credit, have kept trying to revivify it in one form or another,

and then introduced his own try with a call for knowledge of

> the constitution of *regional* social formations, of *regional* articulations and *regional* transformations... it's not difficult to point either to the warrant provided by geography's long-standing commitment to places and the people that live in them or to the regional structures which persist in contemporary space-economies.

It is probably fair to say that many readers were uncertain then how to interpret this. The case for the sort of regional geography that Gregory was calling for is integral to the arguments that penetrate the whole of this book. Quite simply—places matter.

The capitalist world-economy operates a system of imperatives globally, but the implementation of those imperatives is undertaken, in large measure, by people socialized in particular milieux, each in a cultural region with its own language, values and characteristic attitudes. Like capitalism itself, those cultural regions are not fixed, for they are being constantly restructured. But they are interpretations of how to live, how to interpret nature, how to respond to the tyranny of distance. In large part, this place-to-place variability (in may cases as important *within* as *between* countries) is a result of history, of the construction of a capitalist social formation on pre-capitalist foundations. The latter varied enormously, because of their relative isolation; unlike capitalist societies, pre-capitalist ones have been largely unsuccessful in annihilating space by time.

Even minor differences between neighbours, perhaps one the offshoot of another, tended to magnify over time, producing a complicated mosaic of cultural variations - in dialect if not language, in food tastes, in land tenure and farming practices etc.—which capitalism has failed to erase, despite the great mobility of population and the introduction 61 homogenized national and international cultures.

Indeed, the development of industrial capitalism not only to some extent absorbed such cultural variations, it also created more, as in the attitudes to married women working displayed in different UK industrial regions. Capitalism has its history, too, which is deeply embedded in the places created and recreated in response to its imperatives.

So-called 'traditional' regional geography lost favour because of the onslaught that it faced from the 'quantitative and theoretical revolution', an onslaught against which it was powerless because of the poverty of its empiricism and its continued links to an explicit environmental determinism. Some still adhere to it, but their attempts to promote a revival are based on weak rhetoric. Fraser Hart, for example, argued that good regional geography contains 'evocative descriptions that facilitate an understanding and an appreciation of places, areas and regions'.

The region to be described is 'a more or less homogeneous area that differs from other areas', and no standard definition can be offered:

> Regions are subjective devices, and they must be shaped to fit the hand of the individual user. There can be no standard definition of a region, and there are no universal rules for recognizing, delimiting, and describing regions... Understanding is more important than classification, and the core usually is more important than the fringes.

Three key themes should recur in regional study: a sense of time, of continuous change; the relationship between scale and detail; and 'the importance of the physical environment, which provides the stuff that people have to work with, and sets the stage on which the human drama is played'

Certainly, we should be aiming to satisfy human curiosity about how much of what is where and why it's there, about the where and why of places and people about the land and how people have used and abused it'. But to offer no more than superficial glimpses is to do little more than the Victorian pioneer explorers who returned to the great geographical societies with their lantern slides and tales of exotic cultures. Clearly we must *sensitize* people to the variability of places, but we must help them to appreciate the sources of that variability; to use Hart's own term 'our obligation to society' is to promote emancipation, not just awareness. Regions must be presented for what they are: human creations of the contingent conditions within which the imperatives of the mode of production are acted out and etched into the culture an landscape of places.

They are the milieux in which people learn how to survive. Our obligation is to understand them, to show that they are forever changing, and to indicate why. We must do more than satisfy curiosity; we must build useful knowledge.

Systematic fix

The decline of regional geography in the 1950s and 1960s was associated with the ascendancy of systematic geography. For decades previously, geographers had argued that the two were symbiotic, with the systematic geographies(ers) providing the parts that were assembled into wholes by the regional geographies(ers). But in the 1950s and 1960s the assembly line was almost deserted; people became experts on the parts alone.

Most common was the division of geography into topical specialisms. The major split was between physical and human. Within the latter, there was a two-tiered division. At the top level were economic, social, political and urban, and each had its subdivisions - industrial and Agricultural within economic, for example; inter-urban and intra-urban etc. Most human geographers associated themselves with one of the major divisions, if not one of the subdivisions, and the discipline became both compartmentalized and outward-looking.

The members of the various compartments found that they had little in-common with most of their colleagues (certainly those with whom they worked on a day-to-day basis in a university department, except perhaps with regard to methodological, especially quantitative, issues) and much more with the members of other disciplines. (That external orientation rarely became symbiotic, and few economists, sociologists etc. found much stimulus in and use for the work of geographers.) Not all human geographers entered one of these topically defined compartments. Some, especially historical geographers, retained a broader perspective. Others—the true spatial scientists—focused on spatial arrangements, irrespective of the substantive subject matter; Peter Haggett, for example, has focused much of his research on spatial spread and diffusion, using similar models and techniques for the analysis of both measles and unemployment. This was spatial systematics—the study of points, networks etc.—rather than topical systematics. This fragmentation merely exacerbated the problem that the academic division of labour in the social sciences suffers from; the whole - the global world-economy - was taken apart so that the pieces could be investigated, but nobody put it together again.

To study the individual social sciences introduces the possibility of focusing on chaotic conceptions; to fragment them even further changes the possibility into a high probability. Lip service to systems approaches suggested that a framework was available, and would be used to assemble the parts at the proper time, but there was little evidence of what the end-result might be.

The development of a realist approach countered this tendency with, for example, David Harvey's statement that issues of distribution cannot be separated analytically from those of production: economic and social geography are integral parts of each other. Understanding how capitalism operates needs theory which incorporates social (the relations of production) as well as economic (the forces of production) factors, and which recognizes the central purpose of politics (the state) in binding them all together.

13
Quantitative Techniques

Integration seems even more important given the contemporary enthusiasm for empirical study among Marxists and humanistic geographers and also the oddly familiar quality of some recent empirical research conducted by Marxists and humanists. This familiarity could be seen as odd because it is reminiscent of the quantitative research criticized so effectively from these two perspectives as positivist.

For example, this strong sense of *deja vu* is elicited by the work of the Marxist sociologists, Wright and Perrone. They state that: 'It is our hope (to) open up the possibility of bringing Marxist categories into the heart of quantitative research on social inequality as well as making quantitative research seem more relevant to Marxist social scientists. To this end, they present 'a preliminary operationalization of the Marxist criteria for class position for use in quantitative research' and examine 'an application of this *operationalization* in the study of income inequality', complete with multiple regression equations and levels *of* statistical significance. That other Marxists have been receptive to this mode of enquiry is indicated by Patrick Dunleavy's statement that the work of Wright & Perrone is 'the best Marxist empirical work on social class boundaries'.

Dunleavy himself is conducting sophisticated quantitative analyses of political attitudes by housing consumption sectors. Among those espousing a humanistic perspective, David Ley has recently employed attitudinal scales, non-parametric statistical techniques and statistical inference in assessing attitudes toward office relocation. In my own work on the links between home-ownership and political values, we have made substantial use of attitudinal measures and non-parametric statistical techniques, while accepting the weight of the humanist critique of positivism. That something is amiss in this embracing of quantitative technique by historical materialists is suggested by Andrew Sayer's remark that: 'The methodological principles of statistical inference *presuppose* the fatally-flawed empiricist situations of atomism and regularity generalisation'. Sayer's claim is that there is a fundamental mismatch between the use of statistical inference and the philosophical tenets of realism, which he takes to underlie historical materialism.'

The emphasis on understanding the meaning of social phenomena has also prompted humanistic geographers to argue that: 'Methodologically, this requires a move from the principles of statistical inference based on representative random samples, to those of "logical inference" based on unique or idiosyncratic case studies'. The purpose of this chapter is to review several of the central criticisms of positivism (or empiricism) advanced through the historical materialist and humanistic perspectives, and to consider the extent to which the use of statistical inference and quantification is susceptible to them.

Though Andrew Sayer is certainly not the only historical materialist to criticize the type of empirical work conducted by positivists, his criticisms stand out in geography, both because he has been extremely articulate about the specific points of incompatibility between statistical inference and historical materialism and because he has emphasized the necessity for empirical research within-a Marxist perspective. Therefore, special attention will be directed toward his detailed criticisms. As noted above, Sayer has modified his position somewhat so that it is compatible with the arguments presented here. His resolutions of the links between a realist philosophy and statistical inference are, however, developed somewhat differently from those developed here. Altogether four criticisms of positivism will be evaluated in terms of their implications for quantitative research. These include: the critique of theory as empirical regularity and the rejection of an atomistic ontology, both criticisms coming from the historical materialist perspective; a realization that facts are interpreted and, finally, a rejection of the reduction of humanness to physical properties and hence a neglect of meaning, human intentionality and choice, a criticism common to both perspectives.

The arguments in this paper consider the implications of these philosophical criticisms for the *methods* appropriate to historical materialist and humanist perspectives, namely the logical consistency of using quantitative techniques if one accepts these criticisms. In other words, some philosophical groundwork is assumed and this chapter focuses more exclusively on specific methodological issues which follow from preceding philosophical discussions. It will be argued that quantitative techniques are not vulnerable to these more basic philosophical criticisms and that a distinction should be maintained between the logical underpinnings of these techniques and their use by positivist geographers.

Empirical regularity

From the historical materialist perspective, the relationship between theory and empirical research is generally taken to be defined by a realist philosophy of science. A distinguishing feature of the realist position is the rejection of a Humean definition of causality as the constant conjunction of events. For Humeans, causation is equivalent to regular succession; if event B follows event A, we say that A caused B. Humeans do not assume the logical necessity of this temporal relationship. What is at issue here is that nothing is observed except that B follows A.

Realists reject this conception of causality in favour of one which admits of causes as mechanisms, such that properties of A, when stimulated, produce B. For example, from the realist perspective we need to say more about the fact that the match lights after the match is struck than that the former follows the latter. We need to describe the causal mechanisms involved. An adequate causal explanation of this phenomenon consists of a description of how striking the match causes the match to light and this is in part explained by describing the nature of the match and the surface against which it is struck. Causes are conceptualized as necessary ways-of-acting of an object which exist as a property of that object.

Matches light when struck across abrasive materials because they have certain properties. This understanding leads to an ontological distinction between causal laws and patterns of events; whether causal powers are evident in a pattern of events depends on contingently related factors. So, for instance, a realist might say that striking a match causes a match to light but whether the match lights depends on a number of contingently related factors, such as whether the match is dry. It is thus contingent that striking a match causes that match to light but under certain conditions it will do so necessarily. This rationale, as realists point out, underlies the logic of the experimental method, of controlling contingent factors so as to observe the causal process. For social theory, where applications of the experimental method are more limited, the implication is that causal laws refer to tendencies that may or may not be evident in events. This understanding leads the realist, and consequently the historical materialist, to reject two routes to theory development.

First, simple enumerative induction, generalization on the basis of observed regularities, is rejected because theories are not merely generalizations but statements (abstractions) about causal mechanisms. As well as rejecting enumerative induction, realists abandon the falsificationist model associated with Popper, arguing that, if causal laws are *tendencies* and not absolute predictions about events in the world, then the non-evidence of these causal processes in events is irrelevant to an assessment of the truthfulness of the posited causal mechanisms. It is partially on these grounds, the rejection of empirical regularity as theory (with theory here referring to the identification of necessary, or causal, connections between phenomena) and the rejection of the falsification of theory in the *absence* of empirical regularities, that the logical compatibility of statistical inference with a realist philosophy has been questioned. We would like to argue, however, that the use of statistical inference is compatible with a realist view of theory.

The logic of using statistical hypotheses is to generalize about empirical regularities across classes on the basis of samples of these classes. However, although empirical regularities are what statistical hypotheses are about, the use of statistical hypotheses does not necessarily imply an adoption of enumerative induction, as Sayer has suggested in his earlier work. An inference from a sample to a defined population or an inference that an association is such that it is unlikely to have occurred by chance does not imply a similar mode of linkage between the empirical regularity and a theory. It is possible to say that our confidence in theories is not amenable to any probabilistic treatment or wholly dependent on empirical regularity, while maintaining the importance of examining empirical regularities for theory development.

The distinctiveness between and yet interdependence of empirical regularities and theories is widely recognized within the philosophy of science. This recognition has spawned such distinctions as those between inductive evidence and inductive support, statistical evidence and statistical relevance, the latter terms in each couplet expressing a resolution distanced from the enumerative inductive mode of inference. To simplify considerably, Salmon, for instance, presents two steps in the explanatory process. The first involves statistical systemization in which empirical regularities (including those with low probability) are established.

These then *demand* explanation; events and statistical regularities are fitted into a causal network which is largely an abstraction. Salmon's work follows from the understanding that the imposition of 'the high probability requirement' upon explanation-the assumption that only events occurring together with a high frequency can be explained-produces a serious malady that Kyburg has called 'conjunctivitis'. This has led to a reconceptualization of empirical regularities that exclude the high probability requirement, such that one can consider the statistical relevance of improbable events, as well as probable ones, and to an integration of this revised conception of empirical regularity with a realist notion of causality involving abstracted explanation. It is a positive notion of support that is notably lacking in recent Marxist accounts of realist philosophy. An intriguing a priori assumption has been that associations implied by Marxist theories will not be evident in events. For instance, Bhaskar writes that 'laws cannot be constant conjunctions of events, because such conjunctions (1) are extremely rare, and (2) must in general be artificially produced'. One wonders how he *knows* this.

Rather than battening down the theoretical hatches by means of a realist epistemology, it may be more productive, while embracing a realist perspective, to examine the fit between Marxist theoretical statements and empirical reality and *compare* instances of relative fit in order to understand more fully the *conditions* on which the posited causal mechanisms are *contingent*. An explicitly comparative methodology is thus advocated. Such comparisons not only indicate the generality of the associations posited theoretically, but suggest the specific contingent conditions that have led to the absence of conjunctions in particular instances. As an example of this approach, in my own work on the links between housing tenure and political ideology in urban Canada it was theoretically productive to compare these associations across different occupational classes.

Marxist theorists, among others, have argued that home-ownership generally fosters an ethic of individualism and privatism, and that home-owners, as compared to renters, tend to centre more of their interests around the home and fewer toward issues in the workplace. An examination of the associations between home-ownership and political values across a sample representative of the adult urban Canadian population indicated that certain home-owners are indeed more conservative and less supportive of social welfare provisions, but that 'this generalization is 'limited to particular occupational groups.

Specifically, a consistent pattern of associations between political values and housing tenure was found for household heads who worked in low-level managerial and skilled non-manual occupations, whereas virtually no such associations were found for those in skilled manual occupations. This finding was extremely suggestive and the reasons for this contrast between skilled manual and skilled non-manual workers were taken up in a series of in-depth interviews with home-owners and renters living in Surrey, an outer suburb of Vancouver, British Columbia.

These in-depth interviews indicated that home-ownership did not have a critical influence on the political ideology of skilled manual workers because of their strong commitment to their trade unions. The trade unions appeared to be the critical institutional medium through which their political values were formed. In contrast, the skilled non-manual workers did not belong to unions or did not feel a commitment to those to which they did belong. In the absence of an association with a strong work-based organization, housing issues seemed to play a more important role in their political outlook. An association between political ideology and home-ownership thus seemed to be conditional on an absence of alternative sources of organization. As Agnew has written: 'The meanings attached to the tenure differ from context to context depending on the extent to which the dominance of capitalist social relations has been successfully challenged'.

The epistemological and methodological points that follow from this example are, first, that meaningful empirical regularities do exist, and second, that the comparative method is useful, both to document the generality of the empirical regularity and to uncover the contingent conditions which lead to its evidence.

This methodological prescription seems altogether consistent with Kosik's description of the historical materialist method, that is: first 'appropriating the material, in detail, mastering it to the last historically accessible detail , and then 'analysing its different forms of development' and, finally, 'tracing out their internal connections'. The beginning of the investigation is, in Kosik's words, 'random and arbitrary'. Establishing empirical regularities by means of statistical inference can be seen as one aspect of this first step.

The second step involves the comparative method. The final step is an act of abstraction which 'does not amount to reducing "the phenomenon" to dynamized substance, i.e. to something concealed behind the phenomena as something independent of them; rather it is cognition of the laws of movement of the thing itself'. In other words, theoretical abstractions are not removed from the empirical world; they highlight the causal connections within that material world. Granted that theoretical abstractions are not empirical regularities, that they are not always evident as empirical regularities, associations at the level of events give clues to theoretical causal mechanisms and their absence raises very serious questions concerning contingent conditions. Statistical techniques are useful in assessing these patterns of association.

Atomism

A second and related criticism of the use of statistical inference, developed by Sayer from a historical materialist perspective, is that the ontological assumption of atomistic monism, or a variant of external relations, underlies statistical inference (although, as noted above, Sayer now argues that there is a resonance rather than a logical link between atomism and statistical inference). My intention in this section is not to argue for or against this ontological assumption. Rather, questions of ontology can be side-stepped in so far as it is possible to demonstrate that the use of statistical inference is compatible with the alternative ontology, a variant of internal relations, that is posited by Sayer. In other words, it is possible to argue that statistical inference is compatible with a broader range of ontologies than simply atomism. Monistic atomism assumes that the world is composed of an aggregate of distinct things. Given an atomistic ontology, causation is conceptualized as a relationship between separate events, as *external relations* between independent objects. In contrast, the realist conception of causation, that of a necessary connection between events, assumes an *internal relation* between events.

As an example of this type of internal relation, Sayer writes:

> It might. . . seem possible that a capitalist could stop purchasing labour-power, stop accumulating capital and therefore break our alleged necessary relationship between these actions and being a capitalist, but in acting this way s/he would be becoming a non-capitalist. In Marxism, these necessary relationships are 'taken up' into the definition of capital. . .

That is, the propensity for a certain type of action is a *property* of the capitalist and the relation between capitalist and wage earner an internal relation: the capitalist exists only in relation to the wage labourer in so far as the extraction of surplus value defines both. Sayer is fully aware of the standard criticism of internal relations, namely, that if all relations are internally related, it is difficult to see how theoretical priority can be given to some relations over others. As a solution to this dilemma, Sayer argues that the world is comprised of a combination of internal and external relations, so that, for instance, there is a necessary relation between capital and wage labour but an external, contingent relation between capital and the raw materials used to create capital. Furthermore, conceptual necessity reflects empirically discovered natural necessity. 'When we discover such natural necessities', writes Sayer, 'we frequently make what we previously understood as contingently related elements part of the definition of objects; indeed, one might say that progress in-science, in terms of reduction of the burden of facts, depends on this'. On Sayer's own account, then, we approach the world assuming that events are externally related and develop an understanding of necessarily related elements, which are so in fact, through the necessary empirical discovery of regularities and conceptual development. That external relations are presupposed by statistical inference, used to assess empirical regularities in the course of theory development, is, then, scarcely a critique at all.

In evaluating Sayer's specific criticisms of the use of statistical inference given a historical materialist perspective, we have argued that Sayer has tended to conflate statistical inference and inductive inference, and thus the charge that statistical inference presupposes regularity generalization is unwarranted. Furthermore, the charge of atomism is incompatible with Sayer's own account of the method of discovering and integrating conceptions of natural necessity into scientific discourse.

Sayer nevertheless draws attention to the fact that specific assumptions underlie statistical testing. Along these lines, a concern with the assumption of normality which attends parametric statistics has led some 'radical' quantifiers to advocate the use of non-parametric statistics, which do not make the same assumptions concerning population distributions. This suggestion seems particularly relevant given repeated claims that many Marxist concepts, including that of class, are differentiated along qualitative and not quantitative lines, although this has scarcely been considered by Marxists who have chosen to operationalize the class concept. Nevertheless, some assumptions remain using even non-parametric statistics; all statistical inference assumes some notion of typicality in circumscribed populations. But surely this requirement reflects on the need for more careful theorizing about the categories compared rather than on the statistical techniques themselves. This leads to a third possible criticism of statistical inference, relevant to both historical materialist and humanist perspectives, namely that quantification on and the use of statistics tend to direct attention away from the evaluation of the categories employed.

Improverished theoretical categories

To continue with Sayer's earlier critique of statistical inference, he criticizes traditional industrial location analysis for 'aggregating up a large number of very diverse firms in the hope of finding "generalizable regularities" or simply to meet the requirement of an adequate sample size', because this 'has the effect of losing everything in a statistical soup. . . Apparently, making the basic categories less "chaotic" would be unacceptable since it would make the sample less "representative'!. In contrast to this approach, Sayer notes the analytic clarity of the work of Massey & Meegan, suggesting that it is due, in part, to their 'avoidance of empiricist generalization'. Sayer may present an accurate assessment of the way in which statistical techniques have tended to be used in locational analyses, but it is an overstatement to suggest that statistical inference necessarily entails a 'chaotic' aggregation of categories. Statistical techniques are used to measure patterns of association between categories and populations that an investigator defines.

The fact that traditional locational analysts have tended to aggregate diverse firms reflects on the inadequacy of their "theoretical development rather than on any weakness of statistical techniques *per se.* There is no logical reason why a sample of firms must be representative of all firms, rather than, for example, firms that are restructuring to achieve scale advantages. Once -again, statistical inference is analytically distinct from inductive inference. In the former instance one generalizes only to a theoretically defined population. It is the task of the analyst to define the population in a theoretically meaningful manner.

Although shifting the focus from statistical inference to the use of descriptive statistics, it is none the less of interest that Abrams has recently argued that the principal value of quantification in history has been as a catalyst for a radical questioning of received categories.

Abrams further outlines the necessity of going beyond the quantitative base in relation to McFarlane's inability to discover a peasant society in pre-modern English history. In relying on a head count of peasants as a *measure* of feudal society, Abrams argues that McFarlane fails to make important analytic and relational distinctions. McFarlane gives too much *theoretical* weight to the observed frequency statistics and fails to consider the extent to which the relation between lordship and peasant can nonetheless be shown to have been the operational pivot of pre-modern English society. Nevertheless, the quantitative evidence presented by McFarlane leads to a refinement and sharpening of the concept 'peasant' which, Abrams judges, had previously been used 'so inclusively as to deprive it of much of its possible analytical value'. Again, the important interdependence between quantified empirical reality and theoretical development is noted, with the proviso that one is not synonymous with the other.

If Abrams stresses the influence of quantified data on theoretical categories, the other half of the interdependent relationship has been equally stressed. At base, numbers are always measurements of theoretical categories which, in turn, cannot be separated from their social context. This returns to the point that meaningful quantified analysis, even the use of descriptive statistics, is dependent on adequate theoretical development. The point that numbers are produced, not simply collected, has been made forcibly by a variety of authors, especially in relation to official statistics.

Armstrong & Armstrong, for instance, demonstrate the way in which the Canadian census systematically distorts the employment situation of women through the questions excluded, the wording of the questions included and the categories designated to code the answers. For example, the definition of work, which excludes housework and volunteer work but includes unpaid employment in a family business, reflects the assumption that work which results directly in profit and exchange is of unique concern.

The census data on paid female employment must also be Interpreted in the light of the social context. In-depth interviews suggest that certain institutional constraints in Canada, such as low minimum earnings set for daycare subsidies, encourage under-reporting of employment and earnings by low-income women. These comments suggest that quantitative data must always be interpreted in the light of the theoretical and societal context in which they are collected. For this reason quantitative data are usefully complemented by more qualitative understanding of the context.

At issue here is not only depth of understanding but the sheer accuracy of interpretations based on quantified data. Ley cites Brian Berry's interpretation of the increasing correspondence between the city-size distribution of Israel and the rank-size role through time as one example of the erroneous deductions one can make from descriptive statistics which have been removed from their context. Berry interprets the noted historical patterns as evidence that increasing economic complexity leads to a closer approximation to the rank-size rule. Ley points out that the national boundaries of Israel were radically altered during the time period under consideration and that the increasing approximation of the city-size distribution to the rank- size rule reflects the redistribution of cities across political boundaries rather than increased economic complexity. Only a contextual understanding of the Israeli situation leads to an accurate reading of the descriptive statistics.

An understanding that quantitative techniques, including statistical inference, are but one type of evidence and that theoretical conceptions infuse empirical evidence, while neither is reducible to the other, is especially important given the final criticism of quantification to be considered, that it necessarily leads to a neglect of meaning, human intentionality and choice.

Reduction

For the present purposes, a number of complex and somewhat distinct arguments concerning the antithesis between quantification and a non-reductionist conception of human nature will be combined. On one level, it is argued that the precision required by the quantification process serves to restrict meaning to discrete categories and forces a unidimensionality that obfuscates an of relational processes. A related point is that the active and integrated social agent is lost by a perspective that isolates, and then perhaps reifies, particular quantifiable characteristics. Further, in line with the criticism of an overriding obsession with empirical regularity, an exclusive concern with the general over the unique runs against the importance of human agency, however constrained, in effecting social change.

These criticisms point to the profound limitations of measurement rather than an outright rejection of quantitative techniques. For instance, empirical regularities may point to patterns of social activity that can then only be understood by grasping the meaning of these actions in a particular social context.

The weight of the humanist critique is that some properties are not measurable in principle; this does not imply that no properties are measurable or that such measurement is irrelevant to our understanding of social processes. What the humanist critique states is that relationships between measured quantities are one type of evidence, which must be understood and conceptualized, in the situational context. Arguing for an existential geography, Marwyn Samuels has noted that it is:

> broad enough to encompass not only the 'geosophy' of a J.K. Wright or the 'topophilia' of an Yi Fu Tuan but also the geometric modelling and distance measures of a Walter lzard, a Brian Berry, or a Peter Gould . . . Where the one is an exercise in rootedness, the other is an exercise in rootlessness. They are not opposites but correlates; and, in existential terms, the one (a finding of roots) is but the outcome of the other (a loss of roots).

Giddens similarly points to the complementarity of quantitative and more qualitative a more qualitative understanding:

> So however statistical a given study might be, however abstract and remote it is, it presumes some kind of ethnography of individuals involved in the context which is being described. That ethnography is not, of course, always overtly written: in a statistical study, for example, it's largely a tacit taken-for-granted aspect of what's done, but it is

> necessarily there, we think, and it could in principle be written.

Both the humanist and historical materialist perspectives suggest that we must seriously respect the distinction between quantitative and more qualitative analysis, and between empirical regularities and theoretical conceptions, not in an absolutist, either-or fashion but in the sense of realizing the limitations and restricted appropriateness of particular methods and types of knowledge. As Berka has recently noted:

> Mathematization in science has only an instrumental character. The usefulness of this approach depends on its thoughtful usage . . . as well as on its appropriate specification with regard to the concrete object of investigation . . . it is always only a means of helping to objectivize the results of inquiries in the social scientific domain in question.

The helpfulness is this process of objectification must not be lost through a confusion of statistical inference and quantification with the broader philosophical perspective of positivism.

14
Economic Geography

One exception is the recent work of Sayer. In a brief discussion, Sayer recognizes that although economic geography has a theory of agency and structure, it has nothing in between; nothing to connect agency and structure.

Economic geography has a voluntarist account of human behaviour (human agency) represented by the geographically free-wheeling entrepreneur who can locate anywhere, and a structural account where actors become the dupes of the geographical structure of the economy. But as Sayer recognizes, neither the voluntarist nor the structural account is satisfactory on its own. What is required is somehow to bridge the gap between agency and structure. For Sayer, at least, that bridge is realist philosophy.

The first is to add substance to Sayer's claims. Specifically, we will argue that the agency/structure dualism in economic geography results from the adoption of one of two theories of value found in economics. The first of these is the labour theory of value. Here goods exchange roughly in proportion to the labour time contained within them. Such a view is associated with the classical economists, although perhaps its best-known advocate is Marx.

The second theory of value is based on utility. In

this scheme goods exchange in proportion to their usefulness. And their usefulness is determined by both the relative scarcity of goods and their worth according to the subjective preferences of consumers.

Although the use of this hedonistic calculus can be traced back at least to the time of Bentham, it was not until the 1870s with the marriage of differential calculus with utility (and their consequent child, marginal utility) that the neoclassical school, as it became known, fully came into its own. I will argue in the first part of this chapter that the use of the labour theory of value implies a structural account of economic behaviour, whereas utility theory leads to a: voluntarist account.

The second purpose of the chapter is to argue that no kind of philosophical 'ism', including Sayer's own 'realism', can permanently resolve the dualism in economic geography between agency and structure. The argument here is that most of the, kinds of philosophical 'isms' employed by geographers lead geographers away from actually doing economic geography. Rather than approaching the geographical world on its own terms, economic geography is reduced to whatever 'ism' is employed.

Thus even if Sayer's 'realism' can bridge the gap between agency and structure, which is itself unclear, all we have done is to replace one kind of 'ism' with a different kind. Rather than simply playing off one philosophy against another it is argued that there is another way.

Specifically, it is suggested that because the problem of agency and structure in economic geography is a result of the adoption of particular theories of economic value, then what is required as a solution is a non-theory of value. This non-theory of value is discussed in relation to the work of Piero Sraffa.

Marx's labour theory of value

Marx's labour theory of value was contentious from the outset. Rather than examining its problems, however, I intend to examine why users of the labour theory of value are drawn to a structuralist account of economic behaviour. This does not imply that all Marxists are structuralists. As has often been noted, there is clear tension within Marx's own account between structural and other types of explanation. None the less, among Marxist economists, and more pertinently among Marxist economic geographers, structural accounts dominate.

As the economic anthropologist Stephen Gudeman suggests, the labour theory of value is a core code for Marx. By that Gudeman means that labour values are the linchpin for Marx's whole model of economy and society. It is not that labour values are simply a useful way to examine economy and society, but rather that they define what economy and society are. The significance of labour values for Marxist economic geographers is that they are rooted in an exogenous constant-human physical labour. This exogenous quality is crucial because whatever is used to explain the economic system must lie outside it. If it did not, the entity doing the explaining would be changed by the thing that is explained. Thus, as Dobb argues, the central requirement of any theory of value (including the labour theory of value) is:

> . . . that it is some quantity which in any particular case can be known independently of any of the other variables in the system. It must be something which can be postulated independently of the rest. It is some quantity brought in, as it were, from outside the system of events. . . and in an important sense it is on this outside factor that the total situation is made to depend.

Labour values fit the requirement of being exogenous because '(as) used by . . . Marx the concept of labour was an objective one; labour being conceived as the expenditure of a given quantum of human energy'. Given that there are other measures that fit the general requirement of a theory of value, the obvious question is why labour time is chosen by Marx and not some other variable? There have been a number of reasons put forward to explain this choice, but perhaps the one that is most popular and enduring has to do with the relationship between humans and nature.

The argument goes that the human lot in life is to struggle with, and wrest a living from, nature. The only way in which nature is ultimately subordinated, and transformed to conform to the purposes of humans, is through the act of labour. It is for this reason then that labour time is the basis on which a good's value is calculated. Given the centrality of labour values, it follows that the nature of economy and society within the Marxist scheme comes to be shaped by this one external constant.

This will be shown by examining some key features of the Marxist conception of the economy, and of its vision of society. What distinguishes the Marxist view of the economy from other accounts is first, the emphasis on production, and in particular the costs of production, and second, its concern with distribution. That production costs are critical, rather than, for example, demand considerations, stems directly from the broader philosophical justification of labour values alluded to above. For the central fact about commodities is that they have a direct human physical cost. Without the sweat of the brow of the labourer there would be no commodities at all.

Certainly, workers may use tools, such as lathes and ploughs, to assist in production. But tools are themselves nothing but embodiments of 'dead labour', and so their labour cost too must be included when calculating the value of any good. In short, production and production costs are central to the Marxist scheme because goods are valuable only in so far as they are the product and cost of labour. Turning now to the importance of distribution, we find that labour values have two roles. First, they provide an unambiguous measure of the distributional shares accruing to each social class. Although the issue is a complex one, labour values enable easy reckoning of the national income irrespective of how distributional shares (measured in labour values) change.

Second, using labour values implies fixed limits to the size of shares making up the national product. The important consequence is that whatever one class gains in terms of its share of national product, another class loses. This antagonistic relationship in capitalism is measured by the rate of exploitation. It is the difference between the number of hours a labourer works, and the wage s/he receives, also measured in labour values. Having examined the economy, let us now look at Marx's vision of society.

Society for Marx is composed of a number of classes. Although a controversial topic, the definition of, and relationship among, social classes depends on economic considerations. As Keat & Urry argue: 'classes are themselves functions of the process of production. Class relationships are for Marx generated within and by the fundamental structure of the capitalist mode. What defines a social class is its relationship to production. In particular, as Cutler et al. argue, 'economic class-relationships involve definite forms of possession of and separation from the means of production on the part of economic agents'. Workers are workers because all they have to sell is their own labour; capitalists are capitalists because they own and supply the basic means of production, capital; and landlords are landlords because they own a necessary non-produced input to sell to capitalists. Second, the relationships among social classes are defined in the Marxist scheme by the sphere of distribution. As suggested, what emerges from distribution is antagonism among classes, because whatever one group gains another group loses. Specifically, within the context of capitalism, because of the unequal ownership of the means of production, one class, capitalists, always ends up exploiting another class, workers.

Although this is the, principal antagonism, there are also other conflicts such as those between workers and landlords and landlords and capitalists. This is obviously a very brief sketch and cannot do justice to all the complexities and subtleties of Marx's work. None the less, it is sufficient to show why, by beginning with labour values, one is led to a structural account of society. Labour values provide a charter for making production and distribution the central components in the economy. The economy in turn-shapes the nature of society. Social classes are defined by their access to the means of production, and the antagonistic relationship among social classes is given by the nature of the sphere of distribution. What we are left with is a clear social structure; a structure that has the four features that Keat & Urry recognize as being common to all structuralist approaches.

First, there is an emphasis on the relationships among elements, rather than focusing on the elements themselves. In the case of capitalism, what is most important is the antagonistic relationship between workers and capitalists. And more generally, it is the class conflict endemic to all modes of production barring the communist one. Second, the structure is regular, orderly, systematic and enduring. As we have seen, the principal antagonism between social classes holds across different societies and different epochs. Master/slave, lord/serf and capitalist/worker are all variants on the same enduring structure.

Third, the structure is abstract and can only be grasped when the code in which it is expressed is deciphered. Thus only when Marx realized the importance of labour values which lie beneath the surface of prices, was he able to get behind the veil of appearances to 'really' see what was going on. Finally, the structure as a whole determines the roles people play within the system. The result is that individuals need not be referred to. Individuals simply become bearers of the social roles implied by the economy, and more fundamentally by labour values themselves. This is most clearly seen in Althusser's work:

> The structure of the relations of production determine the places and functions occupied and adopted by the agents of production, who are never anything more than occupants of these places, insofar as they are 'supports' of these functions. The true subjects . . . are not. . .'concrete individuals'—real men'—but the definition and distribution of these places and functions.

Neoclassical economics

Around the 1870s the key code was changed in economics. Labour values were out and utility was in. The metaphor was changed from the body, where aching muscles determined worth, to the mind, where mental desires and wants determined value. In the shuffle what was lost was a concern for social structure, and what took its place was an emphasis on the autonomous individual.

As with the case of labour values, utility is the starting point for the neoclassical vision of economy and society. The fact, as Joan Robinson notes, that there are severe problems in defining the term misses the point about utility's role. Like labour values, the usefulness of utility is not in describing the world but in saying how it ought to be. To be recognized as a legitimate theory of value, utility needs to be rooted in a stable exogenous constant in just the same way that labour values are. The anchor that secures utility is the human mind. As Dobb writes:

> To be sufficient anchorage for a determinate theory of value, even formally viewed, it was necessary that utility should be conceived as an expression of some fairly permanent and consistent aspect of human psychology . . . In so far as utility could be hedonistically treated as a fundamental 'satisfaction" then . . . it could reasonably be held to fulfil this condition.

With utility tied to a firm bedrock, utility then becomes the key to explaining the economic system, and for that matter most other areas of social interchange as well. Specifically, because utility is thought to be a 'good thing', and in fact the only thing worth striving for, all human action is dependent on, and thus explainable in terms of, the adding and subtracting of utility. Furthermore, utility provides a purpose to people's lives.

The ultimate goal in life is to obtain as much utility as possible because it is only utility that makes humans tick. Thus, like the teleological element in Marx's conception of society—the ultimate goal is a communist society, in which labour values are finally realized as being the true measure of worth—there is also a teleological strain to neoclassical economics' conception of the individual; the purpose of an individual's life is to maximize utility. The consequence of making utility central is to redraw dramatically the boundaries of the economic problem, and society's relationship to it, as it was conceived by Marx. To examine this issue further I will first discuss the nature of the neoclassical economy, and then look at the type of society associated with it. If for Marx production and distribution are the two main elements of the economy, then for neoclassical economics it is clearly consumption and exchange that are critical. As already suggested, actors in the neoclassical world are impelled to maximize utility.

The origin of utility is, for the most part the consumption of goods and services. Whereas labouring is bad—a source of disutility—consumption is good; it provides happiness and satisfaction to all who engage in it. Although it is usual to think of consumption in narrow terms—goods and services that are bought commercially —one can also view consumption in a broader way. Any act that involves choices can be thought of as an act of consumption. From getting married to deciding when to wake up in the morning, humans are continually making consumption choices. That utility theory can deal with such a wide variety of situations is a result of its being rooted in an eternal constant, the human psyche.

The second component in the neoclassical scheme, which is also informed by, utility, is the sphere of exchange, or price determination. Because utility derives from consumption goods bought and sold in the market, it is possible to specify a relationship between prices and quantities of goods and consumers' utilities taken at the margin. Specifically, utility is maximized when the ratio of marginal utilities to prices is equal. So the neoclassical view of exchange is characterized by a one-way avenue leading from individual consumer utility functions to the prices of finished goods. It should also be noted that the way in which exchange is cast in the neoclassical model rules out exploitation. This is so because value is not determined by an outside measure of productiveness: if a good or factor service acquires a price at the market place, it by definition has its correct value.

Value is determined not from where the good or service originates in production but where it eventuates in exchange. If we now turn to the neoclassical conception of society we find, as in the Marxist scheme, that economic considerations are crucial in defining both the nature of the said actors, and the relationship between them. Specifically, the neoclassical focus on consumption leads to the individual being the basic unit of analysis, and the sphere of exchange determines the relationship among those individuals. There are three reasons why an emphasis on consumption leads neoclassical economics to an individualistic conception of the economy.

First, conceiving of consumption as a source of mental satisfaction implies an emphasis on the individual, because only individuals have minds. Social aggregates such as institutions, classes and societies do not. Second, the satisfaction originating from consumption is not inter-subjective. Although we know how much we like a good, no one else can know. As a result there can never be a 'culture of consumption' because there are never any shared meanings among members of society.

Finally, to ensure that utility is maximized, social influences must be assumed away to allow the consumer to be free from outside influences that may corrupt his/her consumption choices. What neoclassical economics proposes then Is a version of methodological individualism, a version that Boland calls reductive psychologistic individualism. It is a view in which all economic acts, whether individual, institutional, or social are ultimately reduced to the psychological states of individuals. This position is inevitable given that for neoclassical economics, human consciousness is the key exogenous constant.

The relationship among individuals in the neoclassical scheme is given by the sphere of exchange. The problem with the reductive psychologistic individualism that neoclassical economics adopts is that there is nothing to connect individuals. Society could easily be a series of Robinson Crusoes. It is here that the market place, and thereby exchange, is critical. In their desire to obtain utility, individuals are forced to interact with one another. Through selling factor services or buying consumption goods, autonomous individuals are impelled to come together at the market place.

The exchange process, in one sense, is the glue that makes neoclassical society stick together. The precise nature of the relationship among individuals at the market is one of competition, to get the most for the least. This is not the same as the antagonistic relationship in the Marxist scheme. As has been suggested, with value subjectively defined and locked away in the consumer's head, there is no external measure to show whether someone is swindled in the exchange process.

Again this account cannot do justice to all the nuances of the neoclassical scheme. But it is sufficient to suggest why, by beginning with utility, neoclassical economics is led to a voluntarist account of human action. As Giddens notes, the notion of voluntarism originates in Talcott Parsons' work where it 'refers primarily to the purposive character of human conduct, and to the capability of actors to choose between different goals or projects'.

Parsons, in turn, synthesized this notion from an examination of four 19th-century social theorists, two of whom were Alfred Marshall and Vilfredo Pareto. As Marshall and Pareto were both extremely influential in establishing the neoclassical research agenda, it is not surprising that voluntarism describes the neoclassical approach to economy and society. With utility defining the individual as the basic unit of analysis, society becomes simply the sum of the individuals who comprise it. Each of these individuals in turn has one purpose in life: to maximize utility through consumption. This is achieved only by making the correct consumption choices in the sphere of exchange. Thus the hallmarks of voluntarism - purposeful behaviour and constant decision making among alternative choices—are precisely those of neoclassical economics. So in contrast to the, Marxian analysis that has a theory of social structure but not of individual agency, neoclassical economics presents a theory of individual agency but says very little about social structure.

Architectonic and contextual approaches

The argument so far has been that the split between a voluntarist and a structural account in economic geography is a result of making utility and labour values the core code for neoclassical and Marxian economics respectively. In general terms, the use of labour values and utility represents a case of what Curry terms an architectonic approach. That is, by beginning with a set of core concepts—labour values and utility in this case—a complete system is constructed. It should be noted that this architectonic approach is not confined to economic geography but is found throughout human geography. Thus most of the kinds of philosophical 'isms' put forward by human geographers are attempts to lay a foundation for a 'complete geography'; that is, to compile a series of definitive definitions of what geography is and should be. Now, as already intimated, Sayer's solution to the agency/structure dualism in economic geography is realist philosophy. But as will be argued, it is not clear in what sense Sayer's solution is a real solution. For in advocating 'realism' all that Sayer does is to swap one core code for another, the core code underlying voluntanism or structuralism for the core code of realism. To put this another way, Sayer's argument leads to batting around the question of which architectonic approach is best. But this misses the point, a point that Sayer might have realized if he had enquired how the agency/structure dualism in economic geography arose in the first place. For the problem is not which architectonic approach is best, but rather with the whole architectonic approach itself. In particular, there are three problems with any architectonic approach.

First, in building 'complete systems' geographers are often trying to solve problems that confound philosophers. Although it is possible that geographers will solve hitherto unsolved philosophical quandaries, the more likely result is confusion. Second, by adhering to one of these prior philosophies, geographers end up not doing geography, but reducing the geographical world to the philosophical 'ism' employed. In effect, the geographical world is philosophized away. And finally, there are no logical criteria by which to decide which philosophical 'ism' is best, because it is precisely by means of that 'ism' that what count as logical criteria are decided.

Any proposed solution to the agency and structure dualism in economic geography that argues on the same terms as that dualism, that is, by comparing one architectonic approach to another, ultimately falls. For such a solution is pitched at the wrong level. It supposes, as Sayer did, that the problem is to select among sets of core concepts, whereas the real problem is to avoid using core concepts to begin with. What then is the alternative? I will argue it is one based on context. Unlike the architectonic approach that supposes that there are only certain ways of knowing and only certain independent objects to which knowing applies, a contextual approach suggests that there is no 'real' knowledge and no single way that knowledge can be acquired. We simply cannot specify a priori any absolutes about knowing. Rather, In order to know what knowledge, understanding and objectivity are, we must look at how they are used, acquired and verified in the context at hand. Whereas the architectonic approach squeezes the world into preformed philosophical categories, a contextual approach begins with the world intact. It celebrates the richness and diversity of the world, and does not reduce it to something it is not.

As an example of a contextual approach, one that economic geographers may draw upon, the work of the economist Piero Sraffa will be presented. III contrast to the theories of value already discussed that are rooted in the supposed universals of labour value and utility, Sraffa provides a non-value theory; a value theory not rooted in anything, and thus able to be embedded in any context.

Sraffa's non-value theory

Sraffa's publications give no explicit indication of his philosophical position. In working out that position, one can examine the context in which Sraffa wrote or one can examine the written texts themselves. Of course, best of all would be to do both, but for brevity's sake we will concentrate on the second alternative and examine Sraffa's only book Production of commodities by means of commodities. Sraffa's book is unlike any other in economics. There is no introduction, nor conclusion; there is no mention of individual economic actors nor social institutions. All we are given are the equations of production.

Although some have interpreted this terseness as simply a stylistic quirk, another interpretation is that what Sraffa leaves out is more important than what he includes. This is true in two ways. The first is evident when we recall the book's sub-title: Prelude to a critique of economic theory. Sraffa is not offering the critique itself, but rather offering the wherewithal for others to carry out the critique. Specifically, Production of commodities by means of commodities implicitly contains a logical critique of both neoclassical value theory and Marx's labour theory of value. The second issue is that Sraffa's reticence suggests that he realizes that there are definite limits to economic discourse. These limits are not stated explicitly; rather, they have to be surmised from what Sraffa leaves out of his discussion. To understand these limits, let us turn to the substance of his work. Sraffa portrays an economy where inputs, that are themselves commodities, produce other commodities.

The process is a circular one where the output in one production period is used as an input for the next production period. Sraffa begins his discussion with the case of a subsistence economy. What is produced at the end of the production period is just sufficient to replace the inputs used up. In most economies, however, there is a surplus left over even when all inputs are replaced. Thus we might imagine that in a feudal economy most of the surplus goes to the lord of the manor, whereas in modern capitalism it is divided between workers and capitalists. What Sraffa then demonstrates is that regardless of whether we have simple reproduction, or reproduction with a surplus, it is always possible to derive a unique system of exchange ratio that will keep the system going. An immediate thing to note about Sraffa's model is that there are no absolute sources of value that are determining prices.

Prices of commodities are determined by the means of production, and the means of production are themselves composed of commodities that are produced by a' previous set of commodities. At every stage then commodities are produced by other commodities, and as a result there is never an ultimate source of value. Sraffa has been discussed by both neoclassical and Marxian economists. From the neoclassical camp Sraffa's work on production is seen as nothing more than a special case of the neoclassical model, whereas some Marxists seem to think that all Sraffa provides is a mathematically correct solution to the problem of transforming labour values into prices. But both views miss the point. Whereas neoclassical economics is about the production of goods defined in terms of utility and Marxian economics is about the production of goods defined in terms of labour values, Sraffa is only concerned with the production of 'things'.

The word 'thing' is used deliberately because it implies no valuation; 'things' only take on meaning when they are embedded in a particular context, and that is Sraffa's whole point. Napoleoni also recognizes Sraffa's concern with 'things' when he writes: 'A re-reading of Production of commodities by means of commodities has confirmed my Initial impression that it is things rather than subjects which move around in Sraffa's construction . This leads Napoleoni to suggest that what Sraffa leaves us with is a *tabula rasa*. It is in this sense that Sraffa presents a non-value theory.

We must wait to learn how things are valued in different places and at different times; we must look at the context. As there are no ultimate values in Sraffa's system, no form of behaviour is prescribed. The production of commodities by means of commodities must of course be sufficient to reproduce the system, but once this viability constraint is satisfied, Sraffa does not say any more. Sraffa does not lay out a theory of value, nor does he lay out a theory of distribution once surplus is obtained. The values of goods and the way in which they ·are distributed depend on the particular context in which the production system is embedded. Because Sraffa leaves us with a tabula rasa some economists are frustrated. They want a cause for value and a mechanism to explain distribution. But again this misses the point of Sraffa's work. As Napoleoni argues: 'Sraffa forces us to take everything back to the beginning.

We are, now in a better position to understand what Sraffa thinks we can say about an economy and what we must be silent about. At the most general level, Sraffa argues that for there to be continued economic activity, the output of commodities must exceed or at least be equal to inputs of commodities. About the meaning of these commodities, the manner in which income is distributed, the level of consumption, the social institutions present, and the nature of the economic actors, Sraffa says nothing because nothing can be said a priori. It is true that when Sraffa discusses an economy with surplus product, he is clearly discussing a capitalist economy-he uses terms such as wages and rents, and assumes profit -equalization.

However, to conclude from this that Sraffa is now offering a closed rather than an open system misses the distinction between the specific and the general. Although wages, rents and profits are the distributional variables Sraffa discusses, they could in fact be anything from tribute paid to the lord of the manor to potlatch paid to the Big Men. Wages, rents and profits are simply terms used to designate portions of the surplus product. As Sraffa does not provide a theory of profit and wage determination, nor discuss who receives these shares of the surplus product, they might equally well take the form of some other distributional variables. What form they take will depend on the context in which the economy investigated is embedded.

Having discussed Sraffa's work in general terms, let us now turn to its relationship to the agency/structure dualism. In one sense, Sraffa's ideas can be seen as undermining the usefulness of this distinction altogether. Because Sraffa does not have a theory of value that prescribes a priori a particular method of treating individuals and society, the question of whether Sraffa is proposing a structuralist or voluntarist account is irrelevant. It may well be that in one context it makes sense to employ a structuralist approach, while in another context it is best to emphasize agency. Or then again, on another occasion it may not be useful to refer to structure and agency at all, while on yet a different occasion one may want to refer to both.

The point is that Sraffa's work is compatible with all of these approaches because the Sraffan account is not a 'complete system' that has answers to every question. Only by examining the context at hand call we know how structure and agency fit in, if at all. One final point to note about the contextual position implied in Sraffa's work is that it insists that in order either to undertake research or to understand someone else's research we must see such work as arising within a particular intellectual context.

A contextual position not only makes us sensitive to the particular context studied, but it also makes us sensitive to the context in which the person undertaking the study is part. For a researcher always has certain alms, motivations, audiences and methods. These form part of the intellectual context in which the study is carried out. The consequence is that studies often reveal as much about ourselves as about the thing we are studying.

15
Urban Life

The contemporary evolution of geographic work is thus of direct interest to planners, not only as a source of ideas but also as a critique of their work. The same observations could be made for other interventionist occupations where geography and geographers are important. These include conservation and environmental work, resource planning and management, regional analyses and prediction, transportation routing and mapping programmes of all sorts.

The search for relevance in geographical research and emergent theory must therefore include a look at how it is used in other fields. The purpose of this chapter is to review the development and role of theory in urban planning, and to show to what extent it borrows from geography and to what extent it diverges. It is divided into four sections. The first examines the general problem of theory and how it can be judged useful in planning. The second proposes a working classification of planning theory in an attempt to bring some order into a rather jumbled field, and to make subsequent discussion clearer.

The third section then reviews the positivist approach along with the humanistic-materialist debate in relationship to this classification and demonstrates the utility and limitations of the rational model. It endeavours to show that planning theory is the product of the broader intellectual, social and economic climate of the times, and that, theories linger on, coexisting rather than replacing each other. A fourth and concluding section reflects upon the divergent nature of professional and academic work and speculates on future directions.

Theory and its validity

Theory is an abstraction of reality that gives the student of urban affairs both a shorthand and a framework within which to work. Theory can be implicit, as it is in most of our daily lives, or explicit, as encouraged by academic convention. It can be simple and it can be complicated, although as an abstraction, one would expect a tendency to the former. It can operate on many levels or within closely circumscribed parameters. It is always based on assumptions, which in themselves should form part of the theory, but are often not stated.

Theory is often made unnecessarily difficult by the use of obscure language which hinders debate between people of different education, culture and background. In its broadest sense the word theory can be used for any collection of ideas, concepts or intellectual processes. In its supposedly scientific sense it has three definitions: first, a plausible acceptable explanation of observed phenomena, the Baconian inductive method of logical inference; second, an hypothesis assumed for the sake of argument or investigation to be subject to empirical testing and, in the Popperian mode, possible falsification; and third, a guide to action.

The first two, while apparently contradictory, are usually used together in a mixture of inductive generalization and deductive reasoning in most social science research. The use of the third distinguishes urban planning from urban studies, human geography, sociology and other academic disciplines. The urban planner has to look forward, has to propose interventions in the human environment, and has to move beyond prediction into normative theory and action. This fundamental difference between the academic discipline of geography and the profession of planning often seems to escape the casual observer.

The urban planner is oriented toward active intervention in the future through planning, design and the shaping of public policy. The responsibility of the geographer on the other hand has been to the discipline of geography and the advancement of knowledge. Thus while geographers might study the effects of urban planning on the landscape the reverse is not true. Geographers' work is judged by their peers whereas planners' work is judged by the general public and/or their clients. This means that, in general, research in urban planning, unlike that in the social sciences, is geared to specific problem solving rather than to the general advancement of knowledge.

The reason for doing planning research is to suggest a solution, and any scanning of thesis titles or planning journals will show that research initiatives are mostly opportunistic. When the objective of theory formulation is not simply explanatory, but includes its use in planning for the future, we are concerned not only with the conventions of theory formulation, but also with specifying performance criteria. Somehow theory must meet the requirements foreseen to be important in the field.

This immediately presupposes some system of values, if not divine guidance. There are at least four criteria of adequacy which have been proposed for judging if a theory is useful coming from the positivist school. These are: (1) a theory must have a dynamic aspect: (2) it must be susceptible of empirical verification;

(3) it must have internal logic and consistency; and (4) it must not be so abstract as to have no relation to reality. To these, the humanists would add social usefulness and the Marxists, historical continuity, internal logic through dialectical reasoning and a broad societal context in the political economy sense. The Frankfurt school represented by Habermas would include communicative competence characterized by comprehensibility, truthfulness, sincerity, and legitimacy.

The classification of planning theory

At the outset it is useful to divide planning theory into three groups: (1) substantive theory, relating to design and policy in urban planning; (2) theories of explanation of urban phenomena; and (3) theories of process, that is, theory of procedure and implementation. It might be noted that most observers have simply made a distinction between theories of the planning process and theories with, which planning is concerned calls these theory of planning and theory in planning, but this is not particularly helpful in sorting out the descriptive and explanatory from the normative and action guiding.

Substantive theory is that which has to do with creative ideas in policy and design in urban planning. It includes physical concepts such as green belts, new towns and neighbourhood units, legal concepts to do with property and regulation, aesthetic concepts such as fit and congruity, and social concepts to do with the ever-elusive public good.

Substantive theory is concerned with normative ideas about the spatial ordering of the built environment. It is the oldest branch of planning theory, dating from the earliest days of civilization. Substantive theory goes in scale from overall urban form (star, linear, rectangular, etc.) down to site planning and the form of individual buildings. It has evolved through military, political and religious considerations, and through economic, social and environmental analysis. It has always contained a strong utopian ideal, and ail unshakabl'/ belief that the urban environment can be improved. Its major exponents have been, and continue to be, engineers, architects and landscape designers. Kevin Lynch has been the major contemporary contributor to this field, which is succinctly summed up in the title of his last book, A *theory of good city form.* It has been popular, and sometimes with good reason, to criticize physical planning for its lack of human consideration. However since the days of Ebenezer Howard and Patrick Geddes, and as popularized by the English Town and Country Planning Association and the Regional Plan Association of New York, particularly through the writings of Lewis Mumford, social and economic theory have been major inputs into the design theory of the times.

For instance, Howard's theory of garden cities seems to be largely remembered for its catchy magnets and diagrammatic lucidity. However, a casual reading of the text shows that the problems addressed included the overcrowded, insalubrious inner city, economic self-sufficiency, the recapture of increased land value by the community as a whole, neighbourhood units and community control.

The last four are as valid today as they were then, and the focus of much contemporary co-operative theory and praxis. Planning ideas and concepts are much affected by societal and technological change. The substantive theory in vogue at any given time is often the result of a mixture of invention, context and reaction to another set of theory. Opposing theories can be in fashion simultaneously. Thus Le Corbusier, thrilled by the development of the skyscraper, itself a product of elevator technology (high buildings had been known before, usually raising their heads to God), proposed the rebuilding of Paris as *La Ville radieuse.* As a corollary, he denounced the burgeoning satellite garden city movement as an 'assassin' of the central city. At about the same time, Frank Lloyd Wright, conscious of the great open spaces of America, and the power of the automobile in the freedom it brings, was espousing 'Broadacre City'. The modification of substantive theory usually comes about when it is seen not to work in a particular context. Thus large-scale residential demolition for urban renewal (cut the cancer out), was shown not to solve problems for inner city residents, and has, at least in the Western world, been replaced by softer programmes of renovation and rehabilitation.

The spate of residential demolition in Montreal, for instance, started in 1958 with -the clearing for the Jeanne Mance scheme and finished in the post-Expo depression after 1967. The second group, explanatory theory, describes and explains urban distributions and structure. It is the meat of most urban geography courses, although strictly speaking it is not all attributable to geographers. It includes such constructs as organismic analogies, concentric zone theories, sector and multiple nuclei theory, central place theory, economic models of spatial structure, density-distance theory of all sorts, wave theory of metropolitan growth, industrial location theory, CBD and commercial hierarchy theory, urban land markets, land use distribution theory, social area analysis, network and urban systems theory.

Explanatory theory is frequently quantifiable, usually has dynamic aspects and is often used as a basis for building predictive models. It does not say whether any given distribution is desirable or deplorable. It is supposedly built up on value-free empirical evidence, although as Ley has shown, this may not be entirely the case. Almost all of this group of theory comes from the social sciences, geography, economics, sociology and political science, and is the product of this century. Most of it comes from the positivist school of thought, although more recently some comes from humanist or neo-Marxian interpretations. Explanatory theory has two major uses for the planner.

First, as already mentioned, it usually forms the basis for predictive model building. Its use in demography, land use, regional economics, transportation network simulation and for, commercial facility siting is well known. Second, it provides a shorthand for the description and imaginability of the city, a set of rough descriptive tools which aid in interprofessional communication. The third major set of theory used by urban planners is procedural theory, that relating to the process of planning. In fact, in much contemporary American work, the term planning theory is used only to describe this group.

A notable exception is the compendium of Melville Branch, and of course the work of Kevin Lynch, already mentioned. Procedural theory deals with the nature of the urban environmental decision process—how it is and how it should be conducted. It borrows heavily from the policy, administrative and management sciences. Of the three groups it is the latest to receive scholarly attention. This essentially dates from post-Second World War times, although debate on the subject started as the question 'to plan or not to plan?' in the-early days of socialism. In this context it is worth noting that modern planning has oddly contradictory beginnings in socialist and capitalist nations, although they have subsequently come closer together. In post-revolutionary Russia, national planning was the key to restructuring; in fact it was to be the cornerstone of the new state. As such it came to be viewed askance by the West as part of the evils of communism, although after 1945 some countries, such as

France, adopted it as a technique to further reconstruction. Similarly, newly independent colonies have used it widely to guide their development. Meanwhile, planning in England, Canada and America grew up as a pragmatic response to functional imperatives. This was first through public health concerns as developed because of the appallingly squalid conditions of the mid-19th-century industrial city, and later on as a reaction to the extraordinary conditions of the great depression and then the Second World War. Whereas early Soviet planning was largely to do with the location of industry and its infrastructure and the setting of production targets for the various agricultural and industrial sectors, in the West it was focused on housing, parks, schools, transportation systems and social services, that is the domestic rather than the industrial environment.

The great debate about the merits of adopting planning really marks the beginning of the articulation of procedural theory. Four writers typify this debate. For Von Hayek, planning was *The road to serfdom,* and for Karl Popper it was the enemy of *The open society,* whereas Barbara Wootton maintained that there would be *Freedom under* planning and Karl Mannheim that there must be Planning *for freedom.* From this time on, attention has focused on what should be planned, how it is planned and how it should be planned. Scholarly work has looked at the methods by which plans are formulated, how decisions are made, how conflicts are resolved, how policies, plans and programmes are implemented and how they are or should be evaluated. With a few exceptions, geography has not been much concerned with this field.

This classification of planning theory has been sketched out in an attempt to bring order to a rather jumbled field. However, it should be noted that the groups proposed are not necessarily mutually exclusive. Theory relating to citizen participation, for instance, cuts across both the substantive and the procedural, whereas that relating to industrial location has both explanatory and substantive elements. The following discussion will focus mostly on the development of theories of process.

The rationalist approach and the humanist—materialist debate

The rational model has been and remains the basic methodological approach of urban planning since its foundation as a profession at the beginning of the century. At the same time, because of its reform roots, like social work, it has always been ideologically bound. At the beginning it was strongly humanistic, then with the development of formalized positivist approaches in the social sciences it became more 'scientific'. By the mid-1960s the 'efficiency versus people' debate started to shift again toward people, and by the mid-1970s this was being reinforced by neo-Marxist analyses.

The coexistence of several apparently contradictory streams of thought seems to be troubling to purist academics, but to the practitioner, accustomed to trying to reconcile competing claims, this does not seem to be as monumental a stumbling block. This section will elaborate these assertions.

Modern town planning emerged around the turn of the century as a cause, and later as a profession, as an outgrowth of a series of reform movements. First were the public health reformers who saw the problems of social inequality, the horrors of slum conditions in industrial cities, overcrowding, disease, contaminated water supply, inadequate sewer systems, all exacerbated by corrupt municipal administrations. Second was the 'city beautiful' movement triggered by the Paris exposition of 1886 and the Chicago World Fair of 1893, which showed that an urban environment could be glorious, uplifting, green and clean. Wait Disney was a small boy in Chicago who cried when the fair closed.

Third was the conservation movement, precipitated by the fast disappearance of natural resources under reckless exploitation, a movement that grew to encompass people concerns and the parks and playgrounds, movement. Spragge has demonstrated how these social forces developed and how planning came to be seen as a panacea for all urban environmental ills. He demonstrates how these ideological origins can be classified into the earliest goals of Canadian planners, namely, efficiency, redistribution and an aesthetic ideal. From these coalitions of public health activists, municipal reformers, architects, surveyors and engineers, the profession gradually emerged. From these humanist beginnings, ideas of efficiency gradually took over.

The idea of making the city more functional was essentially a prolongation of the urban reform movement. Efficient waterworks, utilities and transportation systems, avoidance of duplication, honest value for the expenditure of public funds, unwasteful land subdivision schemes and salubrious worker housing all became rallying points. Good comprehensive town planning, including orderly street layouts, pleasant parks, minimum standards for housing and the regulation of land uses through zoning would improve residential areas, increase land values and tax returns, and keep the population healthy and contented. That things did not work out that way is well known, but it is from this time forth that faith in the regulatory approach can be dated. The earliest exhortation as to method in planning probably came from Patrick Geddes who summed it up as 'survey-analysis-plan'. This was certainly the method of the first professional planner brought into Canada from England, Thomas Adams of Commission of Conservation fame, and one of the founders of the professional institute.

The idea of the social survey as a basis for town planning is coupled with the ideas of the scientific study of society from the time of Octavia Hill and the University Settlement movement through the early part of the century. The analysis part usually consisted of exposing all the perceived problems of overcrowding, substandard housing, incidence of disease, crime, and juvenile delinquency, distribution of green space (always negatively correlated with the last), traffic congestion, condition of streets and so on.

The plan part consisted of proposing solutions to the problems as they were seen: zoning; minimum property maintenance standards; a parks plan; and street widening schemes. This was then presented to the civic authorities who sometimes acted on parts of it. However, it was during this period of the 1920s that the concept of an overall general comprehensive plan, took hold, and early Provincial Planning Acts prescribed the elements to be regulated, The depression of the 1930s was associated with a swing back to humanist concerns, and in a few circles planning was seen as an important part of restructuring society.

However, even the League for Social Reconstruction, while making an eloquent plea for both national planning and town-planning, did not divine how local planning could be implemented except through compulsory legislation. It was only after the war and in the aftermath of the orgy of building during reconstruction that the rational model as we understand it today became codified. From postwar times up to the early 1960s, belief in the power of technocracy reached its peak. This is also the period in which planning borrowed most liberally, often uncritically, from the burgeoning social sciences. Policy science and management theorists started to examine the problem of how decisions are made in a variety of organizations.

The model for policy making and planning became the one we know so well: the setting of objectives or goals, data gathering, analysis, elaboration of alternatives, evaluation, choice of one course of action, implementation, review and so on. It is of course never used in the simplistic linear form as noted here. Most planning involves recursive procedures and inputs from many different sources. Robinson demonstrates a wide range of techniques for dealing with each step in the process. Although recognizing that the model could be used at any scale or for any sector of activity, its initial overall appeal lay in the promise it held for general comprehensive planning, whether for a municipality or a region.

The other approach of these times, that of 'pragmatic' problem solving (e.g. the housing problem or the traffic problem) was known to be imperfect because of the complex web of variables in the urban environment. Today, in fact, most users of the rational model include in the analysis stage an identification of potentials and constraints and from this, special problem identification. This provides an example of how different perspectives can be combined. In its original formulation the rational model was seen to be value neutral, internally consistent, self-evidently in the public good, and because of the supposedly dispassionate nature of the analysis and projections, providing the 'right' answers to problems. This model, with variations, soon became enshrined in all planning textbooks in some form or another, and with the advent of systems analysis appeared to take on much of the rigour of a more exact science. Even as the rational model was being formalized and incorporated into planners' daily lives, however, it was being questioned, modified, amended, and has come to be seen as an idealistic guide to action which is not attainable but nevertheless useful.

Some of the first questioning came from Meyerson, who looked at the problems of long range planning and proposed a system of 'middle range' planning. This was followed by a whole series of studies of the rational method by policy analysts who came to the conclusion that planning is an incremental process, and that because it is not possible for any decision maker to know all the facts relating to a problem, or to be value free, impartial comprehensive decision making is impossible.

The new descriptions of planning strategies included 'satisficing', 'muddling through', 'mutual adjustment', 'disjointed incrementalism'. These analyses have received much attention by planning theorists. They are very interesting because they describe how decisions are made in the real world. When they are raised to prescriptions for decision making, however, as they have been by some planners, then the endeavour to make real improvement in the urban environment is weakened. These strategies make decision making possible in the inevitable context of imperfect, biased information and competing claims, but do not ameliorate the quality of proscriptive intervention.

The most recent manifestation of this approach is typified in the growth of 'mediation' and 'negotiation' techniques to resolve environmental disputes. While reaching solutions that conflicting interests can 'live with', the central ideal of optimization is lost. A series of modestly acceptable short-term solutions defuses intractable situations, but in the excitement of conflict resolution, the objective of high standards is diluted.

A further problem with the comprehensive-rational model of planning is that it assumes that there is a common good, and that there can be a societal consensus on goals. Davidoff, recognizing the pluralistic nature of society, and with the disadvantaged mostly in mind, proposed a system of advocacy planning. Here professionals would commit themselves to become the advocates for a specific group and press their claims in this competing world. This was in line with the Alinsky model of social activism, and was largely the origin of 'store front' planning offices in large municipalities in the late 1960s, a feature that has almost disappeared. Wilson provides a graphic account of the political hazards in Vancouver.

Advocacy planning represents a conflictual model. It provokes resistance from provincial and local governments, and may disadvantage one group at the expense of others. In the field of co-operative housing, however, it has become institutionalized since the late 1970s in Canada in the form of, Community Resource Organizations. Wharf has describe the problems in detail. An interesting extension of the advocacy paradigm, inspired by Rawls' A *theory of justice,* has been proposed by Kiernan. Briefly, he proposes a theory of positive discrimination, that is, a code where planners would deliberately favour the disadvantaged, or areas of the city containing low income groups. Whether any municipal government will accept such action remains to be seen. Traditional wisdom has it that municipalities are not agents of redistribution. This is the business of the provincial and federal governments.

Reactions to the rational model and its technocratic accoutrements also came because of its distancing from the people it was supposed to serve. The citizens' groups that sprang up in the early 1960s, for a mixture of reasons, made it abundantly clear that they were not interested in efficiency and optimization, but were interested in democracy, open decision making and neighbourhood integrity. This led to another modification of planning theory, the need to make citizen participation an integral part of the planning process. Arnstein has shown how this can vary in practice from plain manipulation to true participatory democracy. In most jurisdictions it is probably somewhere in between, but at least it has become a part of statutory procedure in most Canadian cities.

In contemporary diagrams of the rational process it will usually be indicated during the goals formulation stage, in the evaluation of alternatives stage and in the preparation of the final schema. The environmental crisis of the 1960s and the growth of citizen-based environmental protection groups also precipitated changes in planning theory. As the movement gained ground, fanned by activist authors such as Rachel Carson (1962), Reich (1970) and Commoner (1971), planners began to look much more closely at the biophysical environment.

In 1969 Ian McHarg published his book exhorting us to *Plan with nature.* In it he demonstrated through a sieve-map technique how all areas unsuited to development because of fragile environments could be identified, mapped and, hopefully, protected. A wave of environmental determinism swept through the profession, and this too was incorporated into the rational model, sharpening up the biophysical survey stage. The institutional response to the crisis was to pass Environmental Protection Acts, both at the federal and provincial levels. These all came into force around 1972, and essentially demanded that environmental impact assessments be prepared for all major development projects and transportation networks. Apart from giving planners more work, these initiatives spurred on the development of evaluative techniques. These are usually grouped under the headings of biophysical, social, economic and political. Of these, social impact assessment techniques, with major input from social indicators research and humanist perspectives, have made major advances. Not only primary, but secondary and tertiary impacts can now be unravelled. Social learning theory also emerged in the early 1970s. It postulated that the gap between technical knowledge and personal knowledge could be bridged by a mutual learning process.

Friedmann proposed a theory of 'transactive' planning, arguing that an interactive approach, with a heavy emphasis on verbal rather than written communication, would result in mutual learning, the closing of the communication gap, and ultimately lead to the creation of a 'societal guidance system'. He had no real prescription for the instrumentation of such a theory, but a planners' meetings with a native people's band council are evocative of this approach. The crises of human identity occasioned by the technological age were being pinpointed long before citizen participation became an issue. Lewis Mumford published his warning about technics and human development in 1967.

The humanist tradition, in the form of the slogan 'people matter more' came to the fore along with the flower children in the late 1960s. The planning response to this was to try to develop a humanist model. Friedmann's transactive theory represents one attempt, but the approach is best exemplified in Lash's book, Planning in a human way. In this account of the author's work as head planner for the Greater Vancouver Regional District, he describes planning as a three-way communication process -graphically labelled a six-sided triangle-between politicians, people and planners. His emphasis is on keeping all methods and channels of dialogue open. The planning process, however, still contained the elements of the rational model, the search for a consensus on goals, alternative options for development and so forth. The publication of O'Connor's book on *The fiscal crisis* of the state, Harvey's Social justice and the city and Simmie's Citizens in conflict really marks the beginning of planners' interest in neo-Marxist approaches.

The perspectives and interpretations of critical theory vary widely, but in general can be grouped into three: the mechanics of capital accumulation; the role of the state; and class conflict. Social and property relations have of course been of concern to planners for generations; the early issues of the Journal of the Town Planning Institute of Canada are full of rhetoric decrying the evils of capitalism and equating them with the ills of the working-class society. They were equally convinced that urban society could be reconstructed on a healthy basis through regulation and control, a conclusion still under dispute. The value of neo-Marxist theory is in its analytic insights into social control, the way in which modes of production control those of reproduction, and the role of the state in the process of capital accumulation.

Paris endeavours to show how planning waxes and wanes, not so much because of its own goodness or badness but according to its value to the state at any given time. As most planners are directly or indirectly employed by the state, or if not, by some private developer, these analyses have given rise to some personal anxiety among members of the profession because they are largely portrayed as lackeys of the system, thus perpetuating inequity. More recent attention has focused on the critical theory of Habermas, who, among other things, has examined the question of communicative action, of which planning is one example. He postulates four conditions for communication to operate effectively: (1) that it is true; (2) that it is properly in context (legitimacy); (3) that it is sincerely expressed; and (4) that it is clearly put forward. He argues that if these are accepted, then the social relations of knowledge, consent, trust and attention are reproduced. So far planners have taken these as moral warnings. Criticism of the neo-Marxists focuses on the definition of the state, the perceptions of class relationships and absence of any overt manifestations of repression in Canada.

The existence of three levels of government, which seem to spend much time in heated dispute and jealously guard their autonomy, stands at odds with the given wisdom of a monolithic state. Similarly, state capitalism, in the form of crown corporations such as Hydro-Quebec or Air Canada, muddy the arguments. Further, in these times of encouraged entrepreneurship, it is often difficult to identify the exploiters and the exploited. Although the neo-Marxist analyses of the urban condition are very telling and provide powerful insights, they fall squarely into the category of explanatory theory. This group of scholars is still groping to find a way in which their work can be translated into action without the wholesale structural change in Western society that their perspective demands.

Most radical planners end up with rather timid suggestions for improving forecasting, incremental development, pursuing further research, 'knowing your enemy', and being sure of being aware of the consequences when indulging in any planning activity. They do not present the robust arguments of an earlier generation, for instance Blumenfeld, who has said in many essays that the only way that the conflict between free market forces and human needs will be resolved is through public ownership of all or most of the land to be developed.

Prospects for the future

It is evident that planning operates under conditions of ambiguity, uncertainty, value conflict, shifting understandings and changing societal mores. Though the search for a general theory of planning such as sought by Ozbekhan seems to have receded, the search for an adequate standard of ethics is in full swing. This may well represent a response to neo-Marxist and critical analysis. Two other trends seem to be emerging. One is related to the wave of neo-conservatism, and the other toward the movement for self-sufficiency.

The revival of neo-conservatism, as manifested by the election of Brian Mulroney in 1984, has incorporated pro-market and anti-bureaucracy stances into local, provincial and national policy debates of all sorts. Planners associated with the public sector are the victims of such attack, partly because they are civil servants and partly because they are seen to stand in the way of entrepreneurial activity. The present style of government, whether local or higher, borrows concepts from the business world such as a strategic planning approach, contracting services out and privatizing others.

The emphasis on competition seems to deny any idea of redistribution or of distributive justice. Planners who have spent their lives trying to referee, manage and control the inefficiencies, externalities and inequities of the private sector are going to have trouble in reconciling this with an imposed assumption that the self-regulating market is, benignly efficient. The description by Crooks of the criminal irregularities in private garbage collection in Canada and the United States has become well known. Union-busting may also be a reason for privatization, rather than the stated objective of efficiency.

The second trend is towards mutual aid and self-reliance. Goodman, Schumacher and most recently

Morris have all pointed in this direction for somewhat different reasons: Goodman because of his belief in community, Schumacher to overcome alienation in the workplace, and Morris to counteract economic, energy and environmental problems in the city. The meaning of all this to planning theory is that it will probably take another turn to incorporate the guidance of small groups within its framework. One thing that seems reasonably certain, however, is that it will somehow operate within an again modified rational model.

Alexander has posed the question, 'After rationality, what?', but this belies the evidence from our legislated provincial planning structures, all of which are based squarely on a positivist conception of the planning process. The most recent provincial Planning Act, that of Quebec, which contains in its preamble the recognition that planning is a political act, which gives municipalities the right to choose which regional municipal counties they would join, and which has mandatory citizen participation built in at three junctures in the process, is set completely in the rationalist mode. Further, the latest Canadian planning textbook directly and unapologetically describes planning as a rational activity.

16
Historical Materialism

Many of those who take such a view have concentrated on specific places at particular times, through a more or less modest regional specialization. Others have focused their attention even more narrowly on some specific aspect of a place and time, such as residential differentiation in 19th-century Leeds. Such work may appear similar to that of the analytic researcher. It is distinguished, however, by the concern to identify contextual influences, outcomes and effects, rather than to seek generalizations valid across space and/or time. Always, the synthetic view seeks to elucidate the particular. In North America over most of the past 30 years, however, they have constituted a declining minority within the discipline as a whole.

Recently, however, the synthetic view has begun to find new support within the fields of urban, economic and social geography. In a manifesto for historical materialists, Harvey deplores the fact that geographers have lost their '*raison d'etre* as synthesisers of knowledge in its spatial aspect'; Ley has called for a contextual approach in which the boundedness, as well as the meaning, of human actions is acknowledged; while both Thrift and Pred look forward to a 'new regional geography' in which the complex interpenetration of time and place are brought together. Such ideas are also gaining currency outside the discipline, and Allen Scott has gone so far as to claim that, with 'territorial complexes' as its focus, theoretical human geography may emerge as the exciting research frontier within the social sciences at large in the 1980s and 1990s'.

Albeit in strange guise, the synthetic view is making a comeback. There is no agreement, however, as to how synthesis might best be achieved. The examples offered by Sauer and Vidal de la Blache are in important respects inadequate to present needs. Most people in the developed capitalist societies live in cities. No human geographer interested in the present can afford to ignore the causes, meaning and consequences of that fact. Unfortunately, the works of Sauer and Vidal de la Blache do little to illuminate the issue, as they deal for the most part with rural life in the past. Such biases may still be found among historical and regional geographers. There is a further limitation. It is now widely believed that the study of human geography raises theoretical questions as to the nature of, and relationship between, the individual and society. These questions have concerned, indeed preoccupied, philosophers and social scientists in the 20th century, some geographers included. They inform recent exchanges between Marxists and humanists over the nature and relative importance of human agency and social structure. But they were not issues which either Sauer or Vidal de la Blache chose to discuss.

The great strength of these writers lay in their practice of, rather than in their ability to theorize about, the synthetic method. In his programmatic statements, for example, Sauer cheerfully contradicted himself. A reticence in the face of theory, amounting in some to distrust, is to be found today in the writings of many historical geographers. Even Cole Harris, who has been more willing than most to make general statements about his field, prefers talk of a 'habit of mind' rather than a method, emphasizing the essentially elusive quality of historical judgements. We do not see anything about historical geography which is inherently incompatible with theoretical debate. It is a fact, however, that historical and regional geographers have skirted many of the issues that trouble human geographers today. This, more than their concern for rural ways and past life, will continue to limit the relevance of the message of Sauer and Vidal de la Blache. But the more modem alternatives have not won a consensus either. Strong claims have been made for two views, humanism and Marxism, and proponents of each have criticized one another.

Humanists have emphasized the ways people find meaning through social action. They have been criticized, we believe correctly, for failing to offer an adequate theory of the social constraints upon human action. Marxists, on the other hand, have a well-developed theory of social structure. They believe that material life determines—in the sense of setting limits to—the prevailing character of social ideologies and political organization. Some, and in particular some structuralists, have gone further in arguing that structures determine—in the narrower sense—what people think and do. In so doing, the latter have been rebuked for excessive abstraction and economic determinism.

Jackson & Smith, for example, have noted the 'difficulties' experienced by Marxists in 'translating theoretical categories into active groups of men and women'. Reasonable people on both sides have conceded these points, but have gone on to claim that any failures are those of imagination and ingenuity, and are not inherent in the approaches themselves. Thus, in precisely these terms, S. Smith has recently defended a pragmatist version of humanism. Similarly, conceding that 'the more structuralist versions of Marxism have . . . an attenuated conception ... of human agency', Gregory insists that the fault is not intrinsic to Marxism. Nevertheless, he does suggest that this approach might benefit from 'reconstruction' in terms of the concepts developed by Giddens in his 'theory of structuration'. This, Gregory believes, will make Marxism more capable of 'comprehending intentionality and consciousness'. We believe that Gregory's assessments of humanism and Marxism are sound, but that reconstruction of the latter is unnecessary.

The argument could be made in theoretical terms. Indeed, at least in a tentative form it already has. But in recent years human geography has been overburdened with theoretical statements while being starved of theoretically informed empirical research. In my view there is now a greater need for the latter than the former. The purpose of this chapter, then, is not merely to argue but to demonstrate that an unreconstructed Marxism can accommodate the role played by people in the shaping of events, and without sacrificing the concept of determination.

Marxist synthesis in practice

To rest a general argument on a case study of such limited scope might seem irresponsible. In fact it makes a good deal of sense. Marxists have often prided themselves on their ability to comprehend the big picture. Even their critics have acknowledged a strength in this area, reserving criticism for the Marxists' treatment of smaller events, of particular places and lives. Within geography, Harvey concedes that 'Marxists . . . have had a hard time . . . evolving a sensitivity to place and milieu'. By examining local politics in a small Canadian city it is possible to meet this concern head on. My interpretation of the Kingston New Left places a great deal of emphasis upon the concept, and reality, of class. In the Marxist view, class is viewed as an objective economic relation between groups of people and also between people and their means of production. In these terms, and following the work of Carchedi, four major classes are identified: owners and managers, the self-employed, the middle class and the working class. As those who have written about dual labour markets have emphasized, however, the North American working class is divided into two fractions: a primary sector containing workers who are unionized and relatively well paid, and a secondary sector comprising those who are unorganized, poorly paid and on the fringe of the labour market. In these terms, the New Left was a social movement composed predominantly of middle-class youth. To the extent that it became involved in grass-roots political organizing it concentrated its energies on secondary sector workers, the working and welfare poor.

We argue that in Kingston, as elsewhere, the class composition and base of the movement set limits to its achievement. As Marxists such as Thompson have often insisted, however, class is not only an objective relation but also a subjective appraisal. That makes it a peculiarly rich concept, one that is correspondingly difficult to apply. In Kingston, many of the people that the New Left organized--and some in the New Left itself—did not think of their situation in class terms.

This was important. But in the political alignments and eventual polarization that the actions of the New Left produced, the underlying and divisive influence of class may be seen. It is not necessary for the importance of class to be acknowledged in order that it be felt. It is this characteristically materialist conception of class that shapes the following account. If class was the most important determinant of the role of the New Left, it was by no means the only one. To an unusual degree the movement in Kingston was able to mobilize the support of a broad working and middle-class base, and with this support to win concessions from the local state. To understand why, it is necessary to consider as a whole the historical and geographical milieu of Kingston in the 1960s. Among other factors, the residential geography of the place, local housing conditions, and the leadership of committed organizers all played a vital part in shaping the character and impact of the New Left. In emphasizing the importance of such contextual influences and effects, this interpretation of the character, origins and effects of the Kingston New Left exemplifies the synthetic approach.

Circumstantial origins

The 'New Left' that developed in the aftermath of the Cold War is not easy to define. In a general way this mainly middle-class movement differed from existing communist, socialist and social democratic parties in that it sought to bring about radical change through mass-based political organizing. Ideologically, however, it was diverse. This was particularly true in the early years, when radical populism, anarchism, socialism and religious moralism each contended for dominance. Moreover, its character varied from place to place while always being in flux.

The Canadian movement was shaped by the preoccupations and tactics of the American New Left, these being grafted on to disarmament concerns more typically British. As the Canadian movement developed, regional differences emerged. It has been observed that the American populist tradition and the community organizing strategy of the American Students for a Democratic Society (SDS) appear to have had their greatest impact in Ontario; certainly Kingston's movement was shaped by such influences, especially in the early days. Moreover the movement was never still. In English Canada, the moral attack on disarmament which occupied the Combined Universities Campaign for

Nuclear Disarmament (CUCND) from 1960 to 1964 gave way in 1965 to the broader concerns of the Student Union for Peace Action (SUPA). From 1966, as the movement confined itself to campus, it became increasingly Marxist and sectarian. In 1967 SUPA dissolved into fragments. With the major exception of the women's movement, these soon dropped the New Left's characteristic emphasis on participatory democracy and lost contact with popularly felt concerns. In Kingston, propitious circumstances allowed the local New Left to continue organizing long after the national movement had fallen apart. In terms of its social and class composition, Kingston offered the New Left much potential.

University students, the base of the New Left, made up a high proportion of the city's population, at least during the school year. In the 1960s, the student population of Queen's University grew to 10,000 while the population of the city as a whole remained steady at six times that amount. The size of Queen's in relation to the city helped to ensure that the steady stream of volunteers for community organizing work would have a significant political effect. Organizers were to get valuable assistance from a 'Waffle' group that was also based on campus.

The Waffle developed in the late 1960s as a left caucus of the New Democratic Party (NDP), a social-democratic party roughly equivalent to Britain's SDP. Locally, a Waffle group gave support to the community organizing efforts of the New Left. By the beginning of 1968 it had gained control over the NDP constituency association, which then helped to finance the Community Information Services, a service and advocacy centre for low-income people and tenants. Here again, through its effect on the local NDP, the presence of Queen's gave the New Left a boost.

Of at least equal importance was the fact that the working and welfare poor, the New Left's main political constituency, made up a relatively high proportion of the population. Kingston was (and is) a reception area for the rural migrant poor of Eastern Ontario, and throughout the 1960s its rate of welfare dependency was about double that of the province as a whole. The steady growth of Queen's put pressure on the local rental market. For a city of its size, Kingston had among the highest rents in the province, and by 1970 a survey revealed that vacancy rates in the downtown area had dropped to almost zero. Much of the housing stock in the inner areas was almost a century old, and living conditions in some dwellings were appalling.

Housing, then, was an obvious issue for organizing, one on which middle-class students and poor people could find common ground. The task of organizing was made easier by the geography of the place. Size alone was important. Elsewhere, the New Left became sectarian in 1967. Kingston, however, was too small to support factional divisions, these requiring higher thresholds than the available minorities of one.

Since most places in the city could be reached on foot, it was relatively easy for organizers to get people to demonstrations and public meetings. Social segregation also helped. Kingston was divided into three very distinct areas: the middle-class West End, the working-class North End and a very mixed neighbourhood downtown, known as Sydenham Ward. St Lawrence Ward, in the inner North End, contained a particularly high proportion of low-income tenants. The concentration of the New Left's constituency in this area made organizing relatively easy: this was true both in the summer of 1965 and again with the formation of the Association for Tenants' Action, Kingston (ATAK) in

1968. When ATAK's president ran successfully in the 1968 civic election, she chose St Lawrence as the ward where she was most likely to succeed. If the poor had not been concentrated in this area it is unlikely that ATAK would have secured a voice on City Council. In sum, geographical as well as social circumstances conspired to favour the efforts of the New Left in Kingston.

Actions

The advantages to organizing in Kingston were not apparent to the group of students who set up the Kingston Community Project in the summer of 1965. Outsiders who knew nothing about the city, they set out to 'start an organisation of poor people to solve their own problems'. Having defined a project area in the inner North End, they went knocking on doors. They found plenty of issues, including high rents, poor housing conditions and unsafe streets, but had little success in getting support for reform. Area residents had little sense of community. Indeed, as is often the case, there was some active hostility between the primary sector working class and the welfare poor. Being middle-class outsiders, the students were viewed with suspicion and that autumn, discouraged, they went back to school. Fortunately, the director of the project was able to bring in two full-time organizers to replace them.

Using contacts made in the summer, Joan Newman and Myrna Wood seriously set about the task of organizing. Their first successes were with North End youth. For many years the North End had been the base for a youth culture of working-class dissent. On occasion this erupted into violence, as it had at Hallowe'en in 1962, when a mob of 400 stormed Kingston police station, to be beaten off only with tear gas. Newman and Wood made contacts, and encouraged the formation of a youth-run coffee-house, the 'Needle's Eye'. The 'Eye' attracted many people, and by the end of the summer of

1966 had been hounded out of existence by the local fire marshal and the police. Other clubs were formed, however, and out of these there grew an increasingly articulate youth counter-culture. After a couple of attempts, an ambitious alternative newspaper. *This Paper Belongs to the People,* was set up in 1969 in order to provide 'a different perspective and a better analysis' than the existing media. With the New Left as a catalyst, Kingston's working-class youth were finding a common voice.

At the same time the housing situation had been getting steadily worse. Realizing this, in the spring of 1967, activists began to try to organize residents' associations to press for the rehabilitation of the inner city housing stock. Two associations were formed, but neither was a great success. It was partly out of such failures, however, that the idea of a community information centre was born. Set up early in 1968, and in contrast to the residents' associations, the Community Information service was an immediate success. Apart from service work, CIS became a centre of political dissent. Most of its clients were tenants, many of whose complaints and concerns arose out of their housing situation. As a result, organizers soon hit upon the idea of starting a tenants' association. By September ATAK boasted a membership of over 800.

Apart from the problems of slum housing, one of the more important reasons for the success of ATAK was the relatively high tenancy rate in the city. Less than half of all Kingston households were owner-occupiers at that time. This was about 20 percentage points lower than the rate for other Ontario towns of comparable size. Tenancy rates varied little between the working and middle classes. As a result, those who joined ATAK in the fall of 1968 included a substantial number of middle-class people, as well as students and the working class. The membership drive met with so much success that the decision was made to run three candidates in the upcoming civic election. Two were elected, Newman in St Lawrence and John Meister, a shop steward, on a joint ATAK-NDP slate in Ontario Ward. After more than three years of organizing the New Left had finally mobilized the working and welfare poor. Overnight, Meister and Newman changed the tone and content of debate on City Council. Hitherto Kingston politics had been run by local businessmen, and largely from the Chamber of Commerce. Now this group was challenged at every turn: zoning, housing and welfare policy, the location of parks, all were, dragged out for public scrutiny.

The local franchise, which allowed people to vote In any ward in which they owned property, was singled out for criticism. ATAK kept in touch with its North End roots. The information centre continued after NDP support was withdrawn in the autumn of 1968 and became a storefront for ATAK. Other tenants' groups formed and some affiliated as 'locals' to the main association.

A rent strike was launched against a notorious local slumlord. Support pickets were organized for the electrical workers at the locomotive works. In 1968, and the early months of 1969, ATAK was at the centre of an active culture of extra-parliamentary dissent, reflected in, and articulated through, the pages of This Paper. With its own press, popular support and representatives on Council, ATAK began to polarize Kingston politics. "In the civic election campaign of 1968 ATAK had received support from the NDP, local unions and the Labour Council, while goading landlords into organized opposition. Through 1969 it continued to work closely with the Waffle-dominated NDP, and indeed many people were members of both organizations. In the spring of 1970 a developer unveiled plans for high-rises on the waterfront. It provoked immediate opposition from ATAK, the NDP and a local ratepayers' group. The plans were withdrawn. At the same time ATAK was pressing its demand for rent controls.

The issue had been debated many times. Uncertainty remained as to whether the City had the legal power to enact such legislation, but ATAK, with support from the NDP, the Social Planning Council, the Labour Council and student groups, was insisting that Kingston make itself a test case.

On this issue, students and the working class, along with a substantial fraction of the middle class, found themselves ranged against the small businessmen, landlords and associated professionals who for the most part controlled Council. The issue came to a final vote in August 1970, when a motion to this effect was soundly defeated. As spectators disrupted the proceedings, Council was forced to adjourn, for the first time in Kingston's history. This defeat marked a turning of the tide. Having thrown itself into the battle on Council, ATAK had begun to lose touch with its constituency. Partly as a result of organizers' efforts, several hundred public housing units were on stream, holding out a promise that the housing situation might improve. The FLQ crisis in Quebec that fall helped to give radicalism a bad name. For a combination of reasons, then, when four candidates ran on a joint NDP-ATAK ticket in the December civic election, all were defeated. It was the end of an era.

Achievements

Now that the smoke has cleared it does not seem that very much was achieved. To be sure, the New Left had succeeded in mobilizing some of the poor. This was no mean feat, given the historic conservatism and political alienation of that group, in Kingston as elsewhere. Indeed, with this base, they had helped to provoke a polarization in Kingston politics, which saw the working class and part of the middle class ranged against landlords and small businessmen. Not everyone who took sides viewed the situation in class terms, but it is striking how sharply the class lines were drawn. Only the middle class was divided, salaried professionals (especially those at Queen's) being more inclined to favour the NDP-ATAK coalition, while those associated with the local real estate market lined up on the other side. The effect on the conditions and relations of life in Kingston, however, was small.

The New Left helped force City Council to put up a couple of 'stop' signs on one of the more dangerous North End streets, and to establish a playground in the same area. Better housing by-laws were passed and enforced, and slum landlords coerced into cleaning up their act, mainly as a result of the pressures brought to bear through CIS and ATAK. City government was made a little more democratic and responsive to popular demands, for example through the institutionalization of public meetings to deal with planning issues.

The New Left played an important part in preventing unsightly waterfront redevelopment and in getting public housing built in the far north of the North End. In this way they helped to change the geography of the city. But the consequences were neither entirely fortunate nor particularly long-lasting. When built, the isolated public housing ghetto created as many problems as it solved, while, more recently, high-rise buildings have been put up on the waterfront which are no more suitable to the site than those proposed in 1970. Overall the achievements, if not negligible, were certainly modest. The reasons are clear. As New Left organizers themselves realized from the very beginning, the poor are powerless. Unorganized and often unemployed, they can impose few sanctions. They cannot stop production by striking, because most are unemployed or unorganized. In the sphere of reproduction, rent strikes, boycotts and the physical disruption of public meetings are the main options. All were attempted in Kingston. Unless backed by massive and widespread support, however, such tactics are unlikely to win significant concessions. This is particularly true as long as they are directed at local government. In Canada, more than in the United States, local governments are weak. Such responsibilities as they possess have been delegated to them by the provinces and, in principle, can be revoked. They can make few, and for the most part insignificant, concessions, and even these can be reversed by upper levels of government. Moreover, the prospects for changing state policy at higher levels from a Kingston base were small.

The movement in other cities was not as strong. This might have mattered less if Kingston had loomed as large on the provincial or national scene as did, say, Toronto. But of course it did not. The size of the city, then, coupled with the movement's concern to organize the poor to demand changes in local government policy, set narrow limits to the possible achievement of the local New Left.

People making history

The high level of political support coupled with the modest achievements of the Kingston New Left may be understood in terms of the circumstances in which organizers worked, but not wholly so. The local New Left was created by a group of people determined to bring about change. A full analysis of the movement must examine the active role played by people in taking, and shaping, the opportunities provided by their social, geographical and historical milieu. To some extent this role may be understood in terms of the actions of particular individuals, those whom historians call Great Men. Even so, a variation on this theme must be introduced, for in Kingston most of the great men were, in fact, women. Over the period as a whole the most important person, of either sex, was Joan Newman. Committed, able and articulate, she devoted herself for five years to the task of community organizing in Kingston. Her persistence helped to overcome the suspicion with which middle-class organizers were first greeted. She played a major role in virtually all of the most important organizations: ill the original coffee-house, in CIS and ATAK, and finally on City Council. And yet a number of others played important parts. Giving due weight to the leaders, however, does not exhaust the role played by human agency. It is perhaps obvious that, without popular support, organizations like CIS and ATAK would have counted for little., In that sense, every member, every person on a picket line, every voter, played a part.

Less obvious is the fact that they gave the movement a life of its own. This often took the 'leaders' by surprise. From interviews that I conducted, it became clear that none of the most active organizers anticipated the success of the first coffee-house, of CIS or ATAK. Like the residents' associations, these were experiments; unlike them, they worked. In one sense, then, the organizers were merely catalysts that allowed the real agents of change, middle-class students, working-class youth and the poor, to have effect. But in one respect the metaphor of agent and catalyst is inadequate.

The catalysts themselves were altered. Newman claims to have learned her politics 'on the street' and indeed the views of most activists had been shaped by the experience of collective struggle. The extent of the change can be gauged by contrasting the stated purposes of the New Left at the beginning and end of its involvement in Kingston politics. In 1965 the movement was trying to help the poor to help themselves, and without much idea of how to do it. By 1970, knowing far more about the problems and potentialities of organizing in Kingston, they wanted, in Newman's words, 'to fight for . . . basic change where it matters: in the homes, streets and workplaces of this city'. The achievements were much more modest than that, but in trying to make history they did remake themselves.

Discussion and implications

This account of the New Left in Kingston is synthetic in that its primary concern is to understand local political developments in their context, rather than to establish generalizations about similar movements in other cities. This context, the social and geographical circumstances in which the New Left acted, was in part local. The class structure, the size and growth of Queen's and the size and geography of the city itself, provided a unique (and rather propitious) set of opportunities and constraints. In part, however, the context was national and indeed international.

The unfreezing of the Cold War and the perceived failures of existing parties of the Left defined the distinctive political character of the movement. But it is clear that people were not merely agents of class interests, passively responding to some inscrutable historical and geographical necessity. Individually and collectively they responded to, and sought to change, their situation. This synthetic account, then, assumes and demonstrates that people make their own history, albeit under circumstances that are not of their own choosing. In a general way this formula, borrowed from Marx, is similar to those which are already used by some geographers and historians. To be sure, it is broader in scope than that implied by the terms 'agency and structure" for the latter implicitly excludes the environment. But it does come close to the framework of 'character and circumstance' used by many historians; it bears some similarity to Sauer's treatment of culture and environment and to Vidal's *genre de vie* and *milieu*; it is entirely consistent with the way some humanist geographers discuss action and context. In that respect, humanists, historical geographers and for that matter historians might all provide a broadly similar interpretation to the one offered here. In other respects, however, their accounts would surely differ from this one.

The meaning, as well as the weight, given to 'class' in this interpretation of the New Left is distinctive. The notion that differences in class interests lay behind the polarization of Kingston politics, even though many of those involved would have denied it, is materialist; as such it would not recommend itself to many humanistic or historical geographers. Moreover, the particular classes identified in this account are not identical to those defined by other materialist approaches, for example that developed by Max Weber. It is important to recognize that Marxism, humanism and historical geography share the synthetic approach, for this effectively highlights the common basis from which discussion can proceed. But it is surely misguided to propose, as Gregory and others have done, that these approaches can be reconciled. They share a common denominator but they remain different quantities.

The Marxist approach has much to offer geographers. Its synthetic approach is quite compatible with the habit of mind of the historical and regional geographic traditions. It has an unusually well-developed theory of both social structure and change that sets it apart from recent humanist thought. This theory embodies a materialist conception of determination which most geographers, steeped as we are in environmental modes of thinking, should find congenial. Moreover, as we have tried to show in this case study of Kingston, the theory is not as inflexible as many of its critics have claimed. Indeed it is quite capable of giving due weight to the capacity of people to make their own history, and hence their own geography. Some will object that the Marxist formula is vague and unhelpful because it does not tell us exactly how much power people have to change the circumstances of their lives. But this arises from a misconception.

The amount of power people have depends on the place, the time and the people in question. Those who formed the New Left in Kingston, and those whom the New Left mobilized, were relatively powerless. In so far as such judgements are possible, we might say that they remade themselves more than they made history. But we cannot generalize from such a case, for their situation was unique. That, after all, is a major assumption of the synthetic approach.

Others may object that, vagueness aside, the formula contains a contradiction: it asserts the simultaneous existence of necessity and choice. That is true, but the contradiction is not merely a difficulty with the theory. It is inherent in the world as we know it. As individuals, groups and political collectivities we continually struggle to better our condition. In doing so we define our purposes against the circumstances that we inherit, while facing constraints and sometimes opposition. We are free and unfree.

There are three kinds of activity in a scientific research programme: elaboration and modification of a body of theory, use of that theory to explain actual historical events, and production of a philosophical basis for the procedures in the research programme. It has recently been argued that Marxists adopt realism as a philosophical basis for their research programme, a claim that implies particular links between the use of the theory in explanation and its modification after evaluation. This chapter tries to state and to illustrate the way in which Marxist theory is evaluated by reference to experience, that is, actual historical events. The question of the scientific nature of Marxist geography has been addressed by several recent papers.

Sayer has described a realist basis for science and has attacked the kind of science performed, by non-Marxist geographers. By contrast, Couclelis & Golledge question the description of Marxist geography as science because for them it lacks formal evaluation procedures for its theory. Whereas Papageorgiou enters a plea for tolerance in this dispute, Chouinard et al. have argued that, in practice, Marxist and non-Marxist geographers use very similar evaluation procedures notwithstanding their different 'official' philosophical positions. Our chapter is concerned with a very small part of this debate, namely to show how abstract laws and concrete events may be linked to provide an evaluation of theory. There are many different aspects of a theory that must be evaluated.

First, its logic must be analysed for internal consistency. Second, the theory must be shown to be consistent with existing, non-competing theories and existing knowledge. Third, the theory must not be derived in an ad hoc fashion from existing theories. Marxists also apply a political evaluation of theory: can it be used in the long or short term to enhance the power and position of the underprivileged? In this chapter, however, the issue is empirical evaluation. In particular we have two aims: to show that it is possible in some circumstances to measure the contribution of different mechanisms to an outcome and to show how our knowledge of these mechanisms can be tested by evaluating their use in explaining actual historical circumstances. The essential problem is this—and it is the same for all nonexperimental scientists.

Theory claims that in particular circumstances an event (x, say) should occur. In fact, during one period of observation, when circumstances are different from those postulated in the theory, y occurs. Can that theory be held then to help explain y, the actual history? The second section lays out the argument that, with appropriate measurements, an attempt can be made to use the history to evaluate the theory even though actual circumstances differ from those postulated. The third section illustrates this argument using the example of the development of the current economic crisis in Canada, and the fourth section employs the example of the postwar history of the steel industry in North America to illustrate how to pass from this abstract analysis to examine more concrete events.

Methods of evaluation

Realist philosophy makes several claims that distinguish realist from non-realist methods of scientific enquiry. The three central claims are that a structured world exists independent of human thought, that causal mechanisms generate empirically observable outcomes in that world and that these mechanisms are ontologically distinct from the outcomes that they produce.

Furthermore, scientific laws or causal mechanisms (statements about logical necessity) are not empirical regularities but are tendencies. Even though a causal mechanism is operating, the type of event to which it gives rise is influenced by other causal mechanisms, and also depends on the specific conditions that pertain at different times and in different places. There is therefore no necessary one-to-one correspondence between empirical outcomes and a particular causal mechanism: this is what it means to say that mechanisms and their observable outcomes are distinct.

One of the aims of science therefore is to identify causal mechanisms despite the variety of forms in which they reveal themselves. This is made more difficult in social science than in most physical sciences because of the impossibility of constructing experimental conditions. It is not possible in social systems to isolate, as in a laboratory, the historical and locational conditions within which a causal mechanism can be seen to operate.

Identifying causal mechanisms in, social science is also more difficult because of the intervention of human agency which, among other things, can change causal mechanisms. For the purposes of this chapter, however, it is taken as given that the causal mechanisms central to societies that are organized around a capitalist mode of production are class struggle and inter-capitalist competition.

Our aim here is to show how these causal mechanisms, and the variety of concrete events which are determined by them, can be linked to provide an, evaluation of theory. To fulfil this task we employ the example of the theory of the rate of profit, and in the following sections describe its influence on the postwar history of profit rates in Canada and the decline of steel production in the United States. In order to do this it is first necessary to specify exactly what we mean by a tendency. In other words, why is it that there is no one-to-one correspondence between class struggle and capitalist competition-the causal mechanisms-and the variety of events to which they help give rise: why is it that a given necessary relationship, or law, does not produce a regular outcome?

The literature does not provide a consistent answer to these questions. Bhaskar offers two philosophical reasons for the lack of correspondence between a given law and the variety of its outcomes. First, there exist several different causal mechanisms. In physical science these forces are transcendental: they always hold, though some may be more influential than others in the causing of particular events. Therefore it is not possible to credit to all events the same combination of mechanisms as their causes.

Second, the arrangement of things that make up the material world is such that a variety of different concrete conditions can arise in which laws combine to produce a series of irregular events. In other words, outcomes are not necessarily determined in a regular fashion by laws, but also depend on the way in which the operation of those laws is combined in a particular conjuncture. Take as an example of this view of tendencies the causal mechanism of gravity, which we shall define as the relationship of attraction between objects. (An example from the physical sciences is easier to think about because we can imagine its operation within a defined set of conditions, or in a closure.) The law of gravity states that objects attract each other with a given force that depends on their mass and distance apart. But this does not always give rise to the same event.

First, the conditions that pertain to different places and times vary. So a baseball which is dropped on earth will behave in a way quite different from one dropped from the same height on the moon. This is because the conditions surrounding the ball - the masses that attract it - are quite different in each place, though the law of gravity operates in just the same manner in both places. But on the earth another causal mechanism also intervenes, because there is friction between the air and the ball which slows its progress towards the earth. Thus the law operates in different conditions and gives rise to a variety of events.

In social science, however, the concept of laws as tendencies has not been treated so strictly. This is partly due to a misuse of the concept, but it is also due to a fundamental distinction between the method of science proposed by Bhaskar and that inherent in the work of Marx and many neo-Marxists. In the first place, the concept of a tendency has been misused to describe an historical trend. Jessop, for example, refers to tendencies directly as historical trends, such as those 'towards the socialisation of labour, the concentration and centralisation of production (and) the relative impoverishment of the working class'. These 'tendencies' are thus given an inherently empirical content by Jessop, whereas the term is meant to convey the distinction between abstract theoretical relationships and the variety, not the similarity, of the empirical outcomes they influence. An identified 'Pattern' in history (e.g. people are moving toward the suburbs) alone is not A tendency but a trend: suburbanization is an outcome of causal mechanisms and contingencies, not a law about capitalist development expressed as a tendency. Thus we should speak of the trend toward suburbanization rather than the tendency toward suburbanization; of the trend toward the growth of state power; of the trend toward de-skilling of the labour force.

Equally, throughout the postwar period the rate of profit in Canadian manufacturing industry exhibited a marked downward trend. The second use of 'tendency' in the Marxist literature provides a significant criticism of Bhaskar's conception of causality. This is the characterization of tendencies as forces that lead to contradictory outcomes, a view which acknowledges the dialectical nature of history. Such a view implies that actual history is not simply the outcome of unidirectional or mechanistic causes, but results from conflicts between opposites.

Furthermore, causes do not merely exist at an abstract level, but are embodied within the concrete events which are their outcomes. It follows that within each concrete stage of history is embodied the conditions that give rise to the forms of subsequent outcomes. This argument leads us to modify Bhaskar's account of realist science. It suggests that the conditions in which causal mechanisms operate at any one time are not themselves a matter of chance but are both the outcomes of previous stages, or specific periods of development, as well as the causes of subsequent events, in so far as they influence the degree to which each mechanism operates.

History is therefore evolutionary, not a series of unconnected, specific events. This also implies that in the production of each conjunction of events exist the conditions for their own destruction. We are now forced to accept that events are not simply the result of invoked causal mechanisms in specific historical and locational situations. They are also determined by the course of history, so that particular conjunctions of events are implicitly both the outcomes of previous developments and the causes of those to follow. Therefore, any interpretation of the various forms of outcomes must not only refer to their abstract causes and historical specificity, but must also refer to their place in the course of history.

So, when we refer to realist laws we imply not only

that the forms of outcomes or events are different because causal mechanisms work in different combinations in different situations, but also that the events themselves alter the conditions which prevail, thus providing for the emergence of new outcomes. There are two more things to say about tendencies. First, our discussion does not distinguish between tendencies and counter tendencies, the latter a term used in the literature to refer to some group of events or actions which appears to oppose the effect of the tendency.

Marx's discussion of this issue, for example with respect to the tendency for the rate of profit to fall, is confused; he includes in the list of counter-tendencies both theorized effects, such as a reduction in the value of commodities, and trends, such as increases in foreign trade. But in making this distinction we note that forces which operate to raise the rate of profit are the effect of causal mechanisms just as much as the forces that reduce the rate of profit.

The outcomes of the two tendencies then work in different directions and are concentrated at different times. It is not, however, clear that one force Is necessarily secondary to the other, as implied by the tendency/counter-tendency terminology. In order to clarify these arguments we examine the theory of the falling rate of profit. In a two-department model of the capitalist mode of production, the rate of profit for a given production period is defined as

$$\pi = \frac{\text{Surplus}}{\text{Capital Advanced}}$$

$$= \frac{t(1-\lambda_2 D)}{\lambda_1 K / L + \lambda_2 D}$$

where π = rate of profit per year

λ_1 = unit value of the means of production

λ_2 = unit value of the means of subsistence

D = real wage per unit of labour

K = amount of means of production used per production period

L = amount of labour used per production period

t = number of turnover periods per year.

Thus,

$\lambda_2 D = \lambda_L$ = unit value of labour power

$l_2 DL = \lambda_L L$ = value of variable capital

$1 - \lambda_2 D$ = surplus value per unit of labour power

$\lambda_1 K$ = value of constant capital

$\frac{K}{L}$ = technical composition of capital

The magnitudes of the terms in equation (1) determine the rate of profit. The problem for theorists, however, is to explain how these terms will change in response to conditions in society. To do this, we must explain how the central causal mechanisms of capitalism (class struggle and inter-capitalist competition) produce changes in the variables and so in the rate of profit. Class struggle is manifest in many ways and its ramifications extend throughout society. We may identify, for example, attempts by labour to reduce the degree to which labour power is a commodity, to raise the wage rate and to improve the quality of life, and efforts by capitalists to maintain a commodity economy and to reduce the value of labour power. There are of course many other issues of struggle, but their combined significance to the determination of the variables in equation (1) is that they affect the rate and direction of change of real wages, that is to say, capitalists and labourers struggle over the magnitude of the real wage.

The second mechanism of capitalist society is inter-capitalist competition. Labour produces profit, but capitalists compete with each other in an attempt to obtain as large a share of the surplus produced as possible. There is a variety of ways of doing this. In production, capitalists compete by minimizing costs, by improving productivity and introducing more efficient techniques of production. Some firms compete on the strength of product quality. In the market capitalists compete by attempting to purchase inputs at prices below values and by attempting to sell outputs at prices above the market average. Class struggle and competition do not operate in isolation.

However, these mechanisms may vary in relative strength, depending on circumstances, so the forms of outcomes which they generate vary. There is no one-to-one correspondence between the mechanism and the events, even to the extent that collusion between capitalists and alliance between classes are plausible outcomes. These arguments are briefly illustrated by two examples.

First, suppose that the rate of profit is high. Then the rate of accumulation can be high in relation to the rate of growth of the labour force. This implies that the balance of class strengths swings towards labour and therefore that the real wage tends to rise. It also implies that capitalists have therefore an increased incentive to replace labour with machinery as a way of reducing costs.

Consequently, in these circumstances, the mechanisms of class struggle and inter-capitalist competition produce twin effects: the struggle over the real wage is manifest as a trend toward rising real wages while attempts to reduce costs appear as a rising technical composition of capital. As is evident from equation (1), these manifestations of the laws cause the rate of profit to fall. Suppose, second, that the rate of profit is low. In this case, the rate of accumulation must also be low and some firms will go bankrupt. Therefore labour becomes relatively more abundant in comparison with the accumulation of capital and the balance of class strengths swings against labour.

The struggle over the real wage is revealed now as reductions in real wages. Profits being low, capitalists have a strong incentive to reduce costs but because wages arc relatively low, they have little incentive to replace labour with machinery. In this circumstance, the laws are manifest in changes that cause the rate of profit to rise. Thus we see that outcomes are produced by the operation of a mechanism in a particular context. There is always struggle over the real wage and capitalists are always seeking to reduce costs. But the forms this takes depend on circumstances; this is what it means to say that there is no one-to-one correspondence between a mechanism and an observable outcome.

Class struggle is manifest as a rising or as a falling real wage, depending on the relative rates of growth of capital and of the labour force. Equally, reductions in the costs of production may or may not be associated with a rising technical composition of capital, depending on the relative prices of capital and labour. This example provides several lessons.

First, causal mechanisms provide the structures within which individuals make decisions and their history. These decisions are not predetermined by the mechanisms but also depend on a host of contingent factors. Such factors may include the personal psyche of the individual agents, how they perceive their environment and also how the constraining structures are randomly modified by 'accidental' features of space and time. Second, the causal mechanisms and actions they prompt cannot be considered a historically. Individual responses to forces operating at a particular juncture influence how these forces reveal themselves at another moment in time.

For example, although new forms of labour management introduced in the early 20th century, such as Taylorism and Fordism, were immediately beneficial to capitalist accumulation, they ultimately led to new forms of conflict between capital and labour, necessitating a quite different response in the form of bureaucratic control and collective bargaining.

Realist Marxists begin with this philosophy of causes, construct a theory that identifies a set of causal mechanisms and the events that they produce in particular contexts, and try to evaluate that theory. The empirical part of this evaluation is accomplished by testing the ability of postulated causal mechanisms to explain particular events as the combination of laws, contingencies and historical contexts. Like Lakatos, we require that the continual modification and elaboration of the theory that is required by the partial success of these evaluations shall be creative rather than *ad hoc*. The following two sections illustrate the arguments above. The third section documents the postwar history of Canadian manufacturing performance in terms of abstract forces and relations.

The development of a crisis in the Canadian economy is linked to a reduction in the general rate of profit. The fourth section examines one part of this crisis, its manifestation in the North American steel industry, and traces out the forms of mechanisms and contingencies as events that must be assembled to explain the recent history of that industry.

Rate of profit in Canadian manufacturing

In this section Marxist theory and empirical investigation are combined to explain' movements in the rate of profit in the Canadian manufacturing sector between 1950 and 1981. The first part of this task involves measuring the components of equation (1). The second problem is to interpret the information gathered. Our interpretation of the data is based on Marxist economic theory.

In particular we show how that theory can be used in a logical manner to explain the fall in the rate of profit and the economy's slide toward a recession or crisis. Marxist economic theory argues that economic growth cannot continue to increase at an uninterrupted rate. The basic claim is that as the economy expands faster than the rate of growth of the labour force, workers find themselves in an increasingly advantageous position and can demand higher wages.

Capitalists are then forced to adopt labour-saving technical changes in order to reduce the demand for labour. Innovations of this type, however, cause the technical composition of capital to rise and, in the absence of offsetting factors, the rate of profit must fall. Though individual firms and even industries can withstand such pressures if they are more efficient than average, the economy as a whole is forced to undergo periods of slower growth or recession.

The rate of increase was most rapid in the early 1950s averaging about 5% per annum. From the mid-1950s to the mid-1970s, the real wage increased at approximately 3.25% per annum and thereafter decreased. A measure of technical change in the economy is provided by the technical composition of capital. Our theory argues that this variable should increase as real wages rise. In fact that the technical composition of capital increased by almost 300% between 1950 and 1981.

The process of accumulation in postwar Canada led to increases in both real wages and the technical composition of capital, both of which trends exert a downward force on the rate of profit (see equation (1)). It would be wrong however to claim that a falling rate of profit is the necessary outcome of the underlying mechanisms of class struggle and competition that structure the capitalist mode of production. This is because capitalists can adopt a variety of actions which, in spite of increases in the real wage and the technical composition of capital, may increase the rate of profit.

The routes capitalists may follow are revealed in equation (1). We have seen increases in the real wage and the technical composition of capital tend to depress the rate of profit. However, if capitalists can decrease the unit value of capital and wage goods (λ_1 and λ_2 respectively) or decrease the turnover time of capital, then the rate of profit may rise. To complete our investigation of the rate of profit the changes in the values of commodities and the rate of turnover of capital in the Canadian manufacturing sector between 1950 and 1981 must be examined.

Capitalists also managed to increase the rate of turnover during the period examined, the number of turnovers each year increasing from four to just under five between 1950 and 1981. -The decreasing values of commodities and the rise in the rate of turnover exerted an upward pressure on the rate of profit. The rate of profit is the synthesis of the forces identified above. This indicates that increases in the real wage and the technical composition of capital outweighed the influence of reductions in commodity values and the increasing rate of turnover of capital. We argue that the abstract forces discussed earlier were responsible for the fall in manufacturing profitability, and hastened the onset of a crisis in the Canadian economy. Several contingent factors however compounded the problems of Canadian manufacturers.

First, a history of underdevelopment in the production of capital goods made the manufacturing sector weak and reliant on foreign capital. Second, a decrease in demand for Canadian products on world markets as foreign economies became more competitive meant that the slack could not be taken out of the domestic market.

Third, rising fuel prices in the world market meant higher costs in the manufacturing sector. This explanation of crises is useful at a general level. It begins with a series of logical deductions from our knowledge about the structural causal mechanisms of capitalist production, the central claim being that when the rate of profit in the economy is high we would expect it to fall. In other words there are certain kinds of general outcomes we would expect given a certain set of conditions. We then compared these expectations with empirical evidence of postwar trends in the Canadian economy. Our theoretical arguments were found to be consistent with these facts. Such Investigation provides a useful test of our theory. Had the forces identified led us to believe that tile rate of profit should have risen since 1950, when in fact it fell, we would have been forced to question the efficacy of our theory (assuming no empirical error). Still, the evidence in this case leads us to believe that we have successfully identified the causal mechanisms and a general set of conditions that produced a crisis in the Canadian economy.

The third section, however, only points us to the next stage of explanation. Primarily our argument so far rests on logic. In other words, we would expect the same kinds of events to occur in any capitalist economy facing similar conditions. What this argument falls to do is identify any difference between one crisis and another. To advance our explanation further we need to examine the crisis at a more specific level. This does two things. First it shows how abstract causes are actually produced 'on the ground' by the actions of individual people, firms and political groups.

Second, through historical analysis which traces the development of a series of events, it shows how these events themselves alter the specific conditions within which the causal mechanisms operate. It is in response to these alterations that the outcomes of mechanisms change in form, even though the mechanisms themselves remain the same. The abstract and the concrete are integral parts of explanation. The completion of our explanation of crisis is now illustrated with an analysis of the decline of the US steel industry since 1950.

US steel in decline

However, the analysis here also reveals that a thorough explanation of the history of the steel industry must go further and show how individual agents responding to particular pressures made that history. In 1950 over 45% of the world's raw steel was produced in the USA and at that time US integrated steel mills were the biggest, newest and most technologically advanced in the world . The large domestic market had permitted American firms to scale their operations efficiently, an advantage that was unattainable by other producers so long as their markets were limited by national boundaries.

The European and Japanese economies were still recovering from the destruction of the 1939-45 period, while the US industry enjoyed the opportunities for expansion provided by the Second World War and later the Korean War. Investment in US steel production in the 1950s focused on scale increases, not technological improvement. But in the early 1960s two major technological developments became generally available to steel makers: the basic oxygen furnace, which cut to one-third the time required to change molten iron and scrap into steel, and continuous casting, which eliminated the time-consuming and relatively labour-intensive process of casting ingots.

Thus, the US steel industry found itself in the 1960s capitalized with outdated -and as yet undernourished machinery, while the economies of Europe and Japan were now in a position to invest more heavily in new steel-making equipment. At the same time shipping improvements began to open up cheap sources of iron ore in Australia and Brazil, as well as foreign markets, to producers in Japan. Japanese steel makers also had the advantage of cheaper labour. Barnett estimates that wages in Japan were one-fifth of those in the US in 1964. In the 1970s new steel plants had been installed in various third world countries, particularly Korea and Brazil, where wage differentials were even greater, and such countries are emerging as significant steel exporters.

In 1983 Korea and Brazil were the third and fourth largest exporters of steel to the US, behind. Japan and West Germany. Whereas the US was a net exporter of steel in the 1950s, by 1981 some 25% of the US market was captured by imports. For the first quarter of 1982, shipments from the domestic integrated steel producers were down to 17 million tons from 23.4 million in the first quarter of 1981. Of the 75 million tons of American carbon steel capacity, about 50% was idle at the end of May. Some 20 million tons were in jeopardy of remaining closed and were up for sale or slated for permanent closure in the forthcoming year. By the end of the first quarter of 1982 imports had reached 4.9 million tons, up 34% from the same period in 1981, so imports were actually increasing their share of a declining market. By the end of the third quarter capacity utilization had fallen to a mere 30%. Explanations of decline in the US steel industry typically credit that decline to a misguided government policy or to management decision errors.

Such an approach however provides little more than a description because it lacks any consideration of determination. The government made its decisions in the context of its budget deficit, foreign policy and public opinion it is true, but to provide a complete explanation we have to understand the decline of steel production in the USA in the context of real, underlying structures. In the previous section we established that a rise in the technical composition of capital tends to reduce the rate of profit in the economy as a whole. This does not mean, however, that those firms that adopt a new technology suffer reduced rates of profit. Though the adoption of new, labour-saving techniques causes an overall fall in the rate of profit, it is in those firms which fail to adopt the new technology that the overall fall in profit rates is apparent. This is observed in the steel-producing firms of the United States where technical advance has been slow. Firms which are making losses are located in the United States rather than in Japan or Korea.

The decline in US steel production is not simply the result of intensified foreign competition. There is also evidence of struggles between the steel sector of capital in the US and its labour force which compounded a growing inability to counter a fall in profits. Throughout much of the study period, wages in the US steel industry remained high, a direct result of the actions of a strong union-at least relative to unions in Japan and third world countries-that gained substantial political power during the upward swing in capitalist accumulation in the 1950s and 1960s.

Furthermore, labour in the steel industry was struggling against an increasingly weak sector of capital under steadily rising competitive pressure from abroad. The three-yearly negotiated contract with United Steel Workers of America (USWA) led periodically to labour unrest, most notably during the nationwide strike of 1959. It was particularly during these periods of unrest that imports gained new footholds in the domestic US market, so the contract signed in 1974 was the result of a specific attempt by steel management to ensure an uninterrupted stream of production in the years to come. In this contract, the right to strike was dropped, in exchange for costly wage concessions and improvements in other forms of compensation.

Of course the logical strategy in the face of a high wage environment for US steel capitalists would have been the adoption of labour-saving technology. However, it was becoming increasingly difficult for the steel corporations to attract the huge amounts of financial capital required to regain technological competitiveness. This was due to the declining profit rates in US steel production, the cost of abandoning large amounts of outdated but as yet undepreciated fixed capital, a sluggish domestic market, and competition from cheap imports, produced with cheaper costs, efficient methods and passive labour. Therefore the crisis in US steel production emerged within the context both of manifest failures to maintain control of the labour force and of superior competition from other steel makers abroad. The primary reaction 'of American steel producers in this' situation has been to turn to the state for assistance. But with the exception of the post-1980 period, the relationship between the steel industry and the US government has been, anything but cordial.

Despite lobbying by steel management for protection against supposedly underpriced or subsidized steel from other countries, tariff regulation has been intermittent and predominantly unsuccessful. The 1971 voluntary trade agreements were aimed at steel by tonnage not price, and therefore succeeded only in shifting import penetration to high grade or speciality products. The 1977 trigger price mechanism aimed to eliminate dumping practices by government-assisted steel industries abroad, but failed to stem, the increasing flow of cheaply produced steel from low-cost production locations, in particular from developing countries.

The continued lack of effective market protection represented by these measures betrays a primary concern of the US government to keep steel prices low for other domestic producers, an important consideration for the health of the economy as a whole since steel is a sector of production with large forward linkages. This attitude was also evident in vigorous attempts during the 1960s by the US government to force down the price of domestically produced steel in the light of a perceived oligopolistic pricing mechanism in the industry. In the US, depreciation allowances for tax purposes were between 15 and 18 years until 1981, in comparison with 1 and 2 years in the UK and Canada respectively. The characteristics of a developed capitalist economy in the 1950s and 1960s, including the density of industry and a high standard of life, can be credited with forcing, through the state, the introduction of limited environmental controls. But limited as they may be, their introduction required $4 billion of expenditure by the end of 1979 and according to Barnett & Schorsch a prospective further $4 billion in the following four years.

Crandall has estimated that some 6% of the cost of US steel in 1983 may have been due to environmental expenditures. At least for the steel industry these have been entirely unproductive investments. So state policy, reflecting the interests of labour and, more particularly, the interests of capitalists in other sectors of production, has not been favourable to a steel industry recovery. Profit rates have fallen consistently as wage rates have remained high, as the US cost advantage in raw materials has been eroded through shipping improvements, and as the US industry in general has fallen to the bottom rung on the ladder of technological efficiency.

Index